Peter Riley was born in Stockport in 1940. His education was at Stockport Grammar School, Pembroke College Cambridge, and the Universities of Sussex and Keele, and he has lived since in the south-east of England, Denmark, the Peak District, Cambridge, and Hebden Bridge. His first book of poetry was published in 1969. His poetry has always pursued the intersection of diurnal and exceptional experience, the commonplace and the potential, seeking to inhabit the route where language, on a loose rein, leads the author towards the unexpected recognition. It is also a poetry of result, personal, political, and historical, so it does not exhort and it does not decry: it stands witness. While much of it is a pure extension of the local, Riley sometimes takes up the technique of describing an elsewhere – a foreign, unknown place, a prehistoric grave, a very new or very old music and asking it to declare its hidden messages and singing its song. His several books of prose have worked out some of these concerns in studies of Transylvanian village music, travel notes in Romania, English village carols and improvised music. Since 2012 he has been the poetry editor of *The Fortnightly Review* (online) where the purpose of his reviewing has been to establish a way of describing the appearance and results of poetry without recourse to any of the closed or parochial vocabularies. His poetry is itself the central and generative point of all these possible avenues, and has ventured into intense compaction and expansive narration, hop-skip-jumps and immense rambles, always returning sooner or later to the known percept, the only workable meeting place.

The two volumes of this collection include all the poetry up to 2017 which he wishes to see preserved, and some which he does not. Something like a tenth of its contents has never been published previously.

Peter Riley

Collected Poems

Volume 1

Shearsman Books

First published in the United Kingdom in 2018 by
Shearsman Books
50 Westons Hill Drive
Emersons Green
BRISTOL
BS16 7DF

Shearsman Books Ltd Registered Office
30–31 St. James Place, Mangotsfield, Bristol BS16 9JB
(this address not for correspondence)

www.shearsman.com

ISBN 978-1-84861-610-3

Copyright © Peter Riley 2018.

The right of Peter Riley to be identified as the author
of this work has been asserted by him in accordance with the
Copyrights, Designs and Patents Act of 1988.
All rights reserved.

Note to the Reader

Untitled poems are headed by three asterisks, those which are parts of groups or sequences by a single asterisk, or bullet. Dates are those of first separate publication, unless this is greatly distanced from time of writing.

Cover

Abandoned mineshafts in the Great Flat Lode (mineral rocks under the Carn Brea, south of Camborne, Cornwall).
Image by courtesy of Dt Keith Russ.

Contents

I. Poems, London 1962-1965

Where was I?	19
Privately	20
All Saints	21
High Lane 1964	22
Wanderers Nachtlied	23
Love Poem	24

As If Sonnets (The Lost Pamphlet)   25

and by the way,	28
The Encyclopaedia Office	30
Richmond and Kew	33
'We become extensions…'	34
Burnham Beeches	35

Four Dream-and-Waking Pieces
1. Part of an Inferno	36
2. Summer	37
3. The Return, the Silver Bough	38
4. Dream 29/xi/1966	40

II. Poems, Hastings 1965-1967

Introitus	45
Puisque j'ai perdu	47
Music, wife, snow outside, a lot of old books	50
'I live with the child…'	51
Bus across Mid-Sussex at Night	52

Three Poems after a literary convention in Ashdown Forest
Train skirting the South Downs	53
'To back up…'	53
On Behaviour, after reading Herrick	54
Train	55

'Out into the open…'   56
Sparty Lea Epilogue   57
'About this evening…'   58
An American Photograph   59
Emilio de Cavalieri: Lamentations   60
Further to Cavalieri's Lamentations   62
At Pott Shrigley Brickworks   63

Snow in a Silver Bowl   64

The Twelve Moons   68

Seafront   74
'Wind on glass…'   75

III. Love-Strife Machine

Poems written on 11th May 1968   79

A Day
  1. Getting Up   90
  2. Having Breakfast   91
  3. At the Children's Playground   92
  4. Visiting the University   93
  5. At the Café   94
  6. At the Labour Exchange   95
  7. Having Dinner   96
  8. Visiting People   97
  9. Visiting Other People   98
  10. In the Pub   99
  11. Going Home   100
  12. Doing Nothing in Particular   101
  13. Tidying Up and Going to Bed   102
  14. In Bed with You   103

IV. Poems, Hove 1967-1969

Other Poems written on 11th May 1968   107

The Lost Conditional	110
'The sea is flat…'	112
'The screw that holds the window shut…'	113
Three-part invention for John Dunstaple	114
Five Serious Songs	115
Four Round Dances	118
Two Machaut Songs	120
Strange Family	121
'The wind across the chimney top…'	127
'That it is not so simple…'	128
Victoria: The Shadows	129
Marine Resistance	130
Free ramble over the Archpoet's Aestuans intrinsecus ira	131
'As it might be possible' (The Fighting Temeraire)	134
'A mist coming in…'	135
Getting Away from Wagner	136
'O see like a silver ship…'	137
Memoirs of the Highland Zone	
1. 'which murmuring encloses…'	139
2. 'the mist full of caves…'	140
3. 'very early morning…'	141
4. A story told of Anglesey	142
5. Instructions for morning	143
6. 'angel of the north…'	144
Valley of the Moon	145
'From the window…'	146

V. Poems, Denmark 1969-1973

'Sky streaked with rain…'	149
'Snow is falling…'	149
'Through the day's obscurity…'	149
Blåbærvej	150

Archilochus	152
Wednesday Supermarket Poem(s)	156
'I sit in the café-bar…'	157
White Arrows	158
Slottet	159
'We are at large under the white beam…'	160
'Threats and promises…'	160
To live trying	161
Let us all	161
Northern Harbour	162
Across the Island	170
Grassy Lenses	171
Folded Message	172
'Open the curtains…'	173
'Across the axis…'	174

VI. The Linear Journal   175

VII. Poems, Peak District
(i) (Macclesfield, Harecops) 1973-1978

from *Preparations*
First Third	213
Climacteric	214
Last Quarter	215
Blow Blow Thou	216
Care of the Body	217
The Song Sung	218
The Day Fishing	219
Arbor	220
Edward III	221
Edward IV	222
Edward V	223
A Song to Conclude	224

from *Untitled Sequence*
   In a German Car Park   225
   Bunker Hotel   226
   Is this Düsseldorf or Kiel?   227

Wetton Mill New Year's Eve 1974-5   228
'And again those bright calculations…'   229
'Snowdrops and crocus…'   230

Birth Prospectus. The End of Us.   231

Still and White   238
'In what sense to know'   239
Some pieces of *The Irish Voyages*   240
Essay on the West Window of Killagha Abbey   242
Gallarus   244
Canzon   245

Company   246

Toy Music   251
Polecats' Song   252

VIII. The Llŷn Writings

1. *Sea Watches*   255

2. *Six Prose Pieces*
   St Merin's Church (i)   271
   St Merin's Church (ii)   272
   St Merin's Churchyard   273
   A spring on the upper slopes of Mynydd Anelog   274
   In a white van…   275
   Rhwngyddwyborth 6th September…   276

3. *Poems and notes*
   'fixed points in succession…'   277
   Late autumn, the peninsula on the turn…   278

Porth Grwtheyrn	279
A Repetition of Machado at Porth Grwtheyrn	280
Porth y Nant	281

4. *Sea Watch Overstock*
Pieces fragments and notes	282
Night-watch notebook	284

5. Mornings with a Walkman at Rhwngyddwyborth   288
Things Saying Themselves in Llŷn   291

6. *Sea Watch Elegies*   293

7. *The Translations of St. Columba's Sea-Watch*   298

8. *Overheard by the Sea*   300

9. *Between Harbours*   301

10. Six small prose pieces formerly attached to *Between Harbours*   309

11. Absent from Llŷn 1994-1997   311

12. Llŷn in the Rain, September 1998   314
Only the Song   321

13. Llŷn, Pausing and Going   322

Notes   325

IX. The Derbyshire Poems

Following the Vein
'The sphere descends…'	329
'Unfold the line…'	331
'So, walking down…'	333

Tracks and Mineshafts

I.
Material Soul 337
Eight Preludes 339
King's Field 349
(two poems and a letter) 354
Glutton 357
'A person's single reach…' 363
Manifold 364

II.
'The light alternates…' 365
'Expert hero…' 370
'Wait for the light…' 371
'The flesh, eyestruck…' 381
'Year cap split…' 384
(The cancelled diatribe) 388
'Deeper into stone…' 391
'And there, at this very spot…' 392

III.
'Held in conative energy…' 394
'The city's surface…' 397
'In the dream-shaft…' 398
'Flesh withstands…' 399

Adonaïs 400
'And the miners all dead…' 401
'Full moon…' 402

Lines on the Liver

Spitewinter Edge Lookout Prose (untitled) 405
30 diurnal poems 425
Processional and Masque (The Replies) 443

Notes 451

X. Poems, Peak District (ii), Little Bolehill 1978-1985

The Idea Is	455
Another week on Llŷn	456
Black Holes	457
'The point of generation…'	458
'I depend…'	459
Middleton by Wirksworth 1980	460
'We fall to the earth…'	461
'The blind traveller…'	461
(Postlude)	462
Manchester, Liverpool…	463
'Bronchitis, headache…'	467
Ospita	468

XI. Noon Province

The Night Train Arrives at Avignon	475
Market Day at Apt	476
Fragments at Les Bassacs	477
Les Bassacs	478
Roofwatch 1-2	479
Afterthought	480
Stubborn Interval	481
St.-Saturnin, the Ridge	482
Meditations in the Fields 1-3	483
The Walk to Roussillon	485
Lines at Night 1	486
Lines at the Pool above St.-Saturnin	487
Mediations in the Fields 4	489
Lines at Night 2	490
Lacoste	491
Recalling Lacoste	492
Rustrel and Gargas	493

Up the Big Hill and Back by Ten	494
Counting the Cost	495
The Walk Back to Gordes	496
Numbers at Les Croagnes	497
Just a Song	498
Notes on the Attempt to Visit Lorand Gaspar	499
The Slower Walk to Roussillon with Kathy	500
The Telephone Box on the Edge of the Corn Field	501
Last Night	502
Orange to Chartres	506
Slow Meditation in the Café-Bar *Les Caves du Mont Anis*, Le Puy	507
Notes	509

XII. Reader. Lecture. Author. (1992/3/8)

Reader

Harecops	515
Macclesfield	516
Denmark	517
Bolehill	518
Egbert Street	518
Pastoral	519
Hastings	519
High Lane	520
Through Woods and Fields	521
After a Poem by Nicholas Moore	521
Irish Drones	522
What the Fate Capsule Told Me	523
Golden Slumbers	524

Addenda to Reader

Socialism (Prayer)	525
Aigburth (Howl)	525
Nicholas Moore Retake (Pact)	526

Lecture
'Wie schön bist du…'   529
'Only true passion…'   530
I Wrote a Letter from France   531
'Congress of twins…'   532
Regendered   532
Glow Worm True Worm   533
Heinrich Biber   534
Die Mondnacht   535
Magdalenian   536

Author
In manus tuas   539
'Pure need scores the pavement…'   540
'Voiced consonants…'   541
As with rosy steps   542
E Questa Vita un Lampo   543
Delphine   544
O That Singer   545
Bar Carol   546
'And love alone…'   547

Notes   548

XIII. Snow has settled…

Prelude   551
Wirksworth (i)   552
Wirksworth (ii)   553
Relenting of duress…   554
Further Education   555
North End   556
Poem Beginning with a Line by Nicholas Moore   557
London Bridge   558
Norwich   559
Great Eastern   560
West Side   561
Bolehill   562
Next Door But One   563

Little Bolehill	564
Midsummer Common	565
Cambridge Blue	566
A Shropshire Lad	567
Dublin (i)	568
Dublin (ii)	569
Fontaine de Vaucluse	570
Loft	571
Hackney Loft	572
Parker's Piece	573
First In Last Out	574
S. Cecilia in Trastevere	575
S. Maria in Trastevere	576
S. Pietro in Montorio	577
Dar es Suriani	578
Château Musar	581
Château de Muzot	582
Hergla	583
Djebel Bou Dabbous (i)	584
Djebel Bou Dabbous (ii)	585
Ghar el Melh	586
Saint Louis' Island	587
Saint Médard's Quarter	588
Saint Séverin's Landing	589
Causeway	590
Pascal's Corner	591
Notes	592
Index of Titles	595

I.

Poems: London
1962-1965

Where Was I?

Sipping hot chocolate in a shop window
and the 13th Century dementing outside,
my friend Michael, who will wear
a grey plastic mac to anywhere on earth,
visibly chuckled, his forehead seemed
to sprout architraves we very nearly
missed the train.

In Berlin we met a girl
who only painted fish and took
the professorial Richard home with her.
In Koblenz on the other hand
Nick got in with a very
smart set who didn't have walls
or beds or something.

We drew lots. I ended up with
a small cripple called Lorenz
with one hand and a hook, and
they said, "I hope I don't get
the black dwarf" and I did.
He collected toy soldiers
and was going to write novels.
Totally kind.

Privately

Earthly creature by your
kindness more future

than the stars: we
lose ourselves north

and south and in our
ecstasy forget, as if

travelling. A light
shines from the earth that is

not reflected, a line
unfades over the dark

plotted fields cutting our
unwillingness to be:

we are, our senses parade
the quaking systems by

fleshlight, meeting
head-on a law

of movement in love.
A love of movement in law.

All Saints

By day we walked the city and planned eating. By night we made love and slept. A part of Manchester I'd never known well previously but Tony Connor lent us his "bachelor" room which was a fairly bare space on the second floor of an old office block, not now extant. It had a window out the back over the rooftops of that shabby and about-to-be-redeveloped urban sector, which at several early mornings threw up a yellow infusion of town-haze, in which the dark blocks sat. There was dust everywhere and one naked light bulb. It was our first domestic act ever to go to Woolworths and purchase for, I think, 1/-, a plastic shade for it, pink as I remember. It was Christmas. The twisting stairs up to the room shifted and groaned every time we used them. You stood in the room naked, a black kitten staring out of your arms. There was nowhere to cook or even heat a kettle of water but it was warm because Tony had bust the lock on the gas meter some time previously and we fed the same shilling through again and again – no one had come to read this meter in the last five years, he said. We took our meals in a cheap café along the road at All Saints, which also does not now exist. I record the adequacy of living, with no excursions and no justifying work. The furthest we got was The Manchester Museum, about half a mile away, where we spent an excessive amount of time in the netsuke collection, which also does not now exist, and ignored most of the rest. The labour was one of calm close attention.

High Lane 1964

Snow arrived the day after Christmas,
carpeted the roadway and mooned
outside our window all day.
There was light on the hills
and blue-black lines where hedges ran.

The light of the world lay
on the dark soil,
the king sat quietly among trees
willing at any time to
dissolve away with no fuss,
conscious of a job well done,
smiling his January smile,
promising to return.

Wanderers Nachtlied

We learn eventually
to distrust expectation
and then things happen:
the wanderer in the green valley
finds a shade beside him and light
touches the tree tops. There is
a transposition and then
a fusion: now
we really start waiting.

Love Poem

You weren't
in the streets,

somewhere you
moved or were

still, indoors or
out. The street

was empty
of you, into the distance.

All the possibilities
were suspended, our presence

divided, leaving
no room anywhere.

The missing questions
wanted you back,

the lost uncertainties
begged to be reinstated.

As If Sonnets
(The Lost Pamphlet)

1.
You have gone to Liverpool and I sit
in my room alone. No footsteps
on the stairs, the gas fire hisses. Our future
has become a problem and perhaps
I'll solve it, perhaps not. There has been talk of
choices and amount. You are kind enough
to wait for me, leaving me time
to be alone and worry. But really
you're never far away. I see your black coat
from the corner of my eye
as you turn to close the door.

2.
A future we had vaguely projected
hangs in question in my mind,
a baby you wanted cries
because it's not going to be born.
Furniture, dog, child, cat and canary
all pitched out of doors to fend for themselves
on the cold road, the wind off the sea.
I envisaged a house full of welcome.

3.
The luggage: this we found together,
this you told me to do daily for my health,
a yellow bird of fibreglass and wire
fastened to a pipe near the ceiling and
this was from you. Little tokens of trust,
that sit around the place glaring at me and if
all this is to be redeemed the whole
course will have to brighten, where
have I put the pebbles from Canterbury?

4.
I took the 24 bus from South End Green
to Trafalgar Square and then the train
from Charing Cross ("single", I said) to Bromley
and walked it was a bright rainy day to the left
past the shops and further on
and up the steps of the Victorian house.
I rang the top bell referring to the
loft room you weren't in.

5.
Clearly there were two of you.
Today snow fell, in late February.
I walked over Parliament Hill – children
tobogganing, my shoes leaked and I
stamped the ground. Always this
ghost alongside me in a black coat.
A blind baby tugs at the roots of trees.

6.
An unborn child, a music that will not be silenced,
the trees that grow whether we like it or not,
the elegance of your script, your downward glance.
We met entirely by chance in a decayed house
in a depressed part of the city. We took
the chance of success in each other's eyes.
You are not, I tell myself, for all markets.
The persistent baby starts another song.
Rain falls on the bushes outside, on the
unwanted garden at the back of a rooming house.
I make no case, believing in what will happen,
what will take place. On Tuesday it did.

7.
You arrive from Liverpool full of anxiety.
Our Christian names rejoin. The city
no longer holds us, we shall leave it,
we shall live in a house by the sea.
Somebody teach us patience.

Note.
The only copy of The Lost Pamphlet *was sent to Glyn Hughes in 1965, at the suggestion of Tony Connor, as a proposed booklet in the M.I.C.A. series. It contained some dozen poems, not necessarily including these, or not in these versions, and not under the title used here. These were redacted in the later 1960s and subsequently, from a notebook draft written about 1963. Nothing more was heard of* The Lost Pamphlet.

and by the way,

i

But I *did* hear voices, beating around the room at night. I touched the blanket and a great roar filled the room, a hornet slapped the wall and it stopped. I spoke to the cat and the flies. I haven't got a cat. I spoke to the light bulb and it went out. The last flicker hung in the steam of morning coffee. Doctor, doctor, permit us our trappings: red-hot insurance, flashes of cultural history, impure foods and acts, principles of secondary education. Isn't there a lesson somewhere in this? No. The harp drips dry above the stream. Under a skin of crystal fires we catalogue our stamp collections. White lines on the road, red signs in the air, and us: a mass of plastic material waiting to send out buds of pain, or die of peace. Petals woven over the soil like bridal lace, streams of clear water above and below us, poised. Leaves fall, seep through haze and a thin red officer is in the garden. Blood and bed-lamp. The uncomprehending worm dissolving in God's eye. Live cell: visual Tiger.

A succession of weak days, dithering like grass at the obsolete mill-wheels. Vacant spiderweb on my shoes, fuzz on my hat and dreamwater in my head. I don't wear a hat. Remembering a flame-proof, abiding night or winter sun. The veined sea fetches me, the anthill fathoms, food for sky-worms and the calling dark. I screwed up Parliament Hill and threw it away: no more ice cream wafers. The thread of time lies on the inside of my arm and everything I know lies on the fringes of the blind spot in my eye. My head is full of pink old men in nightgowns, blessed creatures of the equinox.

ii.

Sea. Wine. Till we die or part, no. Generations, houses. I remember. They crumbled. I was. Gone over. The green horizon. The sun, has gone over the green horizon but. Not I. Will return. Decayed seafish and salt, a sharp smell in the. Boats and their rings. In the harbour, their own. To set, sail for. Any known. Island.

The girl and the bottle. The mantelpiece, or the table. Sand on the sill and. Over the roof. Take. And keep it. The sea coiled. And yes, children, with parents. The sea with blue slippery things. Take this. Shell and. Listen. Inside. Throw it.

Wanderer-fantasie. Image of the. The destination. The man playing. The wine. Libraries, shore mutterings. He is mad. He of Europe. Uncatalogued. Sand and waves. Together. A room where a. Waiting for a. Wandering, day and. Nothing. Across the, Importance. Day and night are bound. Whether he wants or. Moves stumbling across the. Libraries of Europe. Crashing stones.

Half an Epilogue. Any known island. Set sail to. Boats on their rings. In the harbours. The sun but not I. Green horizon, has gone. I remember they all. Will return. Wives, generations, houses. Till we die.

The Encyclopaedia Office

(i)
& suddenly I'm entirely alone (Adrienne
is working in a holiday camp in Prestatyn
serving dull food to honest people) carrying
a circular plastic and iron chair across London
to a new room. The taxi driver says if I don't want
to give a tip that's fine but just don't stand there
making bloody excuses that's all. I'm angry
but I'm wrong. The wallpaper is black with
blue and yellow roses, the lino is bright red,
everyone else in the house except a Mr Rodgers
is foreign and my Uncle Arthur saw ghosts everywhere he went.
I took down all the mirrors but there were nasty patches
on the walls some of which looked at times
like faces. It was Vincent Price in *The Masque
of the Red Death*, or *The Man with X-Ray Eyes*,
though I also saw the Beatles film twice and there are
three cheap cafés within fifty yards of Kentish Town
underground station, each with a jukebox. I am
not moving on the earth. I lie face to face
with the moon and next morning there are bedbugs.
In Aden there are empty white cisterns in the hills.
I dream strange dreams and Rauschenberg's
Inferno sketches are on show in the lobby of the
American embassy. I try but I can't remember
the number of Karl Marx's seat, and never visited his grave.
Figures caught in pencilled whorls.

(ii)
Westclox BABY BEN press knob to silence and here we go
with another day which has been all right for ten minutes but
here's Mr Smith at the door saying he doesn't like being defied,
there are rules and he has a responsible job and it's not even
his house. Living above a dry cleaning establishment
seems to make me dream of searchlights in desert landscapes
where crowds arrive with bowed heads to be pencilled out,
dirty steam wafts in the window and on Sunday morning
Congregational hymns drift over the back yard, songs
about glory. The moon turns the waters of men's minds
and surely there is a river running under this road.
To envisage something of the reach, to build forward
a life from the fragments, to act in an image of man
which is Caritas, to owe what is spent.
You almost tremble. "I'm frightened,
they are coming to get me", tap tap on the stairs
"Yes, they hate us." "They want to hurt me." "Yes."
And it becomes a habit to move on, and be as we are,
to stay poor, fall in love, travel by bus.

(iii)
We're very late. We pressed the knob on the alarm clock
and went back to sleep. It's 1964, I've never heard
of Frank O'Hara and he's almost finished writing for ever.
We posit pastoral alternatives, and now we have
Mr. Cuell, who says he knows when everything's
all right here because of it's not he gets
vibrations in Golders Green. I see *La Dolce Vita*
for the fourth time. We're not waiting we're loitering.
The party we vote for is dedicated to change
as long as it is imperceptible. Sky like lead, distant
thunder over the City we have turned away from,
from its financial heart and its work and everything
that holds it together. Was that a big mistake
which is going to pull us down for the rest of our lives?
Ab Hoc Momento Pendet Aeternitas. I've written
some 200 poems about moors and forests and
surrogate fathers and convinced myself that all the strength
lies in what I don't know and can't do and never
think a coherent thought from one week's end to the next and
drift through on a cloud of trusts, in you for instance
and dreamy sensations of warmth towards our few friends,
and my constant amazement at place as a kind of impossible
hypothesis which we nonetheless inhabit while it stands
before us waiting to be coped with. A remaining deposit
after foolishness and waste have triumphed, the start
of a society, and an art. Now we really start waiting.

Richmond and Kew

The gates to the botanical gardens
are shut (we came all this way and)
they're closed. You're strangely
quiet, I don't know why. A far blue
haze lies on the river and we
don't talk. I ask What's wrong? but
you don't reply. There's also a kind of
autumnal depth in the air, built into the haze
and the traffic murmur and a few boats.
Then we find a café, there's a jukebox:
Beatles, things we said. You thaw over
a mug of tea. "It was nice out there" you say,
"blue and amber everywhere and those swans
on the water." I hadn't noticed the swans.
"Nothing's wrong. I was just thinking."
Things we neither notice nor think hover about us
saying what they think will become of us
and our city-sealed promise. Your
colour perception always startles me.

* * *

We become extensions of each other
and fill the living space with act.
Sundays we lie around on bits of
rented furniture or get sometimes up
the road to one of the cafés and
Parliament Hill to feed the squirrels.
We stroll hand in hand past Hampstead Ponds
and sit on benches under the trees at
South End Green. In the evenings we visit,
and sometimes take a little wine.
Much of the time I complain,
about the empty work and the weekly timetable.
But there is a plan, and we are the plan.

Burnham Beeches

for Andrew King

The new leaves spattered on the complex distances.
Noiseless footsteps on moss.
Neither open nor closed dark or light since it's
been that sort of day, no decisions made.

Five
ancient beeches in a witch-clearing
gnarl / stand still / wait / are dead,
are wicked / fantastic / white
fungus on the grey whorls.

Irrelevance of mood requires concentration;
careful listening.

Trace no patterns, touch, forget the name.
The brown wall whispers, shakes and opens
as a curtain to admit whoever passes,
and decides to say yes.

Four Dream-and-Waking Pieces

(1). *Part of an Inferno*

This, he said, bringing me to the place

This, he said, bringing me to the place, is where the negroes come to die.

We stood on the edge of a small cliff, with this scene before us: a bare hill, of pressed soil, a brown lump, and the sky low over it, yellow-tinged on the horizon towards sunset. The hill sloped down towards us from the right and the slope passed under our cliff. It was like a ramp. We stood there and he described the place. A few wooden sheds on the top of the hill, old and ramshackle, the yellow sky showing between slats and through the windows.

The negroes, he said, come here to die. And as he spoke, by way of example, a man stood on the hilltop, and sank to his knees, gently turned over, slowly fell, and rolled down the slope.

As he passed beneath us I could see that there was fire inside his head. He fell below us flashing and sparkling — beams of light shone out of his eyes, nostrils, mouth — close to us, the body turning over — the head threw out comets and fireworks.

It had become almost night, and more came. Hundreds of black bodies tumbled down the hill into the pit to our left. It was darker, there was thunder. And they all had this fire in their heads, and some of them, veins of lightning were netted all over their bodies, defining their shape on the black earth. I don't know if the thunder was in the sky or was the noise of their passing, there was no end to them – it was pitch black night and we were close to the stream.

Three days later I sat in warm sunlight among trees, watching the earth.

(2). *Summer*

    white paper, and
    orange ink in a bottle.
    I dip the pen and
    write, in orange
        (it's difficult, crossed nib
        scratches and blobs)
    I write the word
        Summer
    then knock over the
    bottle and orange
    ink   spreads
        over the paper

    orange
    (through closed
    eyelids
    open window
    onto green leaves

(3). *The Return, the Silver Bough*

Back at the house, the old one, where I was brought up, we couldn't get in at the front because of books – stacks of books in wedge-shaped alcoves where doors and windows used to be. The weather was musty and indoors.

So I climbed over the fence onto next-door's path and went round the back. (She saw me, the old witch, peeping furtively through her curtains.)

Behind the house it was night, and open, and there was an incessant whistle, perhaps from the sky. There were searchlight beams in the sky, moving, forming X's and separating again. The sky was dark blue, without stars.

Suddenly the lights were turned full on and blinded, I lay helpless on the ground. Black insects hopped over the short grass in front of my eyes, and brown moths with crimson bellies fluttered away. I seemed to be smaller.

The windows were blacked out as if for the air-raids, except for one – the big one on the ground floor, our living-room. There was a white figure in this room with a bright point of light at the end of her extended arm. Behind her was a giant moth, dead, fixed to the wall and covering it, its blue wings speckled white. The point of light moved up and down. Above the house there were more searchlight beams, crossing the sky.

I stood in the garden hunched and cowering. I saw myself from about twenty feet away, a dark hooded figure exactly in the centre of the rectangular lawn.

I couldn't recognise the woman in the window, who now looked quite ordinary, and yet I live here, or used to, it must have changed hands. I turned my back on the house, towards the distant moon-lights. Beneath them, if I shaded my eyes, was a row of little yellow-lit house windows, with tiny people in the rooms performing ordinary tasks, tidying up before bed-time.

I considered the possibility of surrender. I could use my handkerchief as a white flag, though it was probably not very clean. But I didn't take my hands out of my pockets.

The light beams in the sky produced only darkness, inside the light, as dust in the white beams.

From the sky I bent down again to the house. I crouched on all-fours like a giant and closing one eye peered at the blacked-out window. I wanted a way out of this enclosed outdoors. I tried to mumble into the back door, "Let me in."

I turned away, into the room as it was

and made some coffee

and went to work.

(4). Dream, 29.xi.1966

It starts from the white houses on the sea-front, which I can identify as Hastings. While viewing them from a distance I walk out of one of them to a small railway station by the shore. I am to take a train to the other end of town. Several trains come in but for various reasons I don't get on: one's too small, one's full, one closes its doors and I stumble back after it's started. But finally this streamlined thing rolls in. It picks up two women off the track – they were just standing there talking and people kept warning them but it's no use the train hits them, and they jump up on top of it (it's a very low sort of train, wide but low, and silver – rather like a river) and they jump about on top, panicking, until it stops. Then they get down and stand on the platform looking embarrassed. The driver gets out, throws back his head in disgust, and enters the stationmaster's office. So I get on this train, at the back, in the last carriage. It's a dining car, where I sit at a white-clothed table with Jonathan (who last I heard was in India in the diplomatic service) and a colleague of his, Sir John something, who's very high up in the government. They are friendly towards me, though perhaps a little condescending, for they both wear dark suits and ties, and I am in jeans and an open-necked shirt. But it is agreed to share the cost of the meal (can I afford it I wonder) and later we'll get on with the conference at the other side of town. We eat. The train doesn't move off, I think it's waiting for us to finish. It's a big meal consisting mainly of starch: rice, macaroni and semolina, served by an Indian waiter whom Sir John treats rather badly, for the poor man doesn't understand much English and Sir John shouts a lot. Perhaps that's why we get all this rice and semolina, the waiter not understanding what we ordered. A letter reaches Sir John. He passes it to me. "Dear Sir John, We're very sorry about Ali but he's trying his best to learn enough English to cope with the job, and attends a night school twice weekly. We believe he's an honest boy…" etc. I glance at Sir John. He sniffs, and leans on the table, picks up his coffee. Next thing the meal's over and I sit at the back of the train looking out through the big curved windscreen, waiting for it to start, which it does, but the wrong way – backwards, so that my end becomes the front. Now there's a driver beside me, motionless, staring ahead: a rough-looking, thick-set man in a dark uniform, his hands on the controls. The train moves slowly and solidly onwards away from the little platform and through the sidings. There's some kind of commotion behind me on account of the direction, businessmen in suits saying, "Now look here…" but I just stare ahead. It's very beautiful, the scene in front of me, the colours all very light, a few variants of white. We leave the tracks without any disturbance and go across a sparsely-grassed field of hard earth as if still travelling on rails, that same steady rumbling movement. Bright, grey-green-white grass and pebbles. Then into an area of sand dunes and at a right angle across some old railway tracks, faint metal lines in the grey-white sand. The noise behind me is now a panic, people shouting hysterically, but I just look ahead as we roll down onto the shore by the side of the bar. It's low tide. We run a little faster, smoothly over the sand. Ahead the sea is very calm, the harbour bar reflected brown on its surface, but everything else sky-blue and white, a deep shining perspective in the reflection. A few seagulls, silence. We glide into the water, pushing up a slight hissing wash. And further in. Silence again. Then the story is taken over into Jonathan's speech. He's describing the event, how the water line rose up the windows of the train. We, the realisation suddenly hits me, *are dead*. Here is Jonathan sitting in front of me describing how he drowned, and me with him, and presumably Sir John something… and this must be some other world. He tells how the water came pouring in from the small openable windows at the top, water lapping round the chin, I remember…

And back to the white houses on the sea-front. I see Adrienne in one of them waiting, wondering why it's taking me so long, getting eventually annoyed, and that fading into worry. And the baby there too, to be fed and cared for. Many years pass. I now see myself in an upstairs room of one of those houses, an all white room with no furniture, and one window looking out to sea, sitting in a big chair looking out, an older man wrapped in scarves and shawls, patiently waiting for Adrienne to die so she can join me. It's very sad, this waiting. Then, presumably, we would go on to somewhere else. Adrienne has at least a life to live, but I have to wait and wait. Grey light of half dawn. I wait. My cold isn't any better. Half light from the window. Seagulls clattering.

II.

Poems: Hastings
1965-1967

Introitus

How it begins:
          it begins with me
walking along the shore at Hastings
just short of the surf line, on shingle.

To walk effectively on shingle you have to
lean forwards so you'd fall if you didn't push
your feet back from a firm step down and
back sharp forcing the separate ground
to consolidate underneath you, with a marked
flip as you lift each foot, scattering
stones behind, gaining momentum.

The shore's long and curves
slightly to the south as you approach the bar.
Winter: a hazy, cloudless day
and cold. No horizon to sea.

Looking up from this.
Stopping and raising the head,
correcting the stoop –
a small sea, its sound
on the stones, of the
wash back. Seagulls in winter
lose the harshness of their bark,
more a mewing, and there
aren't many.

That action, lifting the head,
the skin of the throat unfolding,
air reaching the upper chest
gazing out in no particular direction –
position of receptiveness:
each sense prepared to act, the body
hearkens – the mind is alerted.

That nothing comes
is good. No news
across the shore is
excellent, the truth
is there for a start.

The flesh is full
of what there is
there / then,
has that, offers
back   self, is one
of all that.

I lean again and
press the stones, bend
homeward, for the door
into what comes,
to bring it further.

Puisque j'ai perdu
for Adrienne

Now she cracks hazelnuts on the floor
with a hammer and hands me the kernels
to eat, taste of wood. The town outside
is dark, people are at home. One or two
are bitter-sweet. Yes, some are good
and some are bad. There is music on the radio
by Orlando di Lasso also known as Lassus,
who once sat with William Byrd in a small boat
and they were rowed across the Thames at night.
And all of that is good.

Domini   exaudi
the cat seizes a nut and runs off with it
orationem   meum
the pile of husks on the matting
is greater, at each entry

there is a purity, a goodness:
the generous gift given always calmly
that is my oratio, song and dance
counterpoint and harmony
we stayed up specially for this, it is
my dance tonight, my rhetorick to say
there is a purity which is a goodness
and the generous gift is calmly given
all the time, and I know that out of this
special place it is not given or calm
or good or bad but here it is so utterly
said and heard that it lives on.

The Mass is built on a popular song
which says "Since I have lost" and all the time
in all the specialness we can't omit to notice
that we have also lost, a phrase which is

never far away, tucked into the whole edifice.
I am alone, I have lost, I am not what I seem.
Indeed we have abandoned and lost so much to be
in this observance together the whole of the earth
and our good sleep, staying specially awake in case
a purity exists by which a gift is given not
necessarily to us but as a giving which exists and
we are forced to recognise against our loss
a constancy.

It is the material of this song, movement and shape
breaking into the structure, symmetry encrusted
on stone, the whole theatre of what is set forth
"as if it were natural" reaching to an admission,
that it is ruined in time. The sculpture reverts
to the quarry face: we have lost, we have lost
so much by the time it weaves to an end
that we are hardly where we are and
have donated all our presence into a sung and
danced oratio which reaches its end. Over
the sea or Thames in some dark cave or quarry
is an inscription on a carved tomb
which says again that the utter gift is constant.
Post Scriptum: we have lost.
Appendix: J'ai perdu.

And the gift is of what, of what is,
the human being the person given
to the totality the commonality
given to the continuance over the air beyond
the person in a grand manner of perception,
and here the enclosure of house, room,
group of two assuming ourselves into the future
by a child, so given entire with a clause in
small print: we also lose, we must, otherwise
these things made are of such
colossal beauty these masses tombs and

mutual percepts we might petrify on the spot,
we'd have nothing at all.
A particle, or seed, remains, "lost"
to the immediate city and
isn't this how we survive, how we survive
our own generosity and purity, isn't this
our mark of love?

Music, Wife, Snow Outside, a Lot of Old Books

There was always something wrong with the words,
they were elsewhere, while we sat here in the room
as we are, neither typical nor exceptional
but particular. She talks to me with one hand
touching the wall and it is graceful with no other
in question, no other woman or wall someone anywhere
is leaning gracefully on, no other speech but this.
Then she picks up a cup and crosses over to the window
and sees snow on the hillside. It's there, it happened and
mutual energy resides in the transition, the knowledge held
of snow, simply, for I never said anything about a
blanket of snow; our blankets, you see, are red (ex-
hospital). Snow, cold snow. The light lies on the crust,
the stones under the snow show by folds at
certain places, the music of change and stability
in our presence here, the cold facts. There's also
an albino cat called Rastus, of a strangely
affectionate nature and stone deaf. Language
eats it all up one by one, everything we have here,
we used to have a cat, a lot of old books and there was
snow on the hillside outside the window and language
took at all away.

* * *

I live with the child, remember,
am its attendant. It is a constant condition
not subject to interlude; while the child lives
I am at work there, and owe myself
the same solicitude, as I quit
the alcoholic/electronic heat/throb
and turn homewards late at night. Outside
it is cooler, the sea in white bands to the shore,
noisily, not play of waves but plain succession of.
I move fast   in that presence
resilient   as much as drawn.

Streetlights, pavements, edge of the land, shops and
hotels darkened, the body calm and swift, steps
knowing the way (straight) on, the wind off the sea
stronger towards the cliff, the little night light
burning in the window, home mixed into the
flow of it as much as the sea or the million pebbles
shifting in response, that periodic slow crash,
the concrete groins against erosion as active as now I,
or that seagull which is still there when
I look back, in its territory,
perched on the chimney-pot above the nest
awake at night, calls, we
guard our young.

Bus Across Mid-Sussex at Night

Lit cab of a
parked lorry,
inside the
driver, arm over
the wheel, head
turned side-
ways to a woman,
baby in her
arms, wrapped
in white cloth
she looks
down to it, a hand
under the baby's face
& another man,
fat, in
shirtsleeves standing
beside the open door on
her side
mouth closed
looking at the baby
seen/flash/gone.

Inside, an American,
soft-voiced, drawls
about theatre.

Three Poems After a Literary Convention in Ashdown Forest

(i) Train, skirting the South Downs

What troubles still, what
stops the throat, some
fear?

Great level acres of pasture
before the hills and where
last week was a heron standing
in a stream among reeds in the
rain is none, and rain is
slightly falling into grass.

Fear, then, of loss and closure
of this or any world? Or
failure, making a fool
of yourself / if you could
make a fool like the one in Lear
of yourself or anything…

Leans, as it has before, towards winter,
haggard trees, a line of pylons over the
ditchy wastes around Eastbourne…

What prevents donation what
hinders flow still, someone
enters the carriage I stop.

(ii)

To back up
away from marriage
into the schoolboy
who can't face
the child or its mother…

Barnaby, last night I lay
half waking and knew
I'd heard your cry, its
particular throbbing wail you have
and thought I'll have to get up,
go and comfort him, lift him
up and pat his back

And thought of going home as
a forward thing, venture over
further fields.

(iii) On behaviour, after reading Herrick

No reversal because nothing to turn round,
a holiday without release (November,
approach of the autumn harvest but
no festival) not pagan because not Christian,
no misrule because no order, no
change, a continuum

which we could live with and reach
down to bedrock if it weren't
overlarded with display, unable to accept
that the play of meaning on the surface
is all and enough.

Train

1 hr. 20 mins., no cigarettes left
nothing to read no one to speak to
pitch dark at the windows (a pen,
and a small notebook) which might
show more but for the dirt on them
than a moment's row of orange lights
over a hedge and the names of
stations: Glynde, Westham, Norman's
Bay, the next a nameless halt.

My act continues towards you.
I ask back separation and the
spread of location along the coast, I am
rushed through a technical distraction
and a fondness for categories of
uncertain validity but tinted with age.
Speed on oh speed on bright
line of sheer boredom.

My act continuing towards you,
the line shows through
the paper, slides
across my hand.

* * *
for Andrew Crozier

Out into the open
whatever human frailty
and strength are
together in the light as
being and remaining one

      for that step further, to break down
      the remaining walls between us,
      walls of a house we each
      inhabit but not
      a final home, speak
      what we are: drifters,
      wanderers not in exile
      but at permanent home
      in movement – distinct,
      with our own luggage
      our different treads
      on the same ground, breathing
      the same open air.

Sparty Lea Epilogue

It must be the whole continuance,
of our lives bound through the occasion
it must be this other place given
in return, the small room at night.

The meeting was a specific node
of exchange like a thank-you in a long
conversation, fastening the discourse that
sustains us to a future weather.

I returned to the north and now
I return to the south along a chain
of hills which is also forged
in the eye on such listening

And continue to believe in that
occasion and exchange as a journey
worthy of its extent, capable
of increase as solitude closes in again.

The hope is a trust. The hills
are before it, the trust was offered
against all hope
of locating a centre.

* * *

About this evening, the clear horizon through
the branches, the mild air, the music – I mean
would it help, can you use that? You being,
you know, my real concern in all this
and I don't see how it can, as it stands.
A churchyard, the fragrance, of grass mainly,
some smoke, one tree in blossom, pink and white.
It's a shelter. It moves in time. It's
a music, then it's an architecture, and
a forgotten tale. What's left after it's finished,
as it passes into a new silence? I think we are
in some way, pushed forwards.

Three journeys converge
    1. Winchelsea churchyard
    2. 13th March 1967
    3. Berwald: Septet in B flat
in our presence and we learn again where we are
by the way the music (I think he called it
The Grand Septet) seemed to be a recapitulation
of the churchyard earlier in the day and
there are so many places that offer that sense
of protection which opens to the world revealing
our necessary absence.

An American Photograph

It looks like a lake but is actually a river in New Hampshire. The conifers, and their reflection in the water, a stillness with a sense of flow under it, and of the same objects continuing into the distance on either side halted by the thin white margins. A pastoral dream forms at the centre, of a small boat (and all of a person's being) drifting among islets with trees, on still waters, deeper and deeper into the mesh, lost in corners of the world, anywhere. But meanwhile the sprite, the real mind-work, equally invisible, leaps furiously across the scene, lake, trees, islands, gathering and tightening its frustrations to spring into the abiding world, our knowledge and love of it, also not in the picture.

Emilio de Cavalieri:
The Lamentations of the Prophet Jeremiah
23.viii.1967

I.
Alternation, of single voice and chorus –
dialogue, prose and verse, narrative and song –
the process of thought.

The solo casts forth a hope, a throw
towards the possibility of truth.
It takes the music, the great wheels turning
with the motion of the earth and sky, the shape
and course of it, the voices interweaving and then
it is no longer an occasional intersection with the cosmos,
glimpses, holes through the dome of night
to the unbearable condition beyond, it is constant,
at any given point the whole expanse is there, to-
gether over the surface of the earth, the stars
turning towards daylight, all night long.

The chorus, the company of workers
alive and dead, in space,
"…the sky was white with stars"
with clouds at noon.

2.

The single voice branches out, extra to its ground,
takes risks. It is the chorus that
brings it back home, to our better islands.

The process is prolonged, and difficult
but it flows, melismatic, and holds
the entire condition of light
separately, each its own colour. There is no
loss at the return, there is no spectre out in the cold,
this dance includes us all, this invitation
to this route where we all are, the best road, without
any doubt the best place to inhabit, exactly here.

Ierusalem, Ierusalem, attendite
We call it love, or Jerusalem, something
more than love, that is held
in the mouth, the dialogues.
We say Jerusalem, meaning
the wheel on the road,
touching the earth and
going, illumines the night.

Further to Cavalieri's Lamentations

The conversation is between me and you,
and us and anything that can speak, including
the things we worry about such as
this shouting close to the house at night.

The language of the living, a space forced between
earth and stone, a possibility of transition at
dawn and twilight, forcing us into calm.

We can't ask anyone but ourselves, no one
reads this or waits patiently for it to end, to go
and boil soup or whatever draws us away.
It is ours, the best place, the still moment
when the light no longer flickers the days await us
and peace governs the world. *Ierusalem, Ierusalem,
attendite*: the soup is boiling,
the mouth is expectant, the wheel
on the road bears the children home.

At Pott Shrigley Brickworks

for David Chaloner

Fire by the roadside, along the route
where they bake clay for houses. There was
mist higher up which became drizzle
in the lower reaches of cloud down
the valley, which was narrow, and
mean in one sense, towards the village.

No barriers between the factory and the road,
the hearth and the route in the same space
like those upland paths that go right through
the farmyard, geese, washing, dogs and all.
Casually we stroll through the middle of commerce
and gain a third person, plural.

Our settlement requires heat which is
the sun's domain, we appropriate it,
we control the rage quite delicately,
in a manner quite deliberately light:
the open workshop, the covered home
casually brush fingers in the dance.

                        Ten years later
the brickworks has vanished without trace
and the village has been replaced by a services unit.
All the factories are somewhere else, miles
from any routes but their own, behind steel barriers.
The ceremonies of fire are stamped out
and lie under yards of topsoil, a black band
over orange hardpan. We drift away
into the land in our heads seeking
a forging fire, hung on that slight thread from the hills.

Snow in a Silver Bowl

Verses salvaged from poems written c.1965 based on Set-chö's commentary on the Hekigan Roku or Blue Cliff Records, a document of Zen Buddhism.

   * * *

The truth, and you, and the problem about the truth.

In spring gentle winds
cross the valleys and
rivers and doves sing.
The fish have travelled
upstream to their spawning beds
but downstream someone still wades
in gumboots at night and casts his line and waits,
and sucks his pipe, stares, and waits.

   * * *

The hills lie on one another's backs
and their colours gather towards indigo,
pure and cold unhaunted hills.

Few and simple live up there – when
three move in three move out, not knowing why.
All are made welcome.

   * * *

The tree retracts and its leaves fall.

Cold winds in the great valleys
and raindrops striking the ground.

The visitor sits in the old summer-house
for hours and hours
instead of going home.

* * *

Snowflakes fall separately
into a totality, a one.

Seeking the particular, you fall
into a totality, a one.

* * *

Snow in a silver bowl.

The statesmen and the libraries, the members
of cycling clubs, the builders of
matchstick cathedrals.

The banners flying over the city.

Snow in a silver bowl.

* * *

A few steps outside the door.

White clouds and heavy
sunsets at this time of year
over the hills to the right
as to the left, equally.

Stepping out, further and further,
the way back completely forgotten,
lost in delight and equality.

* * *

A sky containing frost
the moon setting
darkness

Can anyone distinguish
the cold, the clarity
and the distance of these images?

* * *

A pool of dead water
no wind touches.

Prospero renounces his powers.

It is too much – the clouds
coagulate at sunset, mountains behind
mountains distance upon distance
range upon book-throwing range.

* * *

He climbed to the top of the mountain
and the top of the mountain was covered with weeds
and the earth was covered with skulls.

* * *

The mind, a music plucked
on the flowing stream, a new song.

In autumn in heavy rain
the ditches spill over.

The Twelve Moons
After Li Ho

Li Ho, now known as Li He (790-816 A.D.) was a well-connected but entirely unsuccessful young man whose verse has been described as "Dionysian" and so untypical in Chinese traditions. These versions were done in 1965 after those by Ho Chih-yuan in The White Pony *edited by Robert Payne, 1949. A number of phrases remain only slightly altered from this source, including some which were evidently mis-readings, and this is one reason for retaining the superseded transliteration as the name of a partly fictional poet. In 2006 I made changes in the light of the more scholarly* The Poems of Li Ho *by J.D. Frodsham, 1970, and the revised edition* Goddesses, Ghosts, and Demons: the collected poems of Li He, *1983, hoping to engage with the more abstract and complex interpretations of the Chinese characters. This was not a successful venture and the poems were for the most part returned to their 1965 versions, but not unaffected by what they had been through. These poems were written as lyrics, and they supposedly note the seasonal changes passing through the palace enclosures (though it seems always to be cold), with their various abandoned women. The 13th poem was in Frodsham's books only and is different in tone; the thirteen month was the result of ministerial failure to co-ordinate solar and lunar calendars.*

1st Moon

I climb the stone tower looking for spring,
amber willow-buds, palace water-clock, slow drip,
mist spirals wander through the field. In cold
green light a dark wind leans over the grass.
    An embroidered bed bears her
    asleep at dawn, jade-cool skin,
    dewy eyelids closed buds to a paling sky.
On the road willow catkins not yet ready.
The flag leaves perhaps, before long.

2nd Moon

Where they pick mulberries by the stream
we drink wine among dandelions and orchids.
Flag leaves crossed swords clash in scented air,
restless swallows scream at spring's demand,
green patches on rose-mist screening.
    High-set hair and gold bird-tail
    rivalling the evening clouds –
    in pearl skirts she dances on wind-steps,
    at the ferry she says good-bye with *flowing river song*.
The drinkers' spines go cold,
south mountain dead.

3rd Moon

East wind fills our brows with spring.
In flower-city willows darken, deep in the palace
wind stirs through bamboo, new green dancing skirts like water.
For hundreds of miles bright wind on wet clover,
a warm mist blown down to earth.
    Slave girls waiting to follow armies
    apply careful eyeshade, red banners
    flapping on the walls of their compound,
    scents wafted over the river,
    fallen pear-blossom, autumn by proxy.

4th Moon

Cool at dusk and dawn, all the trees.
A thousand mountains, green depths beyond clouds,
faint scent in the rain falling through greenery,
leaves and round flowers beaming through garden doors.
Water sheds green ripples in stone ponds.
Heavy late spring, blossom gladly falling,
old red flowers on the ground, glow in tree-shade.

5th Moon

Carved jade lintel, gauze hanging in the open doorway,
lead-bright water from the well,
ducks and drakes painted on fans.
    Snowy skirts dance in the cooled halls,
    sweet dews rinse the sky blue,
    silk sleeves balloon on the wind,
    beads of sweat on their bodies, precious grain.

6th Moon

Now they cut the raw silk
and split the dappled bamboo.
We lie on bamboo mats in frost silks
cool as autumn jade.

A flame-red mirror opens in the east.
A spinning cartwheel mounts the sky.
On fiery dragons the Red Emperor comes.

7th Moon

The milky way sheds cold across the sky,
round dew-drops on the stone bowls,
flowers appear at each twig end.
Old grass mourns dying orchids,
night sky paved with jade, leaves
on the lotus pond, green coins floating.
    She wishes her dancing-skirt were less thin,
    she feels cold on the flower-woven mat.
A morning wind sighs at dawn,
the Great Bear glittering stoops down the sky.

8th Moon

    Through the night the young widow grieves,
      the lonely traveller thinks of home.
Spiders spin silk on the beams,
a lamp on the wall sheds petals,
the room breathes its light into outer darkness,
tree shadows back-slant across windows.
Easily now dews drift down
and ornament the floating lotus flowers.

9th Moon

Fireflies lost in the summer palace, sky like water,
yellow bamboos, cold pools, water-lilies dead.
Moonlight salient on claws of gate-rings.
This cool courtyard then empty halls then sky, white
dew-drops congealing on the wind,
emerald lacework heaped up on the terraces.
The dawn herald has gone, dawn is ablaze,
a raven on the gold well croaks, plane leaves fall.

10th Moon

Difficult to pour from the arrowlip jade cup.
The lamp smiles in petals, darkness frozen into light,
broken frost-strips diagonal on silk curtains.
    Her high room is lit by dragon-painted candles,
      under a pearl curtain she sleeps, moans, cannot sleep,
      under the gold phoenix dress she feels cold.
Eyebrows that surpass the crescent moon.

11th Moon

The palace walls stretch into cold daylight,
a broken white sky sheds snowflakes.
    Bells! this wine has waited a thousand days,
    drink against the cold, drink to the Emperor!
Royal moats and fountains frozen in white rings.
Where are the wells of fire, the warm springs?

12th Moon

A pale red glow from the feet of the sun.
Some rime still under cinnamon boughs.
Rare warm breezes fight the winter cold.
Long nights ending, long days begin.

Intercalary Month

Emperors show their splendour
as years show their seasons:
72 days falling over each other
ashes flying from jade tubes
extending the year, so why
are we waiting?
Motherly time offers the emperor
the peaches of immortality while ministers
release their dogs into failure.

Seafront
After Montale
(Lungomare, *in* La Bufera e Altro (1956))

The wind is getting stronger, the darkness
ripped to shreds. Your shadow on a thin fence
screwed up and thrown away. Too late now

to want to be yourself. A rat clumping
down a palm-tree, lightning on the fuse,
lightning on the long lashes of your stare.

* * *

Wind on glass clarifies our situation.
We turn and look out. The loss
of old furniture and the life of a field-mouse.
The unprintable migrations.

III.

Love-Strife Machine
1969

Note. Love-Strife Machine was in four sections of which sections 1 and 4 are printed here. The poems in sections 2 and 3 have been dispersed into the chronological and topographical orders in this collection.

III.

Love Strife Machine
1999

Poems Written on 11th May 1968

* * *

And now he swings over to the bitter left
and the other man comes up behind
this could put Blackpool back in the 3rd division
or me right off the map,
        these constant manoeuvres

Cutting a hillside into terraces
has something more to it than supply,
more to it than fun
        or cheating at the supermarket.

The succession of rain and sunshine
wears the structure down
to a desperation resembling pain,
love, hate, aren't in it –
work: to make it at least feasible
that the lines should intersect the way they do
        on the map of it all.

The earth so sweetly goes on without us.

* * *

What condolence the earth has,
the long straight valley up to
Jacob's Ladder in thickening light
blaze of subsoil on the fellside
a flame at the head of the valley,
earthly beacon.

I came in the world's evening
alone, the attendant creatures
sent home, and face to face, clawing
at the scree, working the bone
knowing this stone
also as a city
I underwrite.

* * *

To cut notches in the
green ridge was one way of saying
w/ chalk between the teeth
nothing to this down-land village its
amateur, dramatic, society.

The porous white underlay,
barren, enfolds so much
weather not just at weekends.

    Husbandry of the dead
    notched into the skyline
    above the far from
    dependable condition of meadows –
    the white: the stars: the stone, to give
    a straight answer.

The cliff road over the ridge to Brighton
and nothing holds us, even
by car, at that speed
away from the light in the ground.

* * *

To blaze through language as if blazing through
life   got all burnt-out   a built-in
defence structure is too expensive

(that stone house
fermenting and rotting in the valley
fermenting and rotting in the valley

the valley screams as it rushes past
any world-image
broken.

* * *

O our intimacies
torn apart to the uttermost
ends of the earth and sky
          in this furore
carried off by sea and air
wrenched into music,

fulsome and beautiful
turned bitter in starlight.

We agree, we give ourselves
to the weather.

* * *

I am from language and will return to language
      & no one will know
           what else I might have been.

Storm waves blot out the lights
along the seafront of Hove and Brighton
not the back streets of Manchester or
network of estate roads south of
Stockport not there the
same wind curves across the land
tearing thick grass on the
Derbyshire moors / I wasn't there.

The centre of all this tumult
this plastic material woven into
the rocks and meteorology
of the continental shelf
a morphosis the colour of blood
and winter sunsets   out of
dreams of limestone   consolidates, into

a device capable of speech and silence that can
hold the world in a syllable
for good or ill.

* * *

How can they live
wedged into the curve of the embankment
      as if the threat were not personal
& febrile extension served
        against the creatures of fire?

* * *

      The universe is not contained
         in this machine;
this machine is contained in the universe

is how it could go with some honour.

* * *

Or the house is a mountain
      and the room a cave
open into a remoteness
        measured
in the flight of birds.

* * *

Learning to (speak, listen, dance, be, etc.)
there comes a point when you have to act simply by
throwing out blindly onto whatever surface
seems likely to bear the weight, throw
the whole body forwards onto
the bright substance and hope it floats…

        swimming, in any
        department of the imagination,
        what you deal with is
        surface tension, not
        liquid, not
        depth, not
        mother.

* * *

No one comes to terms with anything

the terms come to us
welcome or not, sought or not
come precise and articulate,
unanswerable.

* * *

The figure of hope is three-fold:
the stance / the turn / and then what
does it come to any realisation but
move on to some new place,
to some kind of home there

the sound of it:
> fanfare   proclamation
> naming   signal   welcome

Here I wrote:

> There's no one in it
> not people
> commands love.

instead of:

> Everyone's there
> dead and alive
> find it.

* * *

Love —   the open air
    or a presence
        like the sea

it is yours, what you have desired,
offered, carefully
to the living as to the dead
    in breathless hush:

trust, between two worlds
what you wanted, lived out, harmed
and healed for

what you found lived.

Terrestrial Home

(after Carrera Andrade, 'Morada Terrestre')

My house folds up and fits
into the figure of lightning
's breast pocket

and the South-East Electricity Board
threatens to cut off the current. We get
messages from the powers of earth,
from the sky, the flight of a
lone wasp or a whip-lash in the night
scattering angels' ashes in the wind.

Notice to quit, to lose
my terrestrial home
and be lost under
                        the stars are my food,
fish swimming up the routes of the night sky
         and the sky turned
inside-out, no more colours: the birds the names
are nothing, a handful of night...

Remember, the body of love
which is fruit and music
and dust, I forget,
falls   at last
like sleep   like shadow.

* * *

for Schubert instead

        I should be asleep
              don't stop
the broken descent
              into Austria
don't stop
I should be asleep

A Day

1. Getting Up

Time comes at us in slabs of light
and the dream calls us, to some
apparently more adventurous sphere.
We turn and find the walls are
highly coloured and the sunlight
fixes them in our minds.

I pick up several pieces of the dream,
pocket them and stumble downstairs.

I collect tokens.

2. Having Breakfast

Noticing the sea draws me
further into the waking world.
It is half-dawn, and the lighted windows
and dark sea are suddenly Europe, fifty years
of broken nights and unwelcome dawns,
knocks on the door, block architecture –
people as mass, people struggling.
Fifty years of bad principles, from which
we barely escaped, if we did.

What can I wrap around myself in this grey
continental dawn, this dawn of too much distance
spread out, across there, full of harm?
Nation, race, spending-power –
cold this morning, displaced,
thrust between two kinds of
half light
       and the sea, a slab of
not exactly light
            enough
to re-direct the mind
               it should
to the centre
       I try to.

3. At the Children's Playground

Some poems, you build one and then
sit inside and it goes round and round.
Others, you have to climb to the top
and slide down in a spiral
or you are invited to jump
onto it and rock to and fro till
you've had enough. When you dismount
or are ejected from the poem you find
you're not exactly in the same place.
There are bits of gravel in the dust and they
catch the sunlight, hurt the feet.
Today, I mean, it grows and shrinks
and a structure of the mind is left,
a stark thing, with no roof and no walls
and the wind sweeps over it and through
the holes where eyes used to be.
Later, at night, it stands there not far
from the sea, in this strange light saying
nothing, waiting for the next generation.

4. Visiting the University

What we need now above all is a few hints
on how to pass the age of 40 without
becoming a cathedral.
We are so beguiled by the golden youth
into a complete distraction from the processes
of the earth and the work of the mind
and no longer know how to sustain the music
beyond the first bright hope.

Confucius, I think, said something
useful about this, the wisdom that falls
like water to its place
                    directio voluntatis
and that isn't in the library either.

5. At the Café

What we want indeed! He comes in
and states exactly what he wants,
a bacon sandwich and a cup of tea.

Though the actual reason I like to come here
is that it offers that strangulated feeling
I get with places stuck in the back streets
of some obscure and complex provinciality –
a certain lift, of amazement that people
live and eat their lives out
so far from the centre

as if all our needs
could settle themselves aside
from the main course, while we, whatever's
left, break through alone

and the tea is 5d.
but re-fills only 3d.

being the substance of desire.

6. At the Labour Exchange

The amount I'm costing the country
in what is called "lost output" by simply
sitting here waiting.

It is certain to me that a country
is not a sausage machine,
but it is maybe not so certain
that anything is created without trade.

I mean what do we get for what we
do or what do we offer for what
keeps us? Nothing? Really?

And I sit here making thoughts with
broken ends as a whole poetic claim
melts away in the air because
there was never any real profit in it
and it's now much easier to breathe.
The clerks and queues of men in
agreement, the whole scene
as light as a feather
touched and it spins off.
We make what people need.

7. Having Dinner

And suddenly it's there,
horizontally, out beyond
the land's edge the sun-spread
restless on the sea and from this height there is
a pointer offered: the headland bearing its
white buildings for whatever they're worth, take
them – on the hand, held out
towards the line of departure,
the sea/sky line

home, we have it about us.

8. Visiting People

Are the stars not
far enough away, is the gap between
distance and contact not plain enough
written in the sky?

The distance apart of two objects
in the room, so that from
one to the other like
turning a page. Shrivelled arcadia.
Green carpet on the floor with frayed edges
and we are not like that,

our hopes glow at various places
as we afford ourselves recognition,
and in something of a frantic scramble
to get on top of the world
or get away from it, form ourselves
neither here nor there in perfect forgetting.

9. Visiting Other People

The distance apart of two
objects in the room so that
from one to the other like
turning a page. And we
are quite like that.

Distance is a great comfort, we
avail ourselves of it like a protective sheaf
it is our right, inviolate against
all the other pronouns

and I sit here with the world wrapt round me
somewhere between start and finish
following earth and weather wherever they go
heading for larger places than warmth
or even succour –

across Europe and pages,
and my own intense difference I certainly
didn't hear what you said.

10. In the Pub

                        There is a bird
called the heron of forgetfulness which hovers
over ale-drinkers. She flaps her wings and we
forget to forget the mean demands of politics,
baked beans and cornflakes we're not
fooled by any such small trickery,
we have our own, we sit here sinking
through the toxic evening as we should.
Our notions of freedom proliferate with the night
but I eat from the table in front of me, no
other, and the rest is always possible
anywhere at any time.

11. Going Home

The bus goes through the dark

and we shall never have any more than that,
I shall never have any more than that,
this, my whole substance
                          borne off
into the night
(all of it) held in its
earth, a number 19, to Portslade.

Though in the mind now
it seems a lesser demand
intersecting with other roads
across from the sea, upland,
than I'd thought, to be aligned.

Network, wild sea air,
no tract has any claim.

12. Doing Nothing, in Particular

The hot water geyser above the sink
demands careful attention. When first turned on
the water comes out cold then gradually changes to
hot or warm whichever the thing's set at. After it's
turned off quantities of *very hot* water and sometimes
steam will continue to dribble out for a while, so
keep your hands away from the spout at this point.
Now,
if it's turned on again soon after this, the water will
come out *scalding hot* (whatever the thing's set at)
then turn lukewarm and finally adjust to requirements.
Furthermore, sometimes
when re-used soon like this, the gas ignites with
a *boom* and a tongue of blue flame shoots
out of the aperture at the front about 12
inches so stand clear. This could also happen
any time the bath in the next room is being run.
Such an explosion usually blows out the pilot light,
and if this is not re-lit then the next time
the geyser's turned on the kitchen will fill with gas,
not to mention the permanent slight leak.
O sweet old geyser, sweet,
sweet old poem, this is where we live.

13. Tidying Up and Going to Bed

So shall my last act be:
settling things in their places, I call out
for the dream again. Everything set
for the next day, fragments
assembled on the shelves for reference,
cast up on the shore. I take off
the heavy coat of distance
and prepare the light in my head
for its mineral twin.
Seeking some token for the future, I offer
this world now, carefully prepared,
up to the starry governor
and quite honestly
turn my head and close my eyes
into the hard, tall, valley,
the strong road, the currents that sweep
across the earth.

14. In Bed With You

Whose presence, unnamed
bears the weight of purpose
much as the world does, in no
easier way.

I shan't know what season it is,
entered into that valley
and any kind of sustenance I can
take in the sunlight
inside my head is mine for now.

As we turn, delicately
for home
the hidden springs support us.

IV.

Poems: Hove
1967-1969

Other Poems Written on 11th May 1968

1.
And all through the day that gentle murmur
as of any metropolis, and this is a big town. Open
the window and it's there. A seagull gliding over
a block of flats on the horizon. When you look for them
they're always there, among and above the buildings,
careful watchers, scouring the surfaces, captains of distance.

Stink of summer and murmur of traffic.
Time children, these things pursue us,
whispering behind us that it's the baby's
bed-time again. Threat and promise, loss
of self, murmurs of a gratified old age
moving to and from us with the tide.

2.
Only a week after their last cleaning the window
glass begins to salt over, takes a white coat
from the sea mists and dust in the wind.

The materials of the universe are alive and active.
Something very questionable floats in from the
kitchen and the heart defends its grip.

3.
One of the screws I took out of the window frame
because spring has arrived, lies on the table.
The thread is corroded, the body stained,
and the head bright where the pressure of at least
two screwdrivers held by two people who
will never meet, has shaved off slivers and
dust of steel, wearing the groove almost away.
One such sliver hangs now, from the scarred
edge. It can't be used again.

4.
Something follows me round the house,
something difficult to avoid, a kind of
dogged angel inscribed "Why don't you just
stop messing around and get on with something?"

I've tried all sorts: amateur theatricals, stamp collecting,
19th Century symphonies, editing magazines,
taking long walks over the mountains and stomach ulcers.

And poverty. Adrienne says I'm getting
that lost look about the eyes, of the really poor.
Well, senses of exclusion and privileged want
are always attractive, and comforting, but
the only real thing is the cause at the centre.

Cause to speak. This angel in the room
makes me nervous, that I try to
satisfy on the page, this
tongue of fire, hardly notices I'm here.

5.
We don't belong in language, it's
a foreign mode. It's night now,
and the curtains are drawn. The old woman
in the flat underneath will be asleep
so I mustn't play records. I glare
at the silence, the town heterophony
muffled behind the curtains. Language is a distinct
enemy – we have instruments – we have
taken each other prisoner, and now we want the truth.

Old woman sleep calm, old
truth keep us at it.

6.

Whatever you do is right.
Whatever you say is true.

Whatever you are, exists.

The Lost Conditional

1.
Local sense that includes the night sky and its
creatures, and resolves in the form of an ellipse,
a bird's egg, the orbit of the earth, accurately formed
and set in stone as a method of directing the will.
We are off-centre to it, rightly, kings of our middle-ground.
We take bearings from the distance-machine we've invented,
in-tent, the men in the rock, the avenue by which the community
moves from its home towards the calendar, the island,
midsummer sunrise. The writing starts where love stops
and beyond is only a cave, midwinter solstice, eastern loess.
But the sun has horns as well as the moon. We erect
the gates of return on the god's head, a planned resilience
that keeps us together, crafted in starshine: the light of the dead
shining in the intelligence of the living, a brilliant green
flash of expiry that clarifies at once the whole
landscape, the factor of our distance that we
finally do descend into, because we are many.

2.
What remains? All, and the potential for "a community
of feeling intelligence" moving severally through the landscape
creating routes, a royal path, re-enacting nothing.

Pink plankton is shifted by the eastern drift of
the gulf stream and the Norsemen stop invading Britain.
Spiritual food-routes that became manic, rushed
beyond Greenland to a cave or an empty vineyard,
advanced technology run by muscle-men.

The old man finishes his dinner slowly before going down
to find out who's knocking a flag post into the foreshore.

3.
Riding the sea and looking down into it, finding
blossom and fruit under the prow, a happy
plain full of flowers. "Do not fall into a bed of sloth
or tank of intoxication, but set out across the clear sea…"
The route is there and back, back before it is there, at
the intersection of home and possibility the light,
the all-consuming crystal, burns.

4.
Running through the fields, plots of the city, running
to the river, running between left and right, opening
the ridge path by the thread of love, like a bird on the wing.
To the source, and the source wants it, the source wants
what we want, but with such urgency we have to run
to keep up with it.

5.
The sky is very heavy. We breathe. We push it back.
Hands fall onto typewriter keys, pushing back
to further and further memories of a clear light
or being. We get tired, holding the present to its promises.

* * *

The sea is flat today, a large bird,
black against the sea-shine, skims
over the water, at each downbeat
wingtips almost touch it.

Clatter of seagulls over the white buildings.
They know what they're doing, they watch
over their young and further their niche,
never settled for long, always off on the air again
over the shore, grubbing in the wrack for what
they have in mind, to bring home, seeking
no further than their span of knowledge and energy.

No further than the end of it, to return with something
saved from suspension in fear, desperation, avidity…
Whatever's brought back is calmly set
on the table and divided.

* * *

The screw that holds the window shut
begins to turn, moves slowly back
out of the hole it was forced into.
Corruption and all comes with it
along the old track as wrist and
driver press inwards with all my strength
but it's coming, gradually easier, acceding
to the turn until the structure gives
the enclosure is abandoned
and the air rushes in.

Three-Part Invention for John Dunstaple

```
1.  The spirit       gives off daylight      the Father of
2.  Comes down,          the dew                              from
3.                            Creation:                        the


Equity       comes quietly,            spreads concord over
                the                        sky
gift             given                      as easy as breath



the fields     comfort      over fields of ice            :rest in work
                            as a blessing      man to god or the earth
o u t          freely             the fountain or         fire of love


the light in the breasts of the company of the hopeful   / Without
as a form of protection to the mind                      / lost
where promise lies     in the hand     and speech        / a star


this    nothing     will wash clean            make fertile
                        without        home    or      consolation
    in    the     farthest     reaches    of     love      a con-


         unfreeze        strengthen        fill the company of men
the condition sways,     re-forms       due to death      forgiven
    cord        that can    in strength         move            we need


with safety             that             heavens             rejoice.
purified         led             towards           the city.
    help      to know     the child       and trust         always.
```

Five Serious Songs

(1)
The condition of rest
is indeed subdominant: *amen* / so
be it, the coda to all from the start.

They shall rest from their labours
    the blessed dead
as the work proceeds.

(2)
Vertical, separated, standing
against the sky, the language
launches into a whole range
of possibilities, the branches
of trees outside half obscured in
low cloud, slowly
and deliberately real

And turning on the world's
spindle always elsewhere, un-
expected, whatever time it
might be; and turned on the
world's expansion back to
this (here) strange persistence
of what lies in the reliance and resilience
of what always is.

(3)
O my little boat tossed in a rough sea
my inadequate sail and no one to
ask or give the word, what can I do but
offer my self, out as far as anyone
needs, over the sea while love
returns us to the walls of our
substance every day "my heart
goes forth my whole life long".

Sets out again my life on a long journey
sets forth whatever the weather my heart sets
out along my life

Again and again
constantly ending
finding a new stone
out of the shore.

(4)
Love, we are not children
and we know something more than the child.

If we could then be sure
what part trust
plays in it, when to
enter that body

    Then we shall know
    Then we shall see
    Then we shall find it all.

(5)
The stars rage in the night sky, path
of the victim struck a
cross them all, that
insupportable otherness in space –
    the distances
white, and deathly.

To the stars, then:
    Illuminate her beauty,
    make her, with your bright resemblances,
    love, as I love seeking.

Four Round Dances
(re Adam de la Halle)

(1)
very beautiful
    swaying
back & forth
    moving
to the music
she is / it does / they are
        al(l)
           together

(2)
Love
    held
together –
    Love,
get the song out of it,
get it known-about,
    joyous is
    love held out

(3)
the gentle look
that passes binding threads across
my eyes
comes round again

(4)
but when shall I again
see that (which) I love
when
    I don't know (how)
to see
    her / half
 (of) the world is
starving (I)
        try
to see

Two Machaut Songs

(1)
our amorous
life extends to the horizon
    the edge of night
I can't forget, having
seen how the day
breaks
    it and we
live with that

(2)
far and close in
our temporary home
a bottle of wine a bowl of fruit
a kind thought a total sense
falls like rain across
the body of
the figure of
my life
without cease
    (your gentle breath, your
    image, your
    movement in the light

Strange Family
for Jeremy Prynne

1.
this morning found
when I breathe in deeply I get a sharp pain in the middle of my chest

and the mountain is there
    (the one I
cut my hand on, Cumberland 1963

the mountain hurts

    as you get higher the valleys
    thin out, scatter across
    the side   there are waterfalls

    become precipitous
    flowers much smaller and no loss

2.
terms of
shadow, the pillar of cloud
flickers in my chest as a whole
range of wish on the edge
of the funnel "for you"
a way of approach
a movement of the eyelids, as
clear as daylight
fresh as the star of

3.
moving across the kitchen we are
crotchety tonight
in guarding who we are
against each other
since otherwise the joker wins &
we breathe into a
polythene bag   suspected of
air traffic: spinning
over the town

          when all the time
we were only smiling at the air
we smile with

4.
it is raining in my head
it is pouring in my heart
it descends like currency in
circus after circus
till the lips swell
and the knees disjoint
it seeps down through
all the strata of sense to
where it touches
the roots of a sneeze

    breaking the cycle
    glass wheel scattered faery on the road

5 (a+b).
he makes the
    sign, of the
  wanderer, sigh of
rain & coming up
  over the bridge
the entry   a mode
    of thinking in
  tune, why not

make it the
    sight, of
  winter, sort of
pain & looking up
  into the arch
the entire air a node
    to fast
  en what to

6.
intending to fall
  into the brightness
bending to touch the leaf
on the ground the drop
  of moisture on the bank
tending to force
  brightness into the soil
    touch of a finger

7.
Do not deny us, hello,
we are crotchety tonight
against nothing, we all
stand at variants, the movement
quickened to a degree of
restlessness then resentment
shakes us   we do the washing up
slowly and drop things
we hate it
             is more than fortune
to breathe it in
                 love I think so

8.
and now another term
begins, be warned, be
wary to the simple
gestures of management
    be before and be
yond the pulse, behind
the bush, these old games
looking for what
             ,get
out of it,
             Henry Lee

9.
who can't trust this silence
& won't have it for good news
there is life and there is
not & this isn't
death but the halt
in getting across   the
step to be taken,
taken

10.
and the hill is a
dusty eminence
unobtainable
Olympic flicker, the thorn
on Madder Hill the people
walking in the street

we are drawn to that
scale whereby
the word becomes its
self, yes beyond
reach of the arm
beyond tree or light, the stone
set in the
medial peach

11.
blood moves quickly
   through the structure
branches across the land
   at the mere thought of it, over
the stream and up the valley, which
spreads into the sky

      air like wine

      into it drunk with us

* * *

    the wind across the chimney top
        vibrates a column of air and a low drone
    fills the room. I think the waves
        are tearing at my chest
    I think the stormwind has my mind
  petrified with its monotonous message from the sky
Keep me warm and hold me intact
        in this rout
  pillow my head away from that monody
      the stars are little sucking mouths
        all over the sky
    they draw my soul out of the house
    into the weather, set to their awful
        tune the air
            rushes over, they pulse
        with pain at the extremes of cold and heat
            where it is one thing / a white
  condition where people of earth cannot breathe
      the ground pushed away under my feet
          the comfortable earth /
    a molecule of water
               charges in from the sea
curves round the house and sets off inland at speed
      hold me to the floor before I cast off
          the rest of my atoms to follow those
    the wind has already sloughed off my face
        and posted to the distant hills
  my arm out: have me here
        bed me in my
  fear of the dead men in the sky

        because I have learned their names
        and they don't like it.

* * *

That it is not so simple a matter of balance, however much
we need it to continue, and it's easy, settled into the flow
but it sets hard into an equilibrium, a statue:
scales and sword, and this too is our delight.

A continuum involving every facet of the person
in constant and sustained attention settles
into a steady confused drone of indeterminate pitch.
And the mushroom-eaters gather round
muttering "expanded consciousness" a term
now used to sell lipstick. No,

it has to be a blazing purpose that throws
all other sense into oblivion, and
moved with, the heart bears it, just,
and afterwards gathers together what it can
hardly knowing what knowledge it has made
dazed, dazzled, remembers the light
    that was, as of some quite
    other world, precise and detailed,
    a scholarly act, loves.

Victoria: The Shadows

The sensual dream of a hypothetical world
fades into the coast road at night.
I open the door
               into the dark hall,
hope and trust asleep now, my body
tired out of discourse,
beyond harm at night.

I live here
in the dark, the shadows
tenebrae factae sunt
the shadows are made
for a purpose.

It is time for my dark agreement.
I open the door, tread delicately, as instructed
bearing a lamp into the night
out of the night, mounting, gathering
the walls round me, the earth
is dreaming and must not be woken up.

& it doesn't change, not
six hours later
to collect the milk again I
open the door.

Marine Resistance

1.
I lean out of the window.
Sun-spread restless on the sea. The head-
land in the distance, bearing its white
buildings for whatever they're worth –
take them – on the hand stretched
out, the line of departure.

2.
The headland bites into the sea with all its force
sharpened to a point as if there is a purpose, an actual
reason for all this stratified culture, a furtherance
of articulation a clarity of what is needed
in such spite of ourselves we can't begin to know.
And I'm left here again, on the shore, at the window,
as the holiday lights flicker in the distance,
and all I have is a geology, a language folded
out of itself, a petroglyphic stroke behind the ear.

Free Ramble Over the Archpoet's *Aestuans Intrinsecus Ira*

In memory of Stephen Rodefer

My intrinsic vehement anger. I'm talking
to my own brain. I'm coming out with it all:
I seem made of insubstantial elements
like a leaf blown around by the wind.

I'm threatened by all the wonderful examples, wise men
who built stone houses, anchored their fundamentals to the rock.
It makes me feel very foolish, like a river,
always on the go, fickle to any particular patch of sky.

I'm pushed around like an unsteered ship,
small bird helpless in the sky roads.
No chain holds me, no key holds me,
I sink to my own level. O my earnest friends,

Seriousness has always been an imposition, I twist it off,
I play games. I skim the honey, driven
by desire, the work that actually is a pleasure,
the lust that won't dwell in craven heart.

I walk down the high street like a youth
heading for imaginary vices, tingling with forgetfulness,
more interested in gratification than deliverance,
dead at the centre, just exercising the skin.

I'm sorry, wonderful examples, really,
I'm dying a good death, mugged senseless by sweetness.
Beautiful girls strike me through the eyes, I can't
touch them but we make love in the bedroom at the back of
                                                              my head.

Well, it's very difficult to overcome natural habits,
to get so you don't gasp at the sight of a fresh young face.
This youthfulness chafes at codes and examples.
I can't stop wanting tender bodies.

But surely to be placed in a fire is to get hot
and who actually is chaste in this town anyway
where everywhere the sexual finger beckons,
eyes cast coy nooses, mouths open for plunder.

What chance does a virgin heart stand
here today gone tomorrow
all roads lead to the bed
it's like an eternal office party.

And by the way I also gamble
yes and it leaves me shirtless,
frozen on the outside but my heart sweats
and it's then I write my best poems.

Thirdly I spend a lot of time in bars.
Actually I don't see anything wrong with that,
I never have. When I start seeing descending angels
chanting the Requiem, I'll turn and go home.

I'd like to die in a bar somewhere
wine at my lips as I drop
perhaps falling off a barstool like Lionel Johnson
and all the saints beg for mercy on this dead drunk.

The inner light is nourished by alcohol.
The heart soaked in nectar flies upwards.
The cheapest bar-fare is tastier to me
than the fodder of institutions.

Look, I am my own traducer, I come out with it all,
all the things everyone probably suspects me of.
But when do they, wonderful examples, betray themselves
and of what? Yet presumably they find some delight in being here.

Faced with the guaranteed object, actual virtuous person,
I suppose we just wait for the stones to hit us.
Is there anyone there? Is the pure mind crouched
behind a bush looking for projectiles or?

I've said everything I can think of, I've
thrown up the poison of my self-mistrust, because
the life I've been leading does annoy me. I want to get out.
People see the signs, but the heart is somewhere else.

If I could talk myself into a rebirth, into
virtue, renewal in the brain,
talk myself into a baby
that my heart may be no longer a vessel of vanities…

You, reading this, what do you think? Would you
exercise leniency at this point? Would you recommend
a course of readjustment, long walks in the hills or what?
I'll do whatever you say.

Is this the point at which the lion
turns from his prey, and lets that one go?
Would a magistrates' court dissolve itself in its own contempt?
recognising that for ever and ever

the absence of sweetness
is very bitter.
Quod caret dulcedine
nimis est amarum.

* * *

As it might be possible
to live in the light of truth
like the sea
         which is not one truth
but, minute by minute, a vast and shifting
progression of truths…

The sound changes,
the friction of the tongue between the teeth
is voiced, the proposition multiplies into
a mark of reality, becoming
extended and useless, becoming something
you can't hide in…

And the entire land is voiced in the presence
of the sea on its shores
the island drifts away singing to itself
spray shoots up round its edges, we are
off, adrift in the Northern Ocean, we
turn our backs on the dream
of a new world beyond the Atlantic,
we head north, we enter the realms
of pure idea, free to cope with the weather
by sense of direction and star-fears.

We are powered from within.
Our intellectual engines hoot and puff
as we sail into the light.

Note. This poem is entitled The Fighting Temeraire *if you like.*

* * *

A mist coming in off the sea
with frost to the lawns, the grass
stiff and brittle and coated as
with glass-powder, each single blade.
No more flowers now,
the fading has started, from out there,
the shrinking body of light.
Sometimes we shout at each other for nothing.
Pursuing our wonderfully broken time
we deny the gravity of signs,
consult the dew on the watch-face
and agree to be tired in concert.
None of these composures will ever instruct me
to quit this work of earth.
or spoil this work of trust.

Getting Away from Wagner

1.
The soft trees. Her *grey* soft arms behind the grey paper wall, and the intransigent stone between his eyes, the slow and scarlet trails of mist before him, and the dangers somewhere above. What seemed to focus was the day-dreamt abstract for several miles, seeking the fierce resurgence of pleasure from the most ancient needles to his weak limbs. Despite the split in his coat and the branches holding his image and the blood that still kept filling him gently, it was not impossible to think of vanishing, *pushing* his foot into night, his son spreading inside the sky. Bright pale birdshit from far above landed in and down the trees like humble gratitude lovingly switched on. It seemed as if he would never stop, but there were no gaps in this part of the forest. She could always redeem his watch he thought, and said aloud, "Oh be near for ever, intemperate lover of the world."

2.
Her tall knees. The *grey* pines beyond the welcoming soft film, and the solid foam between her eyes, the slow and delicate drooping remembrance of enmity between us and branches all over. What seems to make it continuous is the extraction of day-dreams over several years, seeking the power that kept thrusting us from the weakened past back to our swift limbs. Despite the split in my trust and chancre pacing the floor and the floods of light that pull us away, it becomes possible to think of moving, admonishing the forest together, our claws *pushing* towards the fire. Stale white bread from over the road stands on and over the shelf like silent multitudes longing to go home. It seems as if I just walked in, and there are no traps in this part of the house. We might yet reach somewhere she thinks and says aloud, "Oh, take these downstairs and leave something for the milk."

Note: See Andrew Crozier and John James, Getting Back to Parzifal *in* Collection Four and Tzarad Three, *Hove 1969, page 53, reprinted in their* In One Side and Out the Other *(with Tom Phillips), The Ferry Press, 1970.*

* * *

O see like a silver ship, ein Silberbarke
the moon sails the dark seas of sky
and its negative light fills all the valleys.

One birdsong, precisely articulated
measures the gap between night and day
between the food song and the loved one.

Faint touch of a south wind
across the pine forest
the course of a stream, known
by ear in the obscurity, in which
the flower closes and human sense
turns homeward, a-school to sleep.

A thread of the day's commerce
weaves itself towards us across
the moon's path,
we wait to know, how
we fared, what did we make
to set beside this distance and
the mirror in the sky, the little
satellite, the sea glow.

The ground untwines from the fabric of sense
and spreads into the silence. We plead
for the intelligence not of the person
but of the life of the person, a trust,
a distant animal call. The earth exhumes
its batteries of fragrance while an owl
glides over the bleached fields. And look,
the moon like a silver bark on the tree of sky
barks back at us, again and again and everything
we ever said for love or gain is held

in that night click, the moon slotting
into its unmarked track. So another day
becomes possible, our worth is reckoned
and stored, not lost not cancelled not pinned
to our chests, but stored. There it is,
the silver moon buried in the sky the slowly
shifting medallion of each person's empire, that will
crash or not in the last day.

Memoirs of the Highland Zone

1.
which murmuring encloses which
morning encloses in its name…

Language is convex and
slots into the valley like morning.
Tight between them the wind and
fall of water, our bodies…

>We bathed in the rock pools
>naked, erect, full of promise,
>us and the valley the valley and us
>facing each other twice in the morning.

2.
the mist full of caves and niches,
entirely surrounded I worked
the treadmill up Bleaklow
for hours, when
a room of clear air fell upon me
then stopped, and standing on the shale
thought of firelight and The Stockport
Youth Orchestra and all the streets
and saw Jupiter in the sky in
daylight, as if he
were the figure of sky,
including shale and Berlioz.

3.
Very early morning, the drystone wall
shredded the mist, I mean
the wind pushed the mist through cracks in the wall
and it came out our side in long thin streaks.
I was very hungry at the time
& had to light a fire & the wood was green
& made more smoke, which got in my eyes.

It was on the hilltop above Bakewell.

4.
A STORY TOLD OF ANGLESEY

St. Eilian, "white-face" because he walked
with his back to the sun morning and
evening from the eastern corner of the island
to the centre and back.

And the other, Darkface (I forget
the Welsh) bearing no less or less
lovely grace who came from the west
to meet at the holy well
and talk sacred talk.

5.

instructions for morning

breakfast in tin
fold & store blankets & pillows
pack sleeping-bag
tidy bunk
fill pockets from shelf above bunk
check:
    money
    compass
    knife
    map
    pen
    handkerchief
leave bucket on floor to catch rainwater
rubbish bag
milk bottles
put this notebook in rucksack
pay Mr Williams
give him the key

6.

angel of the north 1951

angel of promise in the grace of the human form

with no purpose or plan

the back of the body figuring toil and industry

the front figuring love

how the human form mixes into its elements

and defends itself against them

and longs for them all.

Valley of the Moon
(second version)

Walking the night valley
under the moon, all the flowers
hidden away all the colours
departed, the colourless wind
falls on the grey slopes, the stream
crashes down the rockface.

There is something in us not in the least
concerned for any present want
but working only and constantly against
the shipwreck of an entire life.

There is an elegance in it, a music
continual, relentless as if
it need never stop and then
turns to its close, under
no constraint.

This is the valley, the true one
very difficult and at night
full of strength.

* * *

From the window out across
the bay Worthing looks like
the New Jerusalem: pink
and gold rays piercing the upper
layers of cloud, it is all
wrapped in yellow light and
offered out to us.

Worthing is not the New Jerusalem.
I know this because John Temple
was a secondary-school teacher there
for several months, he paid an
exorbitant amount for bed & breakfast.
TNJ is much further away and its
dealings are fair.

V.

Poems: Denmark
1969-1973

* * *

Sky streaked with rain and wind
weighs on the dull fields far into
distance, birds fly over the pond.
Your shoulder ahead of me, your
soft grey scarf in the vast cold landscape
that spreads round us all the time
like a helpless guide.

* * *

Snow is falling. Are we still
as we were and shall we stay?
Who can say? My heart
packed into your hands
knows roughly where we are.

Apples, cow bells, tin-openers and silk scarves
piled up in the hall. What we were
has just arrived. Do we want it?

* * *

Through the day's obscurity she burns,
through failed languages and the constant
drone that penetrates the window-frames
she burns like a lamp in the night
somewhere close to the sea.

She burns like a red fire
beyond parked lorries at the roadside.

Blåbærvej

1.
Eight rows of small one-storey houses, screened by
hedges, hollyhocks, small pines,
snow scattered, and us foreigners.

2.
Distant woods, lines of
pollard willows
across snow fields without limit.

3.
Slightly raised horizon with trees,
cold wind and snow
direct from Germany.

4.
Empty fields, fields
of snow. Nothing moves,
nothing emerges, temporary home.

5.
Abandoned gardens on the edge
of the town, black and red shrubs in snow,
white powder blown onto the road.

6.
I cycle out before dawn, sound of
dynamo echoes from roadside hedges
clogged with slush it slips and dims.

7.
Northern country, far from old home,
post takes four days, edge of a harder
history. Wondering and sometimes it works.

8.
Every morning I take the snow roads by bicycle
think of all the boots that have trodden this frozen ground
an undemanding job.

9.
Underground hot-water pipes go
by the side of the pond. Passing
birds make the most of it.

10.
Dark with snow outside
beating against the windows we
laugh at each other.

11.
Clumps of snow hang
on the bushes outside. The radiator hisses.
Stay indoors all day, listen.

12.
My breath forms a patch of frost on the lapel of my coat.
Again I cycle before dawn in a white darkness
about my business.

Archilochus: *The Complete Fragments*

Disgraced:
        left my sword by a bush, damn it
but I saved my skin
        I'll buy another one just as good when I

Face-saving, it's my *règle de vie*
this is what I said to her:

        The "opinions" people "have" of me –
        how can you propose that?
        All I do is borrow what I can use
        though I love where I'm loved, hate my enemy,
        dead rats of the world

A voice told me: return to the city
these sea-battles are doing you no good,
find your strength in the city
reign there, exercise your power
be admired

And I find you again, back here
after that long journey on a small ship
victim of nothing and nobody, I'm glad.
Me, I came here wanting mainly a good woman,
I'd already taken her by the hand and we
were on our way to her place when I remembered my cargo
it was lost, irrecoverable
the sea had it all

You have survived the war, you stayed alive
and you've kept your youth. A god has guarded you.
I've fallen on bad times again and here I am
dedicated to solitude, slipping into obscurity
though I was promised to the light

> She likes to walk around with a sprig of myrtle
> over her shoulder so the flowers augment her hair,
> shadowing the nape and shoulders

(now) that the smoke of braziers rises all over the town again
(another war)

> Guard your serenity
> the earth, spread with blood
> the long ships

Well, at the heart of discord even the worst scoundrel
picks up a few bits of humour, death as a gift

> People are dying of hunger in this city
> they should understand

Me, not in the least surprised
if suddenly the deer prefer
the sonorous waves to the land
and swop pasturage with the dolphins
while they hole themselves up in the hills

> Archeanactides
>
> the son of
>
> arranging his wedding
>
> he calcinates

Why have you nipped the cricket in its wing?

> Was transported / in sheer joy (of the act)
> like a wind on the (coastal) rocks
> (she) beat her wings and took flight

Then on that good soil they established
a new place to inhabit, and cleared new fields,
emigrés of so many lands, unnoticed in the world
but with some god's help
this island should be theirs

      That thin boat tossing on the sea
      DO SOMETHING I yelled,
slacken the ropes, catch the right gust
or something, we'll remember you
get us through this and your name will stay with us
      I said to the man

Season follows season, time
extends itself
      I no longer seek your door

I'm not bothered about Gyges and his treasury.
I was never given to envy and I don't get emotional
about the administration.
Power of empire, where is it?
Miles from my eyes

Like the spine of an ass, the island rears up out of the sea
with its coronet of wild forest

Not such a handsome place, not so desirable
as the banks of Siris

      Remember I too can sing the song of Dionysus
      the dithyramb
      if I've had enough to drink

To forget Pharos, the island, its glum fig-trees and the life there
      dragging waves

      Promised, to the light/

       and I find *you*
                         your serenity
   like the wind on
                    rocks, season follows season
It was lost:

My shield, now gracing some foreign war-effort
a beautiful weapon
                  I left it by a bush
but I saved my skin

My heart, confounded in an endless series of insoluble problems,
renew yourself, offer resistance, offer them a resistant heart
don't flinch at evil, in gaining don't exult, in losing don't tremble
supine at home, savour success, lament misfortune but not to excess
learn the rhythm which governs human life.

Note:
*Archilochus: of Paros, c680-c645 BC (?). More fragments
have been discovered since this was written in 1969.*

Wednesday Supermarket Poem(s)

Everywhere you go here you get
Herb Alpert and his Tijuana Brass,
pumping away like rubber kittens.

I sit in the supermarket coffee-bar
Wednesday morning as usual. I read
The New American Poetry

and the labels on the sugar cubes.
They recommend themselves in remote
languages. The coffee is very good.

It is bright here, it is modern, it is bright red
and bright modern, it seems to work well
and how did I get from here to

The rose is a prismatic breaking of light
violent without harm, reached through
conflicts unknown in pure red bars.

* * *

I sit in the café-bar with a headache
sugaring and sipping coffee looking
out of the window at the grey houses
and flats in bright morning sunlight
and their Venetian blinds, thinking
that in those rooms bright sunlight
streams through Venetian blinds onto
white tablecloths, or crumpled bed-linen
or papers scattered on a desk, or a white
cat curled up asleep. And these things are all
factors of various people's lives, striped
by the solar system.

White Arrows

We kiss – our lips unclasp slightly
and we cannot remember, our memories
betray us as to the final quantity
of disorganised speech we have
midwived into the world forcing
a path to this quiet fact through
lost telegrams and drunken
committees while snowy owls
were waiting outside
on the bonnets of our cars.

Slottet

Now milder as she pauses
where the road turns along
the wall thinking it
lesser all the time, the
fiery city of absence

And hopeful as the ridge
curves down to the plough, whatever
time it claims to be
whatever the old woman
has in her hand it chimes
for our departure and the light
that dies alongside.

* * *

We are at large under the white beam, our
talk beside us, the lesser stars receding overhead,
the image catalogue burning between us
and the sea a distant reminder.
Cloud bends over as we turn, cold wind
shifting hair. Ordinary passage wins:
rain and we go home.

* * *

Threats and promises
melt into a dim hedge outside the window,
a silver moth stands on the darkness, feathery
wings closed, and how we have lived or born address
or caught our wish or dropped it, all that we
might have been glances off the silence in the corner,
the thoughtless substance always to hand and
safe in our keeping. There are lights further out
by the sides of snowy fields across Europe where
the words gain daylight on their way home.

To Live Trying

To love as the leaf turns
and opens itself at each
station of the year. Casting
a glance behind we stand
waiting, the four of us:
I, you, they and the child
much more than promise.
The child says now.
Day can no longer be checked.
Luna Park is closed.

Let Us All

The rose turns spiral,
demands more light from
sky to sky it is lost
above and an honest button
is deeper in love, much
further into music.

Decline to surrender
the foolish grin in your hand.

Northern Harbour

1.
Paled in matchless retract he has
fallen away from her to a valley
heavy with crosses who was
so trusted, and now estranged gives
birth to his mother on the distant couch
unnoticed, purple flowers
beside him nodding on their
stems as the world will have it so.
In what state or power he could become
kind he does not know, dismembered by
lotus ants for the sake of development.
Breaking athwart the green cleft and
occluded wavelength he thought he
wanted this pre-human clarity.

2.
But the image box was only on hire and once
alone it is night. The earth indicates
its preference for the lost and faithful
while he, shrugged out of the light, cowboy
sabbath in ruins and the cold lizard
deafens at his feet. Outpatienced he is
scared to look her in the eyes, for the true
horizon is there, in that arc kept, thickening
to cloudy blue beyond the forked inlet.
Well or ill he traces his fault, his razor
snags on the morning soap and
opens an ancient track through fields
of cowslips, sunken to flint, down-
hill every way.

3.
Grounded, and the stream is not clear
and the notch in the skyline fills with snow,
our daily fuse-box, we are half
asleep, forgive us, our daily refusal.
Then lights enter the bay as a signal
long attended, moontrack vibrating on the
stave the choirboy's cue a wooden rod
heading for Lully's foot. A wasp falls
disbanded through the black air, the youth that
emerges in the middle of a life nameless and
meaning no harm but far too late the nerves
connect, the sides touch, he floats howling
out of the window curves over the hill and wakes
up every sleeping vole on the island.

4.
Christmas token at the cottage door, the map
was mapped for the faithful he is
lost on a black moor or study table waiting
for the star to enter its place in the heart,
the hole where the stone used to be.
He is in his chair and the wish waits
in its rusty trap. His offer calculates
while he dozes. His ignorance falters,
flutters in the elements and settles
on someone's shoulder at last. He opens
the door, the night takes his hand
the coin in his palm turned
upwards. Damage laid into the distant
future the hypothesis grinds on.

5.
The bedrock sparkled,
a nightchild came shout-
ing at six the imp-
ending reversals:
hedges aflame with
desire come together
past any wish on the
empty page forever.
Take it in the yellow cup
reluctant as normal,
for the world captains
figured this out
long ago
and called it waste.

6.
Just where the wine is
deepest he walks out
thinking something
needs to be done with these
stacks of surplus affection piled
open on his knowledge of the world.
Mother sends him out for
fish and chips if he returns
with a crown he must be a thief.
But he thought his offer was
black and white and it seemed
like socialism turned
down for advantage, not
for the world will he forget

7.
To keep steady and point
to the farm on the cliff
created as it is in space
as the third space between us
full of worth, the unsold fruit
we follow with our eyes
all the way to the boiler room.
By trust postponed the house is
vacuumed now, the light burns
grey in the fields scattered with
rosebay fluff and bits of fuse-wire,
cancelled gardens with leaning
sheds. Unexpected trope, prize
virgin forehead, undisclosed.

i.
The tongues of flame around your waist
are cold to the touch and new breezes
laden with yellow dust arise from
tombs of kings, we cough our way
through to night. Cancellation
of theory, under the banked and
calling stars pale lines on the earth
pass by the megalith and
down the fields to fields of
shifting grain. Shifting gain
falls from my arm as it rises
to the cheekbone, ashen tissue
that marks me sinking to you,
winding roads I never dreamt

ii.
To know you now I enter a state
of columns, arches, vaults, ruins
of a night and its unmanaged hopes
to continue through any makeshift
dwelling, cosy domestic or costly
protective, charcoal grey.
In a leather wallpapered coffee-bar
with a glass of very cold milk it is
possible to mention the future
and look neither up nor down.
Those to whom we mean something,
spirits we grazed in the open fields
now pass silently in the street
together, will time make all things right?

iii.
Drink up and go, we engaged ruin,
turned our days into ear-rings
and lost the prospectus in the
cold breezes of dawn between
blocks of flats, slowly labouring
the cold pavements to reach
a bungalow with a fridge and cans
of condensed milk in a cupboard.
Small rodents begging recognition
scuttle into the bank, sure at least
of their names. But I was he
and you and you were she or them
if I was him or any
of the four were us.

iv.
As anyone nested in the armchair of
radical but entirely self-fulfilling
action his glance will ever stray,
assuming terminal points, glitter
on a long black dress no woman ever
wore and areas of cloud fuzz
over, two hands on her waist.
Parents will keep children
from the light in their heads,
red and orange, of the year, show them
the ships in the bay but never
the ticket itself, the naked almanac –
there are no guides to love,
or histories of wrong.

v.
Innocence appears disguised as soldiers or
young girls and rips apart the baptistery.
A torpedo packed with sugared almonds
makes for the pier where Jackson's Follies
are waiting to go on with the Funeral Dance.
Innocence arrives in the form
of a look of dazed trust on someone's
face and the whole circus calls it
a day and goes home singing.
The constant bud rocked in
opaque tides survives ages and persons,
ambition and despair, survives body
fluids and uniforms and moves into
meaning sailing forth.

vi.
Ordinary days
begin here and
inhabit this glow
with increasing
relief as it deepens
and darkens over
the town, lights
enter the bay,
take her
down the hill
to the point of highest incidence,
the angle at A,
take her
to the highest harbour.

vii.

Or, sweet comrades, now
that trust is riven
by opportunity into heart
rending waste shall we settle
down to a lifetime's work?
Shall we, stitch and sow
or weep and crow or be
the heroes of our own
uncertainties? It strikes
ten, turn and
look back, that
old man at the gate
full of awesome gift
ours for the asking.

8/viii
People who don't and perhaps
never will exist
tend the ground between us,
their faint falling cries
in wild forsaken places where
the rotten wood leans
against the wall. There
the ring passes to earth
burnished at the field edge
and carolled into years, O listen
to the modest and reasonable plea
at the back of the funeral hall, the
wrapped present glowing with certainty,
the creak of the closing book.

Across the Island

I take a professional interest in your movements
and the back and forth of your mind.

I drive to work in a car with the windows
open on a warm morning

Viewing hedges and grit with something
of a connoisseur's attention,

Knowing it is fearful, work, not knowing
what routes extend through its edges

And the yellow strand is tense in the foliage
as the liquid fire in your sense.

Grassy Lenses

But no one bears their torsion for ever,
it is always worked out in the end,
in decades of patient study, in the stroke
of a fast car into a cliff-face.

And isn't meanwhile a glorious never
to which the starry margins bend,
in decades of patient study, in the hope
of any old vehicle arriving at a meeting.

Folded Message

All I've got is one eye and two brains
to love you with and I'm so concerned
especially at night for your peace
since the directions are uncertain
meagre and costly for two as for one
but to the tune of a progressive reluctance
we shall one day attain some kind of summit
don't you think? These are verifiable things:
that in the presence of two hundred screaming
aircraft known as "the future" our slowly
unfolding certainties keep us upright
even in pitch dark while the alarm clock
in my chest keeps me gentle, where
would you be about now?

* * *

Open the curtains, turn the page, a breeze came and went
in the morning, destroying the night sweat,
brushing at windows where people lie in the dark,
pale, fresh, full of microscopic fragments of natural objects,
new scent newly sent, such a train of events in its wake: light,

European light, and what you can do about it,
such as getting up and, in most places, going to work,
though for those early enough in the mind, perhaps anyone,
it is not commonplace and carries no failings.

Early, the city stirs, in the distance the far watercourse rustles,
a faint scar, scarf-skin or periplast, is gently unfurled,
the embryo's aquatic skin, the angels' song
revives the opening wish.

* * *

Across the axis of the dark machine
he completes his little song, the blossom
springs under our feet. Our stake in earth
is relinquished against his affirmative
for at night the walls are thick
and only the bass of the world
comes through repeating again and again
what we already knew, the fall built
into our measure. Calmly then.

VI.

The Linear Journal

(1973)

Part One

1. *[Tarascon-sur-Ariège*

Someone touches my shoulder and **bang** this
extraordinary thing clapped in my face full of
trees buildings and a river I can't begin
to think about coping with ah these, the
Central Gardens of your presence, your
image, that I hardly know…

A fixed-term loan of variegated parklands
known as "continuing to exist"
or all of the past and all of the present
"Have fun," they say, "Goodbye."
Goodbye goodbye. Our home
is totally unmade, we start departing.

And here we all are, sweaty with trust,
clutching our licenses on the corner.
We flutter we continue to exist we line up
we break our pencils in the car door, the wood
splinters, we are moved, we take up
our memory-bags and away.

My regard, of you, takes the form
of a band of adolescents in shorts
setting out on an alpine ramble
overburdened with tents and calamine lotion
disoriented and thinking, for the first time
of wine.

Out of this scramble no clarity emerges
no government no textbook no map
though the light is everywhere we go.

2.   [*Niaux, Capoulet*

O my eyes hurt and the bottle
is cooling in the stream.
The desired condition flattens itself on the wall,
textual erosion at the river-bend
and calcium accretion, we have
madrigals of love and war
set up in a clearing by the road.

Now there is a hard opaque layer
over all that transportation,
the furthest dark nick of cavern
pulsing through the night sky.
Intently, our madrigals stand in the
gloaming: green and furiously small, they attract
flies and small groups of homeless seeking rest.

O my eyes hurt and a hard opaque layer
is cooling in the sky,
the desired condition fastens itself on my skin –
sexual light on the road and
cancelled glory bring us
crashing to a future state.
We creep into our madrigals and die.

3.   [*Port de Siguer*]

The simple pulse like a train is all we need
to get up this huge pass
escape route (1943)
                    over the top
and it comes easily upon us at this
marginal age that pejorocratic machinery
is at it again elaborating without end
the planned failure of hope. But we
are caught in our own song and the leaf
turns at our feet, there is no harm beyond
the single blade / the cut / the end / get
back. We go by the old routine,
we know the words of command, they are
thrust right into the mountain
where they stand on quaint platforms facing
west, which is not our line today
and the cave slowly clogged up with calcium carbonate
(crystalline) on and on again the leaf turns a
horsefly stings my holiday on its
leg O now my
leg hurts too I sometimes think
a little man in the uniform of
a ticket-inspector is peering through
everything I say and desperately trying
to ask someone something but then we hold
special passes and all the hurt piles
up against the cutting / go
home.

4.   [*El Serrat*

Please don't tell me about your life.
The innkeeper is very pleased to have us here
or rather bemused and the waterfall
does not disturb his rest. Someone
is singing through the ache of
tiny cobbled streets and in the hot dusk
the whole binding of the landscape
folds over, shut. The song
does not disturb his rent. The bottle is half
full I pass it round. We are still here:
they threatened us with cosmic stature
and moral rectitude by turns but
we took the short cut down and settled
grumbling in the clear but thick air round about.
The financial inadequacy of our shoes
made epic excursions a burden hard
to bear and we took our coffee
delicately, in two-handled cups.
For these are honeymoon tents, and the Asian lights
are thus authentic: these are the first steps out
from solitude into two, the social flare.
Then you fell over.
I laughed. It wasn't drink but
poetry and the echo of war.
As a matter of fact I find things
impossible, day by day.

5.   [*Llorts*

Ruthless, you find it ruthless? demand?
so if you can't walk just be carried
it doesn't matter, everyone is sub-standard
that's why we have governments and works
to make it easier, to continue,
                              and one day…

"What a continuous road!" he keeps saying,
and the dust!

We keep to the intensity schedule as best we can
and there is this pulse in the road-line
that sets us aside from waste, that sends us
to you any part of your need.
People's legs collapse, habitually, it's all right
everyone is sub-standard, artistically speaking,
and it's not easy
carrying all this percussion on our backs while
"dreams" flash past and spray us with "dust"…

           There is also
various details of another long valley,
vine fields, stone villages, poppy, ponder
ponder but to what purpose? to what point
there, where the spread opens more out, another
setting point, be carried there.

6. [*Ordino*

Into twilight, settled, exactly so,
which is deep and clearer here than ever,
the stream channelled in a wooden trough
the large white building on the other side
black holes for windows, far-off
far-over beyond the skin of air and now
living in a country slowly turning "fascist"
that could be all right too, with a little help
living in a country slowly turning
pink the cloud fumbles in the west.
England slowly turns,
and we decide to stop here
because the place is one huge crystal, turning
the trees black, the grass grey, a monastery
or a prison, a large white building with windows…
the stream fast the future slow, and in my bag
I have the answer to all your troubles
your tossing in the night
lethal with desire for peace.
This will move you far away,
our determination, in a way fake
but night is almost now
we set up our overtures on the slope.

7. [Andorra-la-Vella]

I'm prepared to believe this thunderstorm
was not arranged as a personal threat,
the development section collapsing on me in the night
it was all lines, and flashed across the sky
from peak to peak, wooden rostrums
floating about under trees
and people are like that – sub their own standard
and missing their own trust, the thin walls
lit up from outside by continuous flashes
and then it collapsed. It was all very enjoyable
and dangerous, our memory-bags squeezed out, crisis
heroics multiplying in the middle of the night and tension
budding through the whole structure while we were asleep
and missed at least half of it.
And now too dark and bright to "know" exactly what
foundered in a sudden extension of the river, checking
that what we hold precious is intact…
        We shall do whatever we can
to avoid greeting death with a cold grin
that we wished everyone well
enough while we took no
more than our share (plenty had more) and we thought
in our heads how it could turn out all right.
We would rather spit on the storm
                              and years later
time, entirely cupped in the palm
and brought here, towards your head.
        There are times
the "visions of night" present themselves
in such a hurry, no answer to it
is over, gentle applause.

8.   [*Soldeu*

And's henceforth much more difficult
of love and war
                              "Goodbye"
and calcium accretion
                                        spread out
impossible, day by

for this is not my life, my
grass by the river, down there, I haven't
felt anything yet…

Fitful, coming and going, since
what we do is elsewhere and so much
waits for us unlabelled all the
time in a slowly turning state,
the squalor photographed
in its folder, under "S".
Well, the air is breathed
in lusty gulps and all
components of the river
furrow out a way of getting there
with least fuss, snap, I never knew

9.   [*Pas de la Casa*

How insistent it can be: is, was,
blue and grey and green, the "panorama"
how it strikes me on the stairs and weaves
hopeful fronds across each hand
and there it is, and shall we
deal with it, now that we are here?

Right then. "Hope", of what
more than getting by
of er um
and then the telephone rings
for three hours
of the cluttered rooms I inhabit
but my fondness dwells in the open grasslands
of not-just-now and my little problems go
up and down
filing across tundra under "T"
the mountain peaks arranged in rows
behind each other, the hikers plodding on
overburdened with compasses, clear as
anything, going
upstairs I welcome him, the
travel agent with his office half-full of
they are so obvious and
brightening I think we came to see them.

10.   [*Porté-Puymorens*

Come together in the fields outside the village
wrapt in full night, warm and dark as always
the air we sniff comes rolling down the valley,
we catch it by the river and keep the brighter sparks
for future use / a fire / in other words, private.
A sense that this, so far away, this darkness
in a foreign place beyond the corners
it is us it is wax again, it floats in the day
completely available. I stroke the edges
of the mind, soft and warm the climate
occupies the vacant cubicle
for the time permitted or required
for self-renewal of a kind, oh you know
how slight a relief the course of events
will take unaided to your
ceiling eye. Or you don't yet know
what risks are involved and reckon
to latch onto this flow whenever
the urge takes us, country and western
and sitting here, cough enraptured through our miniature scores.

11.   [*Barcelona*

Becoming, as time fills out, a polyphony,
involving more and more people.

Children begging in the streets,
dust,
the cupped palm,
of love, war,
administration.

The next picture is again a landscape
not a tree in sight, no river no
repetition and yet it is the same old cathedral,
which we resent, to no discernible effect.
Each dream erects an aerial as it cat-like
flashes past.

These things our adolescents cannot cope with
standing like Greek images in a semi-circle
around the question, the cupped palm
the pursed lip and wider eye, a pulse of light
warfare against the sky, thinking
it is too late we are too old already
and all the better cathedrals are in ruins,
are incomplete, lack power.

And of course we offer something, of course
there is no assuaging, the river in fact
flows, the same valley but no signs of
government
                            our best wishes
are in exile
             they are hiding
behind the trees, the
                     dust
music, the completed air.

Part Two

12.   *[Palma de Maiorca*

So many cathedrals: grey ones black ones red ones
and now another: white
actually light yellow-ochre fading to cream
or "bleached" as the book says.

Like Chinese poets we would travel great
distances slowly to visit our retired teachers
waiting patiently in their huts up in the mountains
but as a museum the cathedral fails:
it is too dark inside and all the colour has been
scorched away. We are left with a white collar
pulled tight on the apple, the infant left in the
car park outside the pub. We return quickly and the sea

is very calm indeed, and blue-green as
usual we simply cross over without event
on a wooden ship as dream-like and empty
as your hand, allowed to fall.

Strange, that such a calm crossing should be
a forward somersault in terms of love.

13.   [Alicante

Then back to the mainland and all the usual
clutter, omit?
nasty little snapshots of
each man his memorials, omit?
Disgorged, we wander through the town –
fleeting responsibilities
hop out of each object as we pass,
deflect, brush the hair from my eyes.
Courtyards at the ends of dark passageways
green and white! There will always be
this abundance of mistakes
sparkle / "riches" / too intimate
stained and scattered I try to keep an eye
on the sea and the sun in the sky
between houses but still I am lost,
three eyes going full blast dreaming
Lorca's blue guitar and still I am
swindled out of ten shillings in some hot corner
and back to the station bar.

The third eye, the fourth ear,
have tempted me away from you
but to love another is
to abase the heart
D'ung aultre amer, nobis esset fallacia,
esset stultitia
where the sexual sense is extended
through all sense of movement
it becomes a condition fixed and integral
to the landscape, and treated as "landscape"
we shall stay where we are.

14.   [*Benidorm*

Out of (quit) the dry coastal plain
(quit the camp) we find a door in a field
which we open and descend to the water-caves
intrepid, our own caves flooding and receding, the pulse
down, step by step. An underground pond (cut).
How did I get here and is this really the sort of thing I
I suck my thumb. If a "new order of feeling"
is to be made compulsory
I think I'll settle for the older one,
the one that goes round and round
and drags a chain of buckets up from the water-table
by a system of continuous linkage, to irrigate
the fields, soften the parched shirt.
Idly wandering in the groves and streets for days
we actually float some 10 feet above that climate
it is there (quick) we bang shout and
arrogantly struggle towards
a mere sense of calm

as it leads us daily further inland

and all those faery distances in the sky
laid out on some board
at night or the late evening when the city grants
us some respite and a ready sense
of mathematics in the air,
generally slow nervous and faltering
but anywhere and sometimes
we reach for our eyes.

15.

And it is true, that we move across
a whole range of intellectual/erotic paradises
Monday, Tuesday, etc.

"I feel an immense calm in your presence"
or "Your presence fills me with a desperate agitation"

The day is calm, the sea and the air,
the traders waiting for weeks and weeks
in the imaginary harbour
or a slow train across the reddish plains
for days, specks of fire on the far mountains at night

ending in
a summer palace, fantastic traceries
in white stone, the light is inside it
and gardens with fountains and dwarf cedars
we say we "want" that, meaning
it is there, we have heard of such a thing.

We bear it in mind, for hours sometimes,
imprecisely, in corridors and offices
that delicate act of transfer keeps us on,
holding out against advantage,
the harm it does our
proper knowledge of heat
that we have it
in the days we move across, the spectrum
held among us.

16.   [*Pinos*

And we do get somewhere, however
distracted, panic in the changing-rooms
dark spatter of shadow on the ground, distant fires
on the mountain at night (a place). No information
for weeks and who needs it?
We came to see a palace
and mostly buy figs from the fig-trees
or get drunk and make strange noise
in the streets, sometimes having to be carried back
down tree-lined avenues to where they sing,
this way making known our presence
fast, the sky slow
and then, and then…
nothing. We proceed.
And there is always someone else, someone
sober, who notices the toad
between the prince's legs in time,
who cohabits somewhere
in mutual trust and victim
or victor keeps open the book.

17.   [*Madrid, the parks*

Cavalry exercising in the early morning, in a circle
among trees, stone kerb around the lake
I'm not trying to remember
each policeman hangs his head
and says nothing.

Ceremonial guard of a capital city we hang about
on the edges of, armed to the tooth, encircling
the exhausted centre.
They fade out. Mist.

The crease in the sky
falls out to the left
and with planned exuberance
I reach up to the leaf it contracts
out.

It seems that what is already known
is casual, and maybe an entire life
is waiting to be collapsed in the next phase, how
can we tell? We set off on trust and find ourselves
duped at every stop but there is no other way,
collapsed alternatives litter the roadside
into and out of the city.

We shall spin off this spiral
we shall begin again, quite firmly on,
to what is next where what is next
is what is nearest.

We can leap right
out of the film or push
ourselves through, either way
the lights reach us, horses again, the dream dissolves
into the mixture, which thickens and clarifies
as we stir.

Part Three

18.   [*Selva, Vallelunga*

Name and place forgotten, thrown into night
all my research ruined in spasms of bulk
maenia and now threading the bewildered mountains,
move in fits and starts, persist, don't forget, go
travel on particularly in the late evening
it is hurtful, a way through the obscure
soup of wishes to what? the last
pink escarpment hanging in the sky, cheap film,
the rose-red towers.

O Mrs Radcliffe! How like living you are,
keeping things from us and attempting to distract us
with a plethora of basically irrelevant detail
such as what has this particular footpath through
fields and fields of invisible black flowers
have any bearing on the flats of terror and love
I fall across when I shut my eyes?

Italian perversities, the yes of no.
This through,
wait for me.
When the light comes
squirming
I'll be there.

19.   [*Valle Culea*

And this is where the colours come in:
blue white brown morning ochre pink
all your old friends are here, a dazzling
white mist follows us up the valley like
cotton wool under orders from the state and yet
there is nothing really to say to them
and we are first to reach the head.

Past explosions and shouts of *Hoy!*
fail to convince me the virtues of stoic forbearance
not choice but accidence is what
dilates my inner chemicals to the point of
no return so I look back and
a country beyond saving
is following me like wadding (beautiful)
(a fine place to be)

20.   [*Il Sassongher*

with its unexpected vistas – look out here comes one now:
the welter of unconditional grandeur
blue pinnacles far away below and around
miles enfolded you could wait for years for this
or never know and not miss it at all
and I never thought of you all the time I was here

but now I do, and I don't know
what will become of us in the stone
wonder-pot I carefully venture towards
ready to sink into a whole compendium of places
ready, to part the air

and you're angry because I trod snow
on the living-room carpet? She thinks of
electric toothbrushes and what it is
that makes us tick so much

it is, persisting and trying to be lost
on the verge of the lesser horizon
O shew me down to the pot of wonders where
we can all fail miserably and it's hardly important.

21.   [*Passo di Gardena*

Stream
cut through rich and
darker grass into white rock
among small pine trees, can it,
cut through pleasure
and set a touchstone on our
social being…
Josquin in the very air, beside which
assertion is lead, endless and
endless distraction.

Behind me here is our New Integrated Settlement
combination of geophysical necessity and sports equipment
set up without much enthusiasm
it flops to the ground expelling noxious gases.
That was a short-lived phase of the world's history.
This inefficiency is due to wine.

And the grass-green gets
darker and merges into the
tree-green, pencil-thin waterfall
on the far mountain rustles,
a dim scar. It is impossible
to hate or even distrust the valley
even the black valley
with its white lines. Byres. You
would have liked it here.

But you are found in a quite different arena
outside the dream and the whole spectrum
and across the red wine I love you.

22.   *[Santa Cristina*

So while it seems we're beginning to get somewhere
such is not actually the case
and another open-air trade-fair has been declared while I
wasn't looking and here they all are again
with their painted figurines and substandard brass bands.
I'm prepared to believe
this was arranged as a personal threat.

I experience distaste
and wash it down.
I have deserted my country
in its hour of need
I have longed for the key
to the field
I have handed the power
to adolescents.

So in this case take the higher track in this case
keep all the secrets close to you as you
head for the dismantled floor.

23.
                                                             [*Alpe di Siusi*]

I feel terrible. I feel like
the bearded fungus on this conifer
and in this rotting state I suddenly sense
immediate victory, no

ironies attached; it doesn't matter
how I feel, ever. I'm through
permanently with immediacy and victory and
being-born and

feeling-around / acres of rich colour
run off from my eyes into the luxuriant distances
where two shepherds are calling to each other
the songs of yes and no

and how can so much warm air
draw itself so loosely through the blue-green crystal
what does it want, shaking the strands and banners of decay
or petrify someone's heartaches into amber globules?

Shepherds are calling translucent cries
in the shattered and untrustworthy distances
from which the wind is due to turn
cold any minute now, from its source

through almost infinite gradations of density
we stand and swivel, continents
apart, defiantly ignoring
the whole crust in beckoning array.

24.   [*Sasso Lungo*

And what do we love anyway (here I am coming up to
a mountain) and would it be some kind of vortex
that slowly approaches holding out its hand
across the Persian carpet

      like a wolf's tooth out of the woodlands

which means what are we doing? what is it that keeps us at it? is it
the note that with all the terrible alterations the hot and cold
and in and out and however much more-or-less at the mercy at a
loss at the end of the tether we still have a marked declination,
a pulse in the roadline, a vocation towards purpose and probably
capable, of. Or quite simply
you do not become a factor of the destruction of Britain
because, oh obviously

(stroking the hairy quarters
of some dog, passive on the lawn, who could have known
or warned anyone what the extension of love involved?
that it cannot be had for a song
or a quick distraction in the colours but constant grind
incapable of holiday whatsoever because no one is going
to complete the self in this field where too much
is to be had at too postponed an offer, set forward and
elsewhere, secured on the loss borne by those people
not seen or thought of, which the music is raising and
drawing closer at every minute / a song is minted
much higher than promissory trellis, and in this hope
I ventured once, groping in the dark, and burnt my hands
on the most amazing things.

25.   [*Valle de Antermont*

O my hands hurt and the man in front
just trod on a wasps' nest so the situation
now involves ducking and places a quite new emphasis
on the "process of ageing" not to mention
the increment of association. This would never have happened
if I'd stayed where I was.

Where I was it was
snowing and there were
steam locomotives queuing
quietly at dawn and nothing to say
what a completion might look like.

Where I was was
where I hardly
began to be.

Then let us go back and try again, this time treading
with some forethought   where the grass is green
broken circle   we file down   under "A"
to our adolescence   our meeting-point.

26.   [Seiser Alm

I shake with the gifts brought to me
to my very doorstep

they mean trouble
as everyone of course
acknowledges, no "dream" ever
rivalled an actual table
a lemon-tree, a glove,
my hand on your shoulder

and here I am in this exquisitely disarranged
open-air art-show waiting to be informed
what to feel next
from you from me from Hector Berlioz
number twenty-six: a very quiet sunset
and a very noisy funeral.

Waiting also, for the next phase of waiting
for the cold wind and dehydrated soup
which we all take as we grow older.

Waiting for what you say, what you bring
into the air
      "So Count Leinsdorf
abandoned himself contentedly
to the enjoyment of his allegory, the
vagueness of which stirred him, as he
himself felt, more intensely than
anything definite could have."

27. [*Langkofel*

O my head spins and the man in front
just trod on the whole spread
I'm breathing, the curved air…

Where does it get you being
a beautiful boy with a stiff prick in 1956?
It gets you to the top of the mountain with the rest of the scouts.

Meanwhile the soup
has boiled over,
this inflationary phase
relaxes and hopefully
the misty pinnacles
threaten no more
as the dead rub their eyes
and ask what time it is.

28.   [*Valle de Antermont*

After which to fall howling into life step by step
the secret risks under every stone we have come thus far
and you don't understand and no one ever will how vital it is
that soon this whole table will darken and be forgotten
while we sit and walk around elsewhere. There is no cause for alarm
kindly get on with your work but nevertheless something is coming
out of the sky into the open air we so rarely inhabit it falls down
across the wooden huts and pine trees across the electric toasters half
the radiators in London spring into life once more and people
are standing on carpets murdering truth. Which recovers.
With some help, and isn't that up to us? Isn't this
what is left of twenty-seven cosmologies while the reels and wheels
grind over and on and I'm far too busy to be important –
call out the dogs, call out the entire office,
forward and upwards to life in the crystal blocks.

Part IV

29.   [*Pesciera*]

Though really I don't (oh I float, I can float!)
understand how it is one person can
become so absorbing I never have (shoals
of tiny fishes pushing between my fingers)
it's as if we should be able to do without
that special substance and of course we don't
it is so hot I'm sweating on the water.
We heard the call: leave the mountains,
tend the fields. Now we have
water and town, intellect and desire. I
float about, I row a heavy wooden boat
into the harbour for food.

If we go around lighting little flames
in an exposed area littered with old furniture
we must expect to have
domestic conflagrations on our hands...

The bread is cheap and good and after dinner
I'll talk or write to you again calmly
I hope, to reach for that pitch where
what is honestly spoken is almost automatically
hope and comfort.

30.   [*Via Appia Antica*

And after the spasm?
and the wider world? –
where are we now?
                        a littered field
what is it? what are we
left with?
           rubbish,
beautiful refuse of the mind,
possibilities, dead poets, monuments
to what? geometrical shapes on the grass –
whose tombs, what rubbish, what
perfected lives?

Mid evening on the edge of the city,
sound of traffic heading for the centre and back,
metropolitan trains, it is normal,
nothing shifts, elegant tombs
standing here and there like
an abandoned game of chess.

It is not what you need
decomposed *ersatz* of myth
except now
which will pass.

Travelled enough, the best minds
shudder at monumentality, there are no
best minds. And nothing is abandoned, we
'll try anything again as needs be,
to refold through and beyond us
the bindings of love, the lives
completed out of sight.

And we pause only briefly
on the perimeter "as though
burnt by acid" the countryside seeping
into the town at the end of each breath
our possible acts come floating towards us like
yes, like doves, white things
on a dark ground and what they say
is transmitted from the dead, such
wonderful rubbish.

31.   [*Catacomb*

It's all going on up there where it's too hot
for anything but anger, shall we fry it for lunch?
Our month's embroiling in hope and focus
has paled from lack of infra-red. We returned to the city
and here we are under the supermarket
where we don't belong. We tend to forget
that no access has been granted, no one
requires to know (it's no use whispering)
and anything we win from the days falls
straight back when we close our eyes.

But we don't fail, we succeed, which is
interesting and rather strange and seems to happen
mainly by default unless we just lack
an adequate reason for collapsing.
It is time to leave the garden to itself
for a while as it needs to be and think
our horned heads into a world if we can
find room for it out there in all that dark noise,
across the land, the social demand, and
nervous tension is what actually,
keeps me standing upright even in pitch dark
while the alarm clock in my chest keeps me gentle.

Lost generation of footsore schoolboys
subject to no one's power and nothing
lives beyond us…

Come up into the day you booked for.

Notes

No. 13, "D'ung aultre amer…" Incipit of a song by Johannes Ockeghem. "To love another would be deceitful, would be stupid."

No. 26, "So Count Leinsdorf…" Robert Musil, *The Man Without Qualities*.

VII

Poems, Peak District (i)
Macclesfield, Harecops

(1973-1978)

Poems from *Preparations*
written with regard to items of
William Blake, Poetical Sketches *(1783)*

First Third
(Blake 1: To Spring)

Eyes westward for the start:
simple courage, or tact, to *invite*
what already is the established
script of succession, called Spring
because it does come

and arrives in a lofty pavilion
of our tongue; its entire presence,
the distinct and shell-like edge
of who we are opens from the throat
onto a building city and a ready throne.

The island sings itself, the hills inform,
our eyes lift to your feet – Peregrine,
the falling bird, travels over the placer
bearing our vocabulary almost as a present
from all we ever could be: take it,

dress her (leaf), kiss her breast (rain)
crown her (light)

Climacteric
(Blake 2: To Summer)

Then the full depth of sky
flames at your nostril and the governor
rears overhead, monolithic as
it's a nice day and we stick to what
we wear and think we spoke earlier.
We are pinned in a sun-shaft: fall
forwards, twist the page as the man-
engine groans and shudders to a pause,
clear from Cornwall to York.

Indeed the die is cast, what
can we do but wear it,
entreat, bend, rummage in the
fragments and lie becalmed. The history
of the form we still are talks us out.

So enter the silver wire, risk beauty
and the offer on it, entire adequacy
bursting into its cone and turning
the bittern's shadow in our former years
on exactly this –

The star is nothing now, the day echoes
clear through water and over distance
protected by song.

Last Quarter
(Blake 3: To Autumn)

Of course it is not ours, laden with
fruit and daughters, juice throbbing
in the vein, gnats and mist on the windscreen
– "The spirits of air live on the smells
Of fruit" – not our November not substance
of our sight. And the fulsome act also
is a departure, and nothing we have yet read
can serve. Leaving for where we are and
turning into a phase of work while
the computerised electricity board
amasses its digits at the negative pole.
So as the year bears downwards we turn west
towards the highland zone, and let
the swallow go because he will,
accidentally omitting to post the invoice.

Blow Blow Thou
(Blake 4: to Winter)

& how soon after we know the limit of wish
at "he hears me not". Northern hedges
tremble, skin clings to silent rib,
sense retracts. The etymology of "window"
      ON *vndr* (silent *r*) the cpd *vindauga,* an eye
        of the wind, an opening for the air to enter…
becomes a problem; we bang our heads against
the mirror as if it were us who froze the tea,
as if we didn't anyway have a yearly increasing
price to pay for keeping warm indoors.
We are owed our meditations (preparations)
in the best stillness of our spirit, when modernity
barely clears the horizon and the off-season
closes the fairground. We stay put, for in movement
the top is faced, and now it is cold,
white, and very cold. The resulting
hesitancy (so far, and then back) is transgressed
in an offered community of act
where *got to* is chosen.   Only there
is the door shut so fast as to fly open
to the light inhering through the sky.
Everything after this is risk.
(Poor little wretch! that dealst With storms)

Care of the Body
(Blake 5: To the Evening Star)

We turn to particulars and it is evening.
The day outwits the year by the honest lust
of the first star at the corner of the road
indicating polar reaches of the heart
in fidelity; the species
gathers its address.

So, an evening bed
is not for sleeping, sleeping
is for flowers and breezes (evening
is for sale) – pluck a promise
from the darkening plains,
on the edge of the silvery wash

and then retire and the dream burns
on in the night, sight folded
back to crimson and maintained.

The Song Sung
(Blake 11: Song ("I love the jocund dance"...)

The sung where: a place
known to us, a fruit where
cliff and kin, keeping their distance
hang over us

The song when: a face
close to us, a coin where
stone and water outcrop together
beneath us

The Day Fishing
(Blake 14: Song ("Fresh from the dewy hill"...))

Pastoral distance runs into biological unknowns
at every point of literary history.

It will be held consistently through the book
that inspiration as breath is also fire, the mirror
along the tongue demands it.

Since the day was squeezed into a segment
by alchemists we have been coasting around
in a sea of particles somewhere between
pessimism and indigestion, O totally,
adrift, and what is the message that holds us?

Textual certainty: the further we come the longer
we go and all of our clog-wheels are rusty and slow

But somewhere we cut inland, somewhere at a
break in the tide and cleft in the shore
steered by a trade wind

Back to the town and all its glorious strangers.

Arbor
(Blake 15: Song ("When early morn walks forth"…)

The bell! the market! our affection
rushes out ahead of us
in the air, burns
as we topple the advantages in
all our honour and potter into the perfect tense.

Edward III
(Blake 20: King Edward the Third)

Come here and note the beginning of a day the gradual
emanation from the surfaces of earth to meet the sky
forming a construct in the air like a new truth
which was there all the time, not enough shed on it
and be where you are, England a beautiful silver-lit shade
the wing opening on her and what the nourished soul
bursts into we call fidelity, something to fight for
to guard the faculties and keep constant watch on the market.
And everything we are is called into this match, we fight
with open and with closed, guilt hesitation and fear,
there is a way of saying that what we seek to preserve
is the best that anyone can be, a wholeness of act
rather than us when we are this and that us when we are right
for the space we occupy here the strange breadth of it
is human movement against and towards, peace and war called
home and however contented we become we never forget,
and this is a trace of anyone's ordinary acts, that beside
the double dome around us and punctuated sky this personal space
is the cleft and battlement from which we boldly or not
defy the sectors, fight aggression without aggression for we fight
wholly soul forth into the risk calmly as we burn the circulars
(calmly calmly to let you know this is calm) and gather warmth
at the surface of extent where our gifts are stored
through night to proffer day into the usual place
and set us even on the ground where we can only be,
again and again to renew and enhance this space we know
by the grace of its limits where the sun rises so often
at that diurnal juncture, the very boundary of our completion
at any time never expands and never contracts and
cosmic terrors whizz through – we reach it at the pivot
of love and strife where the watch is set along England's
shores, and all her families.

Edward IV
(Blake 24: The Couch of Death)

So where is the population, and where is
the palace we built in the spring when we
knew who we were?

You're asleep in the other room. It's
very quiet here. A car passes outside.
Yes, we're continuing and the pause lifts:
we have never known what we are.

Our soul moves among us all
in constant formation, broken and
glowing at each shift of the huge powers
all over the sky and land, the dawn, the
price of fuel and the beckoning of
a visionary hand,
                      a hand that seas
incarnadine.

Every morning I get up and go to work
and one day shan't, without you.

Edward V
(Blake 26: Samson)

Strength is born of contemplation

and fear.

Fear more: fear giants and monsters,
fear snipers' bullets and falling bricks,
bedbugs, angels, Barclays Bank,
not home, not what you have
and are

and fear for.

A Song to Conclude
(Blake: The Ancient Bard Sings)

Delightful child, come here
And see the dawn, very
Image of fresh thought.
England is a beautiful
Silver-lit shade, the wing
Open on her and the heart-
land nourished bursts into
Fidelity. But foolishness is
An endless net and the
Inhabitable globe of feasible light
Remains the cleft from which
Our arrows fly freely,
Shooting and howling up
Around England's shores
And all her families.

Poems from *Untitled Sequence*

In a German Carpark

I trust in the heart-work it becomes
a steady and calm series like adding
the alphabet together, thick stones and
thin stones one after another,
the avenue, the plains.

For the words spoken among us
are still cooling in the sky
and the lights go out
letter by letter, each claim
dies as day folds in.

Black windows, and the depot lamp.
And, really, not such a big night,
not so strong and not so dangerous
hardly worth traducing, leave it
alone, to work its own passage.

Night of thieves and military acts,
we are parked here. Lines scored
on the concrete simulating stonework,
fooling no one. Keep on adding
A to B and the world is ready.

Bunker Hotel

So it should be quite easy now
or at least simple, to slide down
into a whole compendium of places
all at once and remain too dazzled
to locate the route and render yourself
quite incapable and have to be guided
sometimes up rickety stairs to where you sleep.

It's also quite exciting
staying in a hotel without windows.
You could really work here: you could
steer the whole bunker into victory.
The varieties of reflected light
suddenly seem a paltry affair to this
concrete corridor and threadbare carpet,
the tiny, empty, bar, the porter in his
alcove with his accounts. The spirits
that inform us enter through wires, we
listen with closed eyes. The rest
seems merely a promised thing, and
any person is ten times their promise.

We speak of love and point
to the nearest blank wall
and the rest is extra,
deserved, and won, but extra,
my own love of you, and you and you…

When all that was damaged was the map itself
of what lies between us.

Is This Düsseldorf or Kiel?

Is it street-lamps or dawn? planets in the trees
I can almost hear the foliage brushing
under its vaulted courses and beyond that
lights in the kitchen opposite come on.

The room absorbs energy. The further
indices: stars, blood, are carried
equally off with the cruising night
and only the real edge and sheen of
metal stirs, and patches of cloud
cross the bleached sky, as flakes of rust
fall into the garden. Denial and
praise, the cold touch of stone
at the path's edge is not now
my source of you.

So you see there is no solution, this web
of tensions is what we are going to live in
into the future; to talk of breaking it
is to damage more than us. It is also
what we act by, and with, raising
messages to the ends of the earth, holding
intact each working space. A spreading
light moves to the land's edge.

Where a ship is always waiting.

Wetton Mill New Year's Eve 1974-5

The patches of white rock on the sides of the valley float in the frosty haze, mastering the darkness. Like floating verses, like verses of songs which move from one story to another, and follow you around. Amazing grace in the freezing dark. And the songs say that death is a beautiful thing, like a floating stone, like a thin coating of frost and moonlight on limestone (*rilievo schiacciato*) or Orfeo's despair in little repeated choruses, choirboys singing and dancing in the side-chapels of 15th Century cathedrals by candlelight, without audience. A music that moves straight back home from any point, waiting to be linked into another music, that seeks to know, and will never relinquish the quest for enlightenment. The light has departed from everything except the stone.

* * *

And again those bright calculations under the hill
where love descends as total governor
demanding the closure of the circus in the sky for ever

and again that trace of acute sense spread over the townships
to which love is a source and cardinal, marking
the whole band across the sky for future reference

and again that pearl of inalienable truth set
into the cortex, match-head at the end of the vein,
sighted with such rigour and ignorance. But sighted.

* * *

Snowdrops and crocus in the grass,
marks of the year's spring
traced on the ground, leading us on.

Day's spring is a splash of frying egg
and eternity's cubic fluorite crystals
the colour of Madeira.

And none of these is human enough
where spring does not arrive
but is brought, across a division…

The theatre we make of living,
quietly burning toast as the pale early light
from the yard crosses the window.

Birth Prospectus. The End of Us

for Michael Haslam

1.
Little spinner, you are too clever
and connect right over. That is
the end of you, lost in ardour.

Because of this (which is natural)
a surplus of energy builds into the
grass and the trees of the forest
elegantly describe themselves as
interim customers, under contract
to the oceanic combine. It all stays.

Or begs to as the level light
sinks in strata over the slight curve
of land, the stars edge past us
to shoot off behind and our azimuth
declines to the east of south. In ways
of which I have no understanding it is
an act of beauty to occur at all, the end
of us too.

2.
I operate with a lumpen-vocabulary
on a soiled page, clusters of day
to day. There's not an ounce in it,
but the tenacity and stored size
of a wasp trapped in the instep.

The modern produces this buzz, in-
tensed, the wing beats accelerate
until the body renounces its extero-
ceptor and shrivels, this we all know.

It began late in the alphabet and left
such a wake of drowning sailors
adhering like fury to a denial of
social intercourse, further and
further in to a black unbreachable
doubt, open solitude, a knob
of congealed blood.

Quietly,
reading the sun.

3.
Brought so often to vacuity the mind
trembles on while we shift out of it
and busy ourselves with flannel, less
than a kind wish away. This whole crevice
of delusion folds back on itself and
no one has any better space than
the details you find inscribed
on the walls of your cell.

You read the book,
you trace the call. All you know
is human kind, appointed
to the furtherance of love
so there cannot be a decadence
so our loss burns in the yard before us
to a residue of corrosive albumin,
old gold. You tap our distances.
All the innocent prospectors
scrambling on the interface
they all love and
justly to be alive, and say so.

4.
Gliding onwards, the difficult
things of the earth, and how we re-
learn to call them. This evening
five crows move over the garden:
leave it there as much
as to say that the earth
is as a matter of fact adoration
in its slightest hint of length.
Many have borne witness to this
and never known an instruction to
achieve or not make blobs and
scratches, in French *écriture*.
Designed to omit almost everything
we do if a hand can touch with such
sweeping gentility the upper of
any known thing.
Omitting to mention,
love, our ungainliness against
the possible gain.

5.
Or only that it is worth writing
for no eyes to see and as dully and
imageless as it comes (like a swallow
between the rustling and complaining
roots of our patience) as
flat as that, that living furthers.

6.
Further life, a clear and
darkened horizon, a lens
on middle earth and its
conceivable error.

7.
Birth prospectus blanked, a blood-mist
of over-stimulated cell energy,
a bipolar arc breaking into spasm
which destroys the child, has her
for dinner in the night without
a footfall without a touch of remorse.

And we insist, in spite, that the turn
of the sphere is at worst hopeful,
and still, living in the failure, metal
retakes its charge, foot down at the
bend no idea where we are bound to.

7A.

Apparelled in earth we hear the wing
beats behind us and don't turn.
The child dies into what we call birth.
We call it birth and furrow on.

§

Wing, petal or placenta, construct
of the oceanic tides, emissary
of a luminous world we fringe
in our absence, but in real light
know not; which was all to get us here,
here is on the ground.

§

We have two eyes, the bird swoops
over the lawn (black) and is gone.
There is no pathos in this provision,
no seeking in a fold of skin for
recoverable deposit. It hangs
on the dome, the rush and claw
of terrain, here is where we live.

§

And are securely wrapped in it,
being only where we can be;
the rest is a prosperous nation
of its own speech.

§

And also that we can't, don't,
shan't, and cease. That can only be,
to know everything. And you,
that must be you.

§

We in our partial and twisted end
to end time have the vulgarity
to debate various degrees of your
expendability from all sides while you
live an entire nation of observances
and suffer honestly your coronation
to the furthest reaches of the globe.
Your wisdom coheres your slightness,

§

Daughter, be still.

Still and White

Yesterday's paper
glows in the hearth,
friable and
almost air.

The news is behind
the heart, beside the lung,
the news remains, left behind
in the rush to quit.

So long studied, and
all of fidelity,
there is no else
where to apply.

Unconquerable page,
still and white, bearing
its own
exfoliation,

Really all my life is
blocked out from this telling
except by certain
"mysterious" cracks.

* * *

In what sense to "know" more than
acknowledge or refer to, the wrong
and its cruelty, so that

the void it creates is moved
gently to the front of our sight,
a window onto ruin.

The whole band is then held taut
across the forehead and rather
than bow out in disdain

if we raised our shoulders onto the
plane of event, a tension, in which we
are no more than item, could then

extend to the child a promise which
is more than verbal, which she recognises
at once as entire and textual

and if we do take on the hurt
it follows that we bear it
before us all the way home.

Some Pieces of *The Irish Voyages*

i   Sky blue and turquoise
       lichens on the stones
       and pockets of green-black fern
       in standing water.

ii   A tiny bird, a stone-
       chat on the sea wall.
       A spill of hard
       resonant flakes
       down the side of the air.

iii   Snow burns into the film of earth
       thrust by the wind into pockets
       and crevices of the promissory mass.
       Cold: traces of fern
       on the electric kettle.

iv   The path is lost
       among wet stones.
       What we called the doubts and
       cracks in the marriage were
       grains of fortune folded in
       our hands below the cliff.
       The sea takes
       up the light and
       casts it on the sand.

v   Huddled together on a rock in the ocean
       for an actual belief, a lost
       point. We walk again the thin line
       of scattered debris to where we are,
       with no mention of anything modern, no
       doors in it. And no other light
       but the light of our countenances each to each
       no other light in the whole island.

vi   Green ideograms on the white sand
       where horse and rider passed in the night.

vii   A wrought-iron cross bearing a polished disc
       over a lump in the grass.

viii   Remember us, ragged
       petally ghosts,
       slips of flesh that
       crumple in the wind,
       outspeaking stone.

ix   I am tired of the new words
       for the old fears
       and the narrow escape.

Essay on the East Window of Killagha Abbey

Uncertain and yet managing the journey,
able to return and tell, if only an echo
or shadow of what he had seen, what
he had seen through. He's up there on the
eminence now, telling it all. It flickers behind
him and twists back into time, and really what
's left? We pay, settle down, check knife
fork spoon, switch off the main light. He
persists. He won't have it any more closing
on its own vector. He shifts northwards
into the beam. We begin to see through him.

> Look, there is no such thing, no self
> country; you recognise your terminal as
> the heart-needle spins. There are points of
> light in the water of the rotting deep and
> you sail over on a frail craft smeared with
> currency as long as it holds. Then you are set
> forth into love where the contraries touch
> in closing distance, which ends us.
> Surely the rising sun is constant, it is
> our postmark as we walk again the thin line
> of gathered debris to where we are.

Telling-it-all, which is only another and
complete departure from here where nothing
but the skeletal body remains to be said,
hardly worth an ear. Truly the flesh
is blown off him onto the east wall, the map
writhing in the heat cuts perspex panels
across the heart-space, following the vein,
purpose burning blue to the final signature:
green ideograms on the white sand, where horse
and rider passed in the night. Mythoi
burn across the earth towards us

and arrive to be taken by the arm:
a process, not a residue or a fall but an actual
trade. Orange and blue-green lichens spread
over the stonework. Such is the journey, wall
to wall, ground in, intercepted at truth.
Night by day the cavities in the graveyard
transmit their messages across our workspace.
We stand at the entrance, a tree of petal flames
in front of us through which the sky is this
and that, darker and lighter than it was but always
parcel to the furthest wish we are completely
determined, to finish.

Gallarus

O sweetest scholarship love-tasks, to restore the errors in the transcript, to reinstate the cracks under the gloss paint, rebuild the house into ruin. For it is complete, ruin, and poetry stands in it, fully housed in the ramshackle shed, the dry-stone oracle bridging a sea cleft on the west coast of Ireland, holes in the walls, mud and straw between the floorboards. Poetry squats inside it with scabs on its face, waiting for news, wine, "inspiration", distant gunfire, moonset. Star through cell window, the person dispersed, scattered and re-integrated, magnetised at both poles, lost and found. Photograph of a ghost as a column of warm air on an infra-red plate. Solidifying. Living in ecstasy, waiting for the milk-star.

Canzon

If you will trade me for constancy I
will seal the compact with my whole
expression, my figure etched in the
die my life sunk in the eye leaving
nothing behind, not a trace. If I were then
given fully might I be complete, un-
merged or hard bound enough at least to be
a spoken fact before the child of our love.

Company
(for Derek Bailey)

1.

Starting from everything we could possibly have been doing a line tends out in the morning hurt, a sustained spark. A quiet and lonely thing in the grey forests of the world.

As far as to the fringes of beyond us a lamp on the horizon scores its intentions as inexorable, starting to turn towards us. Electric or elastic tension starting from an arrow-shot. Listen, it wavers and dies.

The path closes behind the light. And it multiplies and disperses, opening into a spread, an enclosure, a bed-sitting-room in the mountains. We are drawn towards it and cowboys and falconers turn to look at us as we pass by and the moon sets before us and hermits leap out of tombs in the cliff face and read us treatises of love and death, and up there on the far plateau is a plate of light, spreading…

The broadening of the world in our absence, affection hovering over the well squawking with hunger while we sing and fade.

Techniques for keeping the flame alive, the sound in the air against the inertness of matter. Continual praise, the faithful orisons every day in tiny chapels on remote Irish headlands, cupping the fire or burning the flag…

Wound music. And the vast solitude in the echo, threading the streets looking for a partner, the spaces between the musicians full of invisible fire.

Trance music, moving towards and away from the world. Abrasion and salve converging. Forming a company.

2.

Carefully, feeling the way, like a slug, testing the ground with our horns, retracting and proceeding, and, as the day gathers force, opening out, breathing in a wider and wider landscape. The full and chiming biomental sphere, bright with trees and mice and nesting orioles…

Song at the pitch of hunger, the blackbird in the late evening, breaking his time across the stones of the valley by the slight rain for the truth of it, lost for the furtherance…

This "we" is no more than a trust, and an audience.

And the mice, what about the mice? They are gnawing holes in our hearts,

To let through the light.

3.

Through the heart-holes of our corpses when we turn the handle we witness a clown show,

a mime, a puppet theatre, in dim flickering where Laurel and Hardy get trapped in all the fine objects we've invented and fall over in tears.

The tears are real: a dew on the lens, which casts our vision like a fly's all round us to the world

in bits, in clarity,
we recognise the graceful stupidity
of our survival. The simplicity
of our complexions.

4.

When you speak to the trees
the leaves drop off.
You collect feathers.

Slowly something, a feather or a leaf, flutters down
and hits the pavement with a deafening crash.
A defining crash.

The shock, and persistence,
of sheer gentleness, the
unrelentingly human, the
cutting and stroking edge
of anything that's sheer

And surrounds us
and breaks through all our delays
as waving logs we drive full-tilt into the snowbank.

5.

As if your life depends on it?

Play as if our lives depend on it.

Not on its urgency, but on its being there,

a bastion of sound between us and wrong,

cohered by speed.

Note: The poems of Company *1-5 and* Toy Music *(below) derive from twenty such poems in* The Musicians The Instruments *(The Many Press 1978), which originally derived from the music of ten improvising musicians taking part in* Company Week *in London in May 1977, convened by Derek Bailey. This work has existed in many different redactions, each one moving the texts further from specific engagement with the event and the persons and attempting to unite them sequentially. I don't now acknowledge the individual musicians for fear of disrespecting those named in the pieces I no longer include, but retain gratitude for their impulsions. All of these redactions remain equally definitive.*

Toy Music

We are caught in a commerce
And wring our fingers:
The nurse is terse
And the gypsum lingers.

The examination
Is only a game
That starts at the end
And begins again.

So play with the toys
That reflect the stars
And suffer the noise
That bites at its bars

Like a broken clock
In a school of music,
Smiling back
At whoever views it.

Father has locked
In stone and bricks
The key to the clocks
And covered with sticks

The hole to the heart
Secure from rival.
We're waiting to start.
Method: survival.

Polecats' Song

What is wrong
With sitting long
Waving your tongue
At a passing song?

What is right
About staying up all night
Trying to fight
The absence of light?

What's the matter
With the hurried hatter?
Toast on batter
Would make him fatter.

What's amiss
With an honest kiss
Against the hiss?
Think about this.

What is so
Wherever you go
Is how you know
The glow of snow
Will never leave
The back of your sleeve
If you believe it.

Note: In the narrative from which it is extracted, this song is sung by two polecats, North Polecat and South Polecat, in a clearing in the forest on the Equator, to the accompaniment of small percussion instruments.

VIII

The Llŷn Writings

(1977-1998)

1. Sea Watches

I. Cliff-Top Annuals

1
Almost there we hesitate, and turn, high on the soft
Edge of Britain, to view the whole story: the sea barking
Up both sides of the peninsula to the point, top
Crest of land, pilgrims' goal or final extent
Of a life's coming and going called together when
There is after all a focus, an intellectual love.

2
That we shall not reach today and is quite
Obviously already all we are, and warns us
Not to postpone the issue for a quiet bed
Or any other future. The car gentle as a hearse
Takes sunken roads through fields that carry
Sea-glow, yellow scatter, proud, tall and thin.

3
Grey concrete road down old stream cleft
To the bay, white sand, slab sea, guard dog barking,
Chug of generator engine at the beach shop:
Unchanged items. And the same us with different
Surfaces, year after year we are here again.
Alternatim to eternity, if our love is proven.

4.
Wide and bright sea spread in the great daylight,
Dividing behind to the isolated fires that warm us.
Stone shore where the light breaks. A marble boulder, red
Veins in the white mist, smooth watery surface
Half sunk in grey sand, so hard and clear a thing that
We are put to guess what harm we could be in.

5
Shifting slow and vast extent viewed from the cliff
Top, so large as to raise questions talking
Of the whole of a life not just now, and never to stop
Forgetting the recent deceits of resentment.
So calm and clear a thing as not to be around when
The earth is lost to those of mere power.

6
Closed earthlumps that collide together and fight
In the dark we seem, and the seeming harms us.
Yet we retain moments of casual success as we feed
The family in the caravan at a meal-time close to others',
Hid from the noisily munching ocean that
Thrusts behind my ear like a jewelled hat-pin.

7
Pyramids of light flickering on and off
On the sea surface, wedges of light, and us walking
Back to sleep on the abandoned table-top
Like the horizon's dinner. But instrumental
Day and night for intercourse of love and pain.
The hills bend their heads to the hollow, homely hour.

8
Half crying sea birds above us in the night,
The constant breath of wind and the farmer's
Wife comes out with a little torch to feed
The geese. Baffled at yet another mother's
Triumph the sky stamps its foot and raises its hat
And charges out to sea rattling its tin.

II. Sandlogged

1

A double track, a furrow in the groundswell
From the house down to the sea, a corrugated breach
Between fields of sheep and wheat, down to the great sink.
Lined with hawthorn, bramble, blackthorn, bent
Gorse: Look how the wasps wallow in their graves,
Bathing in ripe blackberries, drinking their blood!

2

On either hand the seething fields and the full sea
Like life and death (though which is which)
And stark on the margin between them crowds
Of people, blurring over the sands like brush-
strokes, shouting and lying. You'd never believe
The cadences, the successions of fall.

3

Fields of wheat and pasturage halting at the level
Sea, where the fish shoals move in and out of reach.
And the beach crowd fills the bay with truce flags, pink
Blue and yellow, choral energy, manes iridescent
In the sunlight. And voices over the crashing waves,
Calling us out to face our enemies, gods of food.

4

Beyond the pleasure zone the cormorants skim steadily
Over their door to success crying at a pitch
Of failure (this is the solitary walk between crowds
On the clifftop pastures) and those crazy birds rush
To and from their island capital, unable to deceive
Themselves out of constant pleasure, constant thrall.

5
Souls of the crowd chorusing like a bell
Of a clifftop church, clear over grass and rocks, each
To each extolling what we have and like to think
Even despair is a shrewdness, a gesture meant
To spread the load. But, *das einsam,* ah, he craves
Gem-like contraries in the wrack, eyes in the dark hood.

6
Cooling and getting hungry we slowly
Walk back along the long sands carrying beach-
balls, blankets, fish-nets, binoculars, crabs,
Two small girls, books, towels, pebbles to keep, brush
And comb, bucket and spade; we carry what we conceive,
We carry carrying, being carried, fear and fatigue, we carry it all.

7
"I was ill, I couldn't sleep, I couldn't tell
What I was doing, so I came to this remote stretch
Of coast to fight the falsest persons I could think…"
And the sea this evening calm, a seething tent
Of blue-grey down smeared salmon and thick with caves.
Duplicitous, occultly tumultuous, screen of blood.

8
Almost asleep in the thin walls, undeliberately
I send my soul out like a night bird or a witch
To fly over the dark roads now silent of cars
And kids, skimming over the fields and black bushes
Over the white line that the wild waves weave
To settle on the headland, with your moon I fall.

III. Sailing, Sailing Away

1

Cold and wet, shout out the morning news:
No unit of life's pain will be eased this day
Or by being out here. The wind and the rain
Comb the field grass and units of time past
Rattle in our heads like pellets. Then space
Partitions and new warm promises crackle in our beaks.

2

Hell's Mouth. We scuttle across it in pairs.
We are traders: offerers, losers, those who
Claim to be givers are the worst of all.
Vast arc of shore where the sea never stops
Pounding the sand, days nights and years away.
Drear infinity. We cluster back to the car and lunch.

3

Next we stride across acres of jagged wet rocks and bruise
Insteps through the rubber. We get across the bay
Limping from shelf to shelf. There are departments of pain,
I suppose, and stores and garages. Our memories are massed
Against us but we slip them by in the trusty face
Of the arched instant. The car engine sputters into ticks.

4

Up and down the small valley the slow soft airs
Come to and fro, the stream purls and slips through
Old manganese workings: here and there a ruined wall,
Black holes in the valley sides. A stone dropped drops
Through nothing to distant water. And remember, far away
From here management decides hurt. Thank you, Mr Punch.

5
Why do we roam the land as if finding and lose
Everyone's time? There is nothing, but a grey
Gravel, a lost horizon, and a winding rain.
The slightest construct of care would cast
It all behind us like salt as we turn to face
A clearing sky to landward and a truly human fix.

6
Out on the open sea in a small boat there's
Suddenly nothing that isn't obviously true.
The sea top is a shining cloth. A dying gull
Sits in it like an old man in an armchair, props
A wing on the meniscus and joins the lift and sway,
Slowly giving himself to the one truth for ever head first.

7
The boat glides up the cove and grates on the loose
Stones. We mount the side cliff and wind up the day
In wet shoes with fishscales in our hair. The fisherman
Winds the boat up the shore, grinding slowly past
Heaps of marine detritus and wrack, to a safe place.
The light is almost gone. The sky curtain stirs and leaks.

8.
Lying dozing late in the dark caravan, slight glares
Of lighthouse in a square on the ceiling every few
Moments, I send my consciousness out like a gull
Over the sea, away from the wasteful and gaudy shops
Of this life, away from my own tricks, indeed away
From the untruthful land. This dark divided church.

IV. Forth Out and First Back

1
Driving up the coast road alone, a strange sense
Of being already dead, suspended where I pass
Over hills and through villages, incapable of harm
Or good to the people. My wish is neutral of course,
Provisional good sincerely upon unknown heads.
At a bad cliff corner the family leaps in my throat.

2
And on up the side of North Wales to a town
Selling death back to the lost people from industry
As coloured wrap with glims of distance, toffee stick,
And here-we-are-before-we-were-again (pastoral) that slides
Off before you can suck it. So buy quick and go,
On by the cool straits, the calm woods, and railways.

3
A country is no one's playground, no one's absence.
The mountains gather towards the sea, touched with thin grass,
And the coastal strip sweeps under in a curling arm.
A country must be sure to be more than a pause
In a life or a year. Pecking at the scattered threads
Of a remote history, small salt crystals stick to my coat.

4
The car park at Bethesda is roof height on the first crown
Of the valley side. I get out of the car and am instantly
In a large arena of lost industry, black scarp, headline nick:
Broken backed mountains and the sky stock full of clouds slides
Constantly over. Fears and promises flicker across us glowing
Like shadow angels. We cleave between. Oh razor-sharp days!

5
Returning shortly to the car park at Bethesda the tense
Distance of farms and cottage rows on high shelves
Of the slate mountain, hit by the late sun, calm
And empty one senses an enemy. There is a torse
In the pastoral disc, an incision at the quarry beds
Letting through the dark. The day's width offers a groat.

6
There is an exit, a return. The road leads down
Into the valley, up and over this shifting, sliding geography.
The car shoots past chapels and fortresses as quick
As a thought about where the enemy bides,
The false person I wanted to have a go
At. Cloven hillsides and the gulls flying sideways.

7
Nothing but evasion. I am in the men's
At Tudweiliog, a tourist pub, thinking alas
I cannot define the root of harm without alarm
But I'm glad we sit together at the tables among gorse
Bushes children's swings and flower beds,
Brave harmony, from heaven's blast remote.

8
I squeeze my eyes and I'll blow your house down
Says the wind banging all night with blustery
Threat the tin panels of the caravan I'll kick
It to bits says the wind and life it rocks from side
To side and my mind is miles away in the still slow
Garden at the roots of the wind the voicing maze.

V. Performing Dogs

1
Triangular field, pointing out to sea
Like an open beak, grass crown, feathery cliffs,
Grazed thin, scattered with white flecks:
Feathers, wool, thistledown; I walk you this morning
End to end wondering how a new day won't reach more
Than an inch or two forwards or raise its head above shame.

2
So hive off on an excuse. Green road, hilltop ruins.
The solitary on the top track, fearful of farm dogs,
Pauses before the uninhabited, holiday cottage.
The wind is everywhere, the house another family's
Mindstock: childhood coin and wedding gift and
Promised past. Curtains closed. God save us from death.

3
Or the great shore empty as far as you can see
Curving away, the waves grinding the quarried cliffs,
Roaring into shingle. Difficult walking, slow steps
Across the wind. Which if it led or were pointing
Anywhere would be a happy place, if the stones bore
Down the chute and rattled into boats under a trade name.

4
At Nefyn the travelling circus chimes and spins
The same old tale with its ropes and its dogs
As any other twisting mirror: that age in age
Out we detest what we become, and were, we hiss
And bark in the big pointed tent, we can't stand
Our ends and gladly hoot a fearsome breath.

5
God save us from half-life, it is also necessary
To note, sitting on the rocks eating fish and chips
At twilight, on the edge of the great curve, six
Mile bay watching people zooming and spinning
And riding the meniscus to what point or
Purpose we don't know, but working all the same.

6
To their renown, for each is a space that wins
Its own centre, to which you and I are just dogs
Perhaps, just a circus game on the far edge
Of visibility. And some spin quietly and miss
Reward, but turn an acre of inhospitable land
Into a terraced garden, richly flawed, flowered, brief.

7
Love is where centres meet, I think I see,
Gathering mushrooms at twilight on the high cliff
Pastures, those white domes glowing like clocks
Here and there on the dark ground and the dawning
Sea light over my shoulder. And they don't just grow or
Gravitate. But beam and echo name to name.

8
Lying awake at night, my focus climbs
To the caravan skylight, barking dogs
At the farm, slowly, like old age
Mounting into a mortgaged tower, to kiss
The ghost of distance behind a shadow hand
And watch the sea, and stick there, weathered leaf.

VI. Eaten Zero

1

Sometimes pasts are satisfied. It's like
Sitting on a café terrace over the deserted shore
In the evening sunlight sipping coffee in the thin
Savoury smoke of a barbecue as the waves reach
And reach in white fuss the great length
Of brown sands, where no claims reside.

2

The man who runs the beach shop and café at Porth Or
Decided one year to stay open in the evenings
And run a barbecue. No one came but it was
A gentle evening of deep sun and enough wind
From the sea to ruffle one's hair and move
An empty cardboard plate across the table.

3

It was a quiet summer, the concrete track
Bending down the fields to the pale shore
With no cars parked, no shouting, no one in
Sight but me and the man tending his beach
Barbecue which no one wanted and at length
Sitting motionless, staring at the incoming tide.

4

No sound but the beating of waves and the generator
Engine behind the shop chugging away, things
Of residual time worn lightly because
A long past means a sure future and twinned
To the extent beside us is a sense of love
Where centres meet and agree to become unstable.

5
And the Centre of Anything is a Hell of Lack
The Mouth of Which is a Wide Shore
Feeding Generosity into a Rubbish Bin
Called EAT ME: a Country where Each
Has his own Centre and Swells there in the Strength
Of Winning, a Hole as Deep as it is Wide.

6
These Spenserian periods passed before
My mind as I sat there thinking things
I cannot now recall, and through my binoculars
Distinctly saw my father in a large winged
Armchair floating on the sea about half
A mile out, heading north and singing Handel,

7
"Gentle Morpheus, son of night…" so like
A winged deity crossing the sun's red core
As it descends to the sea our senses move in
Traverse to the world's pull, that downy peach
That gets us in the end, and surely a strength
Of purpose survives the lapse of will, a sleeper's guide

8
Across the drowsy shore where centuries before
Hundreds landed daily, peasants merchants kings
Barefooted and lost, ghosting the outer rose.
The man in the white coat went and turned
The engine off behind the shop. The lamp above
My head flickered in the wind like a palmer's candle.

VII. Eight Seaside Chapels

1   *St Beuno's at Pistyll*

A place where people can shelter from one dream
In another, the finished dream, the walls hung
With medicinal herbs, the light dim and opaque.
Here you could silence the press and begin to address
Directly the separation of desires. Through thick
Stone walls the fruit trees rattle like the sea.

2   *Llangwnadl*

Where travellers rest. I sit in the silence,
Doing and thinking nothing for as long
As I can bear it. Triple aisled light in which
I lose my name. But my stomach hurts, my nose
Bleeds, isn't that enough self for today or
Anyone? The lark turns, rest your shadow and belief.

3   *St Merin's Church*

Grassy humps in a clifftop field. A sunset beam
From the sea spreads through the stalks, among
Nettles and cow-parsley faint turf lines, dim shape
Of nave and apse. Here I lay my self crest
To rest, I hope, and crowned commoner O quick-
ly, turn north, where distance makes free.

4   *Bryn Celli Ddu*

Gentle Orpheus, son of light. You are the sense
At the centre, the mechanism through which the long
Beam passes at morning and evening, the bridge
Across the heart in the darkness that grows
Daily finer as the body ages and at the core
Of which a line of light writes final relief.

5   *Llandudwen*

What is that relief? O wait and see, the cream
Of liberty is not to know, the prize is the sung
Response echoing in a stone room the shape
Of a person built over a grave. Cornered. So dress
Your anxious head proudly in the thick
Brightness. Be that engine which learns to be.

6   *Capel Anelog*

And this site of which nothing at all remains
Was where the final question was asked on the long
Pilgrimage to Bardsey. "Did you remember to bring
The tin-opener?" or "Did you really expect the rose
To be an inner answer to unwelcome law, or,
If now is almost time isn't it far too brief?"

7   *Ffynnon Fair*

Now is over, over the hill. The waves scream,
The waves crash. Here on the brown rocks hung
Over nothing, here at the impossible landing, cape
And hood gathered close, distance is set to our best
Sight –for we saw people prepared to stick
To their truth. The island lies before us on the sea.

8

The salt raging within, the ravenous remains
Of the earth running in the vein, reaching the tongue
And bursting into courtesy. An everyday thing,
Far removed from the sickness and errors that bring
Every day of self to a weary and troubled repose.
Far away on the night shore the salt wings close.

VIII. Seawatch

1

Sunk in a grass hollow in the cliff, my station,
A grave green chair. The sea is blue green white,
The sea is grey and folds, the sun is split
And the clouds are a fire. Truth is never
Quite the same, its quantum cracks but
Like a three quarter moon hands down adoring stead.

2

Which is a pulsing certitude, a gently
Wavering assurance. The sea throws
Silver coins at the rock. The whimbrel, that shuns
The sight of man, passes down the coast
And a heron follows, for if we are still
We are welcomed, if we are one we are met.

3

A wind up the coast, scent of a milling nation
Traverses the brow, so calm a bright
Disposal is for a moment carved a bit
Above his hand and for a fraction the ever
Fractious lark curves over his head. He says I am but
A shepherd of the plain, without ambition, later dead.

4

Stuck in the middle of life, that ungently
Grinds of ruin while the sea is a knife thrown
Across the earth. This evening it darkens
From grey to white and draws at what cost
I don't know the light from the fields until
Swathed in shade I let it go for sixpence net.

5
My O my I thought I had a notion
To validate with truth this brittle
Spending, at every smile and every bite bent
Closer to the ground, shifting the weather
Onto my back and wearing like Canute
A crown of clifftop grass and soil all the way to bed.

6
Now it is the middle of night. The empty
Waves continue to knock on the land, down
There. Still some light clings to the sea and the floss
Flickers on the rocks. Human will bearing its star-crossed
Ensign haunts the black interior for good or ill. Spots
Of rain on my coat, are you with me yet?

7
And it will be good. The clouds open: a true equation
Dominates the eastern sky, bright Queen of it:
The shadow of the earth rises across the firmament,
Proving us truly here. And working hard, wherever
Some portion of true hope lies open in the cut
Of a single life (knife, wife, strife, head).

8
When I get back to the caravan it is twenty
To four. Stumbling in the darkness I hear a moan
Of blame, a sleeping urge to die and quit this mess.
But there is no speed at all, no wily ghost.
I tuck the blankets round me heavy with dew,
Closing on sea moon and all, but alive in you.

2. Six Prose Pieces

St Merin's church, 7:30 p.m. 2nd October 1977

A chrysalis clinging to a grass stalk. Foundations, lines of shaped stone, green granite sunk into the turf. There was never any final sermon, advice, lesson, instruction – the truth was on its way to the boundary of the sphere and, as it were, intercepted here, and speech was made possible. Marking the ground, leaving a grassy hump in a field with traces of stone edging. The sun gets under the cloud on its way down the sky and will soon settle into the sea, without the hiss heard in heroic times. The peninsula funnelled human souls to a final stadium, of which there is nothing left.

No oracle. You could hardly commit questions to a grassy hillock with a lump where the altar used to be. Answers are not to be expected from a texture of nettles, brambles, and autumn grass stalks. Indeed it is very difficult to live on this earth and you should avoid getting stuck in all funnels except the one that leads to the realisation of hope, the sundering shift to love and its reward. The ground is pitted with holes and people do not know how they got to be where they are; it is fruitful also to forget. Skin tremors on the brink of independence or fight the question-mark back to its cave.

And it doesn't matter, that too will bury itself in time and be forgotten into a monument. A chrysalis on a grass stalk at the west end, sunset out on the sea and within this relic of a purposeful enclosure it becomes feasible to hinge on time as a progressing scan and welcome the faintest chime of reciprocity. We are not alone. Cheep, chirr, whatever is out in the darkness. Faint cries. Populations skimmed by love's edge.

St Merin's church, 7 p.m., 9th September 1978

The wren darts under the thorn and a piece of wind pushes a stinging nettle onto my hand and I hear you as clear as a bronze bell over the sea. We live for what we truly know, slight as it may be, letting go of time in gratefulness. All the green boxes are open and casting their words, a healing scent in the air, a slight recognition, a treatise on what we live for, entirely alone as a few drops of rain patter on my shoulder as if requesting my attention, and strike the open page, and refresh the stinging nettle.

These constantly made and re-made pacts, the gulls flying back to roost through low cloud, the eye sinking down the page in search of the earth's blackness. And a constant distant roar, sea or traffic, what difference would that make? A constant distant roar.

There is no lack of wealth but there is a lack of prosperity. There is no lack of ideas but there is only one thought on the ground tonight, that the person bears a radius beyond the earth, and everything s/he does is the literature of that nation and no other. The crown writes itself into the forehead and the whole structure stands squarely but awkwardly on a disavowal of superior understanding, balanced across the earth on comical tripods. And the thief makes off at dusk with the gain in an understood version, leaping the rocks, ringing the silver bell into hell's mouth. The drops increase, I shelter the page under my mack, where it is already night. The sun's lower orb stands in the pulpit again, the condition is inescapable. He burns in my face across the rain.

We don't add up to what we are, logarithms of grace.

St Merin's churchyard, 7:30 p.m., 9th September 1978

Hurriedly extemporised sermons in long grass are less than half the pilgrim's map, as it gets dark.

Get back to work, however ill you feel, prise the event out of inner sanctity until the ground opens ahead.

Poetry is such a personal thing, but meshing the surface into parcels of time and the edge glitters.

Break these trusts and it is a reign of terror: civil engineers conduce our lives, love is an official secret, ignorance is funny bliss.

The sun bears down on the sea, its royal road a narrow path across the wide sound, constantly changing.

Save us, sun, me, anything in this physical garden, from the automatism we die of, the unbeing we try not to wish.

A spring on the upper slopes of Mynydd Anelog, 11pm 6th September 1979

Stepping out of the bracken into a still circle and all those questions and urgencies mounting up for weeks and weeks disappear. Dry spring, scattered with stalks. As there is no reason to be here, there is no reason to leave, but only to sit in the grass in a circular clearing in bracken and open the mind's box to its own ends, free as the wind, to enter that state of children and old people, having all the time in an exact clearing.

Out there the sea is a dreadful confusion of directions with no boundary, horizon washed-out, a grey ghost in the wardrobe of the sky. Here in the image of protection, there is no need for advance.

Then if there were to be in someone's life a direct and "final" questioning or coming to a point, the shelter found under this bright bank says it will always be postponed, as long as there is any working format of hope.

The return to the main road will be a dream manipulation. Up here in the twiggy cirque it is wide awake and slightly chilly but simple and clear as it can't be on waged ground. For anyone, this winning light. The house on the horizon is called Mount Pleasant.

In a white van on the road outside the site of Capel Anelog, 11:40pm 6th September 1979

There can be very little against us except fear. Sometimes we can mend our errors in dream. I had an aged aunt who died when I was thirteen, before I had learned how to make myself welcome to her, though I knew I was a surrogate grandchild.

The sermons are muffled under tufts of yellow grass between slate-roofed stone sheds. Too many questions and no answers. If nothing occurs to you try occurring to someone else.

Push open the door of the dark cottage in the evening, enter softly, feel across the small room to where the old woman sits among her guardian furnitures, nodding half asleep in an arm-chair near the fire, take her hand, rouse her gently and whisper in her ear under the tuft of yellowish white hair, "Hello auntie, it's me, it's your nephew." Forgive her sudden tear, and her pretence: she had forgotten you were coming.

Rhwngyddwyborth, 6th September 1980 in a terrific rush in the middle of packing the car to go

Rusty tramlines carry us into the hell of resentment. To the end of a life signed with a list of dead factories producing nothing but their own smoke. Stupid work, O stupid focus while it is a beautiful morning it really is. O what a beautiful morning as if the sky and planet played bouncy-ball together, played any lived nonsense in bright intellectual ardour… "Put the table out," she says, "Put out the table."

3. Poems and Notes

(a)   (1982)

                                          fixed points in
succession, a chain of stations through the land,
tumulus on a metallic vein, hill fort on a volcanic dome
a processional sequence, that breaks
the disorderly obstructions to desire
and needs constant renewal – a well in the
valley, homestead under the hill, sermons
along the route... grave stone.
Gather up the silver threads in the rubble
that twine together to a gleam in the distance,
the world's treasure at its final section.

So it is from side to side the cloth of gold,
bright and dark with gorse and hawthorn
patchwork of farms and volcanic domes, thick
with fish and wheat and leading somewhere,
to a point, the roads sunken below
head height gathering closer and joining as
the land narrows, pushing towards the distance
or end, the island, the saints' repose,
the logical outcome.

(b)   (1983)

"The constant glow of light all round the horizon that bespeaks the presence of the sea".

Not through rich fields, but through fields of world to the rich point, is the good path.

Late autumn, the peninsula on the turn, about to become the winterland impossible for foreigners.

Humped shape of Bardsey on the sea, blotted out as another grey rainstorm sweeps over it.

Home, and the small head-glow round it, the working sphere of a life. Occasional lights in the windows of some of the cottages on the headland.

Rain curtain draws over the sea. The bitterness between the object and its image.

Sweeps up towards the mainland heading for Mynydd Anelog. The bracken slopes, St Mary's the erased chapel, the old woman living in a Nissan hut with about fifteen dachshunds, rope and wire stretched from shed to shed, vibrating in the shout of climate.

Porth Grwtheyrn, 21st August 1985

Yellow poppy, groundsel, carlin thistle,
Tangles of metal rope, rusted iron cogwheels
Sunk in sand. Slate, granite, aggregate, shale.
Flung wiremesh, rails, bolts, rivets, grills,
Axle, roller, valve, beam, plate.
Rustle of water down cliff-face. Hawk, goat,
Wild shore strewn with lumps of concrete.
Mermaid's purse, crab-shell, sand-hoppers, boat.
Plastic bottles, rope knots, tin cans, bird bones.
Oystercatcher, little gull, wave smacks gravel.
My hair a thin cushion against the stones.
Concrete telegraph hut, bits of copper cable
Still dangling from it. Monster ruin of loading quays.
My family, my lunch, my erratic, growling days.

A Repetition of Machado at Porth Grwtheyrn

The soul creates its own shoreline.

Mountains of ash and lead.

Little arbours of spring.

Porth y Nant

Exposed slate beds on the road down to the deserted village, grained vertically, blades upwards to the feet, and slippery where little watercourses spill onto the road.

Vast bent shore, heavy brown gravel crunched under the long waves.

Derelict machine-buildings in the cliff, bracken and bushes on decayed concrete terraces, big iron cog wheel half-buried in the shore.

Part of a wooden pier thrust into the sea from a concrete filtering-shed, sea pebbles falling out of concrete walls, shreds of corrugated iron, lichen, sea mulch, encrusted strips of copper wire lying on the shingle outside the roofless telegraph shed.

Wild goats on the cliff terraces, among the stone chutes.

One of the "ends of the earth". Passages to something else, something not-earth? A new language? A moneyless economy? Remote unvisited stretches of shore where people gather to launch themselves on the sea in bids to escape, in frail home-made boats hoping to avoid the eyes of coast guards and storms. Victims of other people's wealth. Desperate prayers, overheard by the sea.

4. Sea Watch Overstock

I.
Pieces, fragments, and notes during the writing of Sea Watches 1984-7.

So calm and clear a day you could turn and face it.
"My life is a mince of pain."

An earth tremor, a low rumble, the little grocery shop
at Rhydlios trembles and the tins rattle on the shelf.
We thought a heavy goods vehicle had passed by.

The farm: earthen banks separate the fields, the fields
scattered with goose feathers dung and mushroom stalks
to the cliff edge, furrows of white rock.

Hollow bone, porous tuff, delicately poised at the land's edge,
an industrialist's wink could crush all of it

Except the calm clear factor
spoken trembling in florescent stone.

* * *

Insane hilltop citadels on igneous outcrops,
heather filling the air with sweetness, stonechats perched
on swaying bracken fronds, patches of broken stone.

Sphagnum grasses, bilberry, insane citadels guarding
nothing, ravings of old men, actor-politicians,
the body preserved and guarded in the mountain-top house
pride of intellect, spasm of power

but wishes all shall fail thee.

* * *

Crossville Bus Company, Pwllheli 2458 or Caernarfon 4631
Route Llangwnadl – Nefyn. No go the circus.
Telephone box vandalised. A fritillary at St Mary's Well.
Buzzed by a RAF jet from Anglesey, the herd runs towards the sea.
Enter a bald woman leading a blind child.
"The world can only be served by the extraordinary" (Goethe)

* * *

Walking in the dark night, sea sky and land
confused together. Loud sea, dim, clouded flickering
of house windows… again an earth tremor.

> Nothing but the total glimpsed in facets
> and so the fish eyes in the tree
> the cars honking each other
> the ground thick with crossed bone.

Phil Davenport died this week in Mozambique.

No return, a single light ahead across the cancelled fields.

* * *

Waking in the night
I see the door-light through your hair.

* * *

A faint cry in the night, of sandpipers
through the steady wind and rain on the roof

> "brine stings the window" (B.C.)

The faint piping of oyster-catchers in the morning
like an aeolian machine behind the steady
rain on the roof and the wind on the corners.
Collect these details. Pick up your wages as you leave.

2. The Nightwatch Notebook

Texts prepared in 1989 for Sea Watches VIII, *then called 'Eight Sea Sunsets' and the whole work 'Shining Cloth', written at night out on the cliff or on returning to the caravan, in either case in the dark and not entirely legible.*

A. Saturday

Between insistence and response a sudden crack
a report of unknown origin
three-quarter moon low over the farmhouse.
Imperfect circle, perfect fear.

Saturday (2)

The world-sheet folding the line through time
as the arm turns inward for protection
against the spread [? against the speed]

A land hump black against the silver turmoil
that advances greedily but wants no reward.
A long stone against the star, a theory that works
that predicts reliably and declares its limits
and opens the door for the singers, who come every year.

Sunday (B)

Cloudy complicated sunset, patches and layers shifting
against each other on the horizon, a dark underlay
moving gently from left to right. Family of three choughs
on the headland, their hollow cries…
Sitting so still "a god might enter him" (Rilke)
Sitting so still an equation might settle on his arm
[…]

Patchwork of yellow cloud-wisps carpeting the sky.
Like a night watchman his freedom
disperses into echo. A proof might
pass through him […]

C

Cirque of rain clouds. What did we see today?
A wet moth clinging to a grass stalk.
An ancient church in a clump of elms.
Dark grey turbulent sea pounding the land, you
cannot love it "To love the sea is only
to love death" (Mann) still head
still head in the passage of weather.
A wet moth clinging to a grass stalk.

D

Light is torn from us.

To end up alone in a grim seaside bungalow
(homo fragilis) smelling slightly unsavoury
and burning the night light as the spray
hits the window in outer dark, harbour [?harvest]
of the extraordinary, eyes turned back in.

The horizon blurs, a flock of jackdaws black rags
against the sky, waiting, the dark will come in
and the light will go out, the light will be restored.

The strange animals in the head will dine [?die] together.

E

Never stop. Pause and protract. Withdraw
and separate. Lay items together in order
like a stone wall on top of a cliff, a spider's web
across a culvert. Listening for an answer.
"Death should not be a problem. If all goes well,
you pass into dreaming and the world vanishes."

Waves, wing-beats.

[F and G are lost except for one word, "lucifer" or possibly "dulcimer"]

H

Back at the caravan I switch the light on to a chorus of complaints.
I make myself some cocoa and read Chinese poems.
The "I" of these poems is always alone.

* * *

Soul tangled in wires [?violas]
serious, uneven, alone, not-alone,
worried about the gas cylinder
the fire that flowers at the end of breath
worrying florescence that might
suddenly go pop. And the head fire
fall into dream leaving everything unfinished.
A string band playing in the farmyard in the middle of the night?

* * *

Later the blur intensifies, moon over a black shed
glows like a light bulb through ice
thin strips of cloud in streaks across the sky
like something very fast photographed
but there is no speed. Waiting to pass
into company.

* * *

I settle comfortably into bed
by the small caravan window
onto grey field edge, black shed
and streaks across the sky. Legible,
heartening lines. Too dark to
write, I write. I fill the pages.

* * *

Filtered moonlight on the bed,
serious words, some of them,
about nothing much, the head of a tree
against the sky, a wish for sleep,
serious breathing in the room, like a lighthouse.

* * *

And so calm and clear the shining cloth
curvature of [?thought] which
passes, becomes cloudy, spreads
into a width of mental movement
also in [   ] of largesse for
tomorrow [   ]ing what we keep
when we lose the moon and the sea and the whole
[two lines written on top of each other]
saves terrestrial events from waste.

5 (a)
Mornings with a Walkman at Rhwyngyddwyborth (1989-90)

Never relenting creation of event, at the still point
in the world sheet, the whirling sheet.

Butterflies: blue, white, yellow-white, pale brown
dry thrift tenacious to the stone,
lichens: orange, white, cream-brown.

The city occluded in distance
but speaking clearly on a good wire.

A tern plummets to the sea and curves back
at the good moment / a cormorant hangs
on the meniscus and slides into the music.

Their rate of expenditure is low: we need them.
A whole flock of whimbrel.

Sea wind across his voice,
a paralysed man in a wheelchair on the sea-front at Llandudno
requests the Eroica,
all of it,
and insists on period instruments.

* * *

And all calm, all clear, crisp, all Cs.
Nothing can close this light,
passed on, generation to generation
it is everywhere.
And to bear it, to take it in hand
we make it a dark light
a light spread over
the dull gleaming acres of sea shifting
this way and that, a constant light
worked through the dark seething land
forking and crossing and burning at points
in living rooms and supermarkets
the light the line the lineament of love
longing for its lost spaces, the departing air.

* * *

A bush full of sparrows.
Spearmint by the roadside.
Small flocks of oystercatchers and one curlew, disturbed on the cliff top.
Martins round the black barn.
Dark cloud band, dark sea circled in light.
Ink sea.
Cloud band breaks at edges, grey theatre.
A light moving on the sea.
The farmer has died and his boat lies in its shed all summer.
Pleasure boats edge into the cove and sail away.
Gorse bushes clicking in the heat.
Massed clouds over the mainland.
If you abhor privacy, you abhor history.
Wrest the emptiness to the bone, play knucklebones with it.
Peace exists as an inner turmoil.
Two families of choughs on the cliffs.
How many more years, this holiday?
I get heavy and toil up hills.
Events are repeated a tone lower each year *[cantus firmus]*.
Corrugated sky, thickening towards the horizon, stretching beyond sight, streaked with light.
Cliff edge walks. Little flocks of passerines, the ordinary folk of these demesnes.
Clear pools in the rocks, gently rising and falling.
To be engaged with the world, from the house onwards – strictly in that direction, kindly.
On all our queries and requests for assurance the world maintains graceful impermeability
which keeps us going, year after year.

5 (b) Things Saying Themselves in Llŷn

Late evening at the caravan. Very quiet, slight wind in the bushes outside, darkening, faint plash and grind of sea beyond the field. I finish a bottle of rosé with some herb-flavoured Welsh goats'-milk cheese, which I take with a small coffee-spoon from a sheet of foil spread on a saucer. It signifies nothing, waiting to be written-over and replaced, as we work a life through in the earth's terms and are replaced. The earth continues, the sea keeps on breaking on the shore for centuries with hardly a shift of tone, storms come and go, the calm clock-like breaking continues. As everyone knows. I was fifty last week. Grey hairs dominate my headscape. I move slower over the cliff paths. Inwardly I am still that scowling child in the photograph, wanting to know what keeps it from the world, deeply resenting the tension between bosom and horizon. I sit in a corner and frown at all the light and horror that passes the window. It is a relief when the evening wraps all that away and settles like a blanket over the earth, and the sullen child reaches his rest: there is really nothing out there you need to know, but gently whispering grass and a white sonorous border where the land falls to the sea. For the moment tenable, held in trust for tomorrow and another puzzled, resentful infant being shown the sea and told to make the best of it. To return at fifty to the same distant coast, cleared at last of guardians.

(a) We climb Carn Fadrun and picnic on the curved ledge near the top among heather and stones and bilberry. A palomino pony comes over to share our lunch. Then we walk over to the area under the crest, sheltered from the wind, and stumble around awkwardly on the broken surface, tracing prehistoric hut circles and eating the bilberries. The children play at "estate agents" and sell the hut circles to each other.

(b) I walk round Mynedd Careg looking for pieces of jasper in the long grass of the old quarries.

(c) We buy a bottle of goat's milk from the two old women who live in the white cottage in the fields at Rhydlios. A small house standing in the middle of a collection of structures which have accrued to it over the years – two caravans, various sheds, pens and paddocks, kennels, fruit trees, a veranda, and a long earthen mound with goat bones sticking out of it.

(d) We walk over Uwchmynned towards the sea in the early afternoon. It's a very dry summer, the slopes grey and brown with thin grass, the tracks baked hard. It would be very hot but for the constant sea-wind. The vegetation on sea-side fells is always stunted, clings to the ground, constantly halted by wind and salt: low firm heather patches vibrating in the wind, gorse bushes clenched and bent. Dust falls from the ground as our feet break it at stony lips. We walk over the dome and down a small valley towards St Mary's Well, the slope increasing as we descend. We mount the far side a little, and stop to sit on a small rock outcrop and have our lunch. Opposite us a National Trust warden is strimming a patch of bracken near the site of St Mary's chapel, perhaps. Why is he doing this? In the base of the cleft below us are two wheatears moving around on the path, foraging and returning. Then we walk down towards the sea, a huge blue plane tilted towards us, Bardsey Island riding it in the middle distance like a roosting seal. We mount to the right onto the lip of the cleft and out onto the cliff shoulder hanging over the sea, then down the stone steps hewn at some time, by someone, in the granite cliff and finally onto a pile of rocks at the edge of the sea. This is where the well is, round a corner to the right, a long stoup on the cliff face in a lichened crevice with fresh water dripping into it and trickling out at the other end. One by one we creep along the rock ledge over the breaking waves to reach the spring. One by one we scoop up the water in a green plastic cup and drink it.

6. Sea Watch Elegies

The world-sheet breaks time open –
we are the waste some of which gets called back
curved back to surround random events like
a shell and offer the future a site
a line that stands, a long stone
against the star, a trust that opens
at its point – we are set again, we are
daily beings, yearly ideas, we stick.
The silver turmoil warns and arms us,
Passing home.

*

Cloud-sheet lit from below
orange bands
wind in grass
a man walking on the cliff
passing measures
serrated perspectives
accumulated lives
replaced persons
measured thoughts
choired land.

*

Like a night-watchman over the sea
a shepherd of the plain, not without ambition,
I stay still enough for the balance to rest its
question here.

———

Cirque of rain clouds to the west
a wet moth clinging to a grass stalk
questioning welcome.

Dark grey, turbulent sea, flecked waste,
quick moving air on the cheek,
hater of governments, lover of order,

world order – Answer it, this
mindless power. There is nothing to stop us
loving in peace and constancy.

———————

To end up alone in a grey house
grim grey seaside bungalow
a few gathered belongings
persisting with a work
of uncertain provenance or future
dark wine in the evening
a collection of tapes
without you I am nothing,
a leaf in the wind, an old fox
walking unhurriedly to earth.

*

Black rags cast in the
grey sky, light infused
with meaning
meaning take your stick and go
everything is busy without you
and so he does
to a room, and lights a lamp.

Wave noises through the walls,
black scraps cast on a page
defying passage.

*

Alone in the house
a green shelf over the sea
the few things needed
work to be done
certain and necessary
dark wine in the evening
various musics
always with you
wherever you are
set on earth.

Waves (dim things) pushing at the land
all night through the thick walls
begging, thoughtless begging
suddenly stops and we agree
we agree to live in a world
to live in a world
that does have worldness.

*

"As he lived so he died,
in mild and quiet sort"

like a night watchman or a
welsh farmer steadily

binding the fences
calming the afflicted

and his belief
in worldness.

———————

Leaving me alone or worldless
up here on the cliff top at night
everyone asleep behind me
stop pushing, roll over.

*

Two hundred and forty-fifth wave
rolls over, two hundred and forty-sixth
everyone busy elsewhere as I
watch nothing on purpose
and worth every second too, as the vast
haul of dark earths our core.

*

Night winds hugging the coast
and night birds sailing
over the ground-light, over the sea.

One lit window, over there, along the cliffs
attending day. Let me
too be nothing but

*

And never stop,
lay the pale stones together

on the edge of the land
that warn the traffic and
shepherd the stray
thoughts to their purpose.
Set aside a tenth of the profit
for the commonalty.

And at last, pale streaks across the sky
thin cloud televising dawn
ice crystals
float over the house
and black shed.

*

The grass again.

*

Always saying more.
There is no more to say
but to beg release and
order it down, world go
under, go under world
for we hate it. We've
had enough. Enough world,
enough wine. Enough cold/hope.

*

And creep into bed at last
into darkness in the day
and peace and closure in the plains of loss
and the pains of lessness fall.

7. The Translations of St. Columba's Sea-Watch

1.
To be enfolded bodily in a summit
Like the ink in a letter
And witness the sea's entire calm.

2.
The heaving waves riding the glitter
A continual singing
Addressed to a cause.

3.
The clear headland with its smooth strand --
We are established at the outer edge
Cloaked in brightness, smeared in birdsong.

4.
The local waves beating on the rocks
The [...][1] from the graveyard.

5.
Great flocks of birds hanging over the sea
Rare mammals[2] passing down the coast
Gods of food, gods of want, human centres.

6.
Watching the tide rising and falling, my
Back to the land, I attain my secret name.

---

[1] *possibly* shout, call.

[2] *glossed* whales

7.
And recognise my failings, so difficult to speak out.
A contrite or empty heart, watching the sea.

8.
Honour the movers of these powers --
Sky messengers, earth lumps, ebb and flow.

9.
Read books good for the soul
Learn to avoid power of lies
Meditate silently, sing aloud.

10.
I gather dulse from the rocks, I go fishing
I share the food in the community
Alone in my room.

11.
So to think further the simple heights of physics
That redeem our term, and the necessities become
Lighter, and life is [prized.][3]

---

[3] *query* priced *or* prised

8. Overheard by the Sea
An abandoned poem

Earth rises to the foreplain between love and understanding.
It takes the gull path, you can almost feel the tremble,
the surrender, the flare of passage. How can we wait here,
how can we not be there where the waves break on the horizon
to announce a new island? The fields fall to the sides
of the sky like words in transit to a new tongue
in the hopes of the townships. Vast bay, sea hauling gravel
like a thousand typists bone to metal, wheel against
wheel at the land's edge – our lives are milled out:
all we have left, pushed against earth's lock.

Earth light cast into the sky over the sea,
raised in a hand that arches back to home, and where
is it now, the faithful turf, a fractured line in the sky,
the whole massif plunging westward into sunset.
We lose what we want and get what we are: a coat to wear,
"woven of thorns and nettle stems" someone
shall no doubt wear us for a while in memory
of socialism like a shadow on the skin.

Home is a green caravan tucked into a corner
of a wheat field, its windows glowing dimly
as evening drains the day. A lost photograph
blown over the pier railing, the nation as it might have been.
We tend our scattered fires in clefts of the
coastal rocks as if waiting for a transport, and what
was that noise? What was that sudden planet-like rasp?
The tall grasses still hold the light and the ruined cottages
glow in the evening, someone's home "a small cell
among many graves…" and the heart knows, the boat
will come in one day and a bonny boat swift with the tide,
set by the stars. Sons and daughters, listeners, factors
of the receding pulse, am I there in that treatise did I win a place
in the log of love? You seasick sailors I want to go home.
[…]

9. Between Harbours

I

Long and tiring journey
through car zones

Arrive "washed out" –
back of neck, eyelids, shoulders

Walk down to the sea, where
metal stays sheathed.

All the stones are rounded
and form sentences together – it

Doesn't matter how you feel and think it
matters how the heart answers, dying dying.

2

It matters when, the heart questions,
dying to finalise these taunting distances

And be where you live. A wild home
or a protecting distance, where

The stones beat against the sea
growling and grinding together to form

A musical sentience, darkening as the
earth turns and the gulls descend.

Wine, supper, silence and sleep. The stones say
every breath is kept safe to the end.

3

In the little cove the stones rattle and squeak,
a thin stream comes down to the sea and the
slight waves tonight tap idly on the rocks.

My night camera, favoured site, journey's end.
Between driven earth and halting sea
the tide like a little washerwoman scrubs

The pebbles smooth and grades them in strata
and with Beckettian astringency repeats
what little she knows every eight seconds.

Further out the real sea, a vast self a vast unit
that pulls away from time and sorrow and knows
only its own sense, and picks at the shore

As at the edges of an itchy scab. Its own hero,
its own journey its own faint curiosity at
otherness and love. I walk back up the cove

To the fence that separates all this from
the possible, and traverse it at a 5-barred gate,
waking the farm dogs. I head for the small

Window-light across a vast indigo haze
belonging only to the world, pebbles
in my pockets, arguing about the waste of days.

4

The sea seems to breathe slowly, and to fall
one step at a time, because the universe

Is what it is, calling and calling and calling,
attracting everything to its path, death.

A red mullet falls out of it and I
slit it with a sharp knife avoiding

The poisonous spikes, setting aside
the blue liver and shiny bowels.

I make rather a mess of it, failing to clear
the smallest bones, but it makes a good meal

Eaten with care, with world trust
under the conflicting messages.

5

A minute or two on the shore, in the small cove
the body complaining as the stones roll

And shift underfoot and the substance
of the sea changes with the light.

Lies told proudly by the Thames change the sound
the sea makes on a small Welsh shore

More than they change the welcome behind
the lit window. Something more than the earth,

Some priority, cuts the haze and clears
the difficult ground the failing

Body tracks to the end. Head wobbling
on top of it saying I've lost my watch.

6

A figure standing on the little shore like a statue
a post sunk into the shingle as night slowly falls
the noise of breaking fills the air and little

Wave rims ply around his shoes. All the white lines
and pale fences of dark England snaking through
his body as he stands there like a notice board

At the water's edge, all the roads and service stations
of his way there abseiling down his digestive system
like the belly-dance down a Cimabue crucifix from panel

To panel to the end, the foot, the fixed point on which
the horizon spins into reverse and the midnight special
shines its ever-loving light on me.

7

The length of anyone's life, a gathering of traces,
dim ghosts on the dark surface of memory swaying
from side to side like a boat coming quietly to harbour
crunching on the stones and stopping.

To bring back what is gained, to climb the steep
track up the cove, the sea growling below and the wind
combing my hair. I smile back and head for
something less permanent, and much more clear.

Back the twisty path up the cliff to the headland,
and cross the dim field towards a known condition
and a short time, that sees a long way and is
over before you know it, I can't wait.

To deny eternity and lie under blankets between
thin walls while the gas cylinder growls and,
asked the question, answer Yes: this brevity,
and separation, is what I came here for.

8

Red gas-fire glow, dark space, blankets firm on
cheek and shoulder, slight wind noise outside

And that thing standing down there on the shore
like a life-belt holder, scratched and marked

With the colours of earth, full of
twisting cloud and longing for peace.

By the water's edge where the first life
on earth floated idly towards the stones

Or gods and goddesses from the curvature of the earth
rode to shore in a wooden boat called Absolute Certainty

And met a notice saying Welcome. No Parking. Pay
at the kiosk. And saw a waterfall twisting down the cliff

An old man warming his hands at an electric fire
and a list of indulgences pinned to a door, which opens

And I wake up in earth's brightness. Smoke
rising from the harbour, wet grass, hunger.

10. Six short prose pieces formerly attached to *Between Harbours*

1

Noticing the Holyhead lighthouse several miles away across the fuzz and remembering a wet evening at Dalkey, strolling among the captains' retreats, thick-walled one-storey houses set at angles among the coastal rocks, after staying too long in the Queen's Bar, when a strange little crowd gathered at Forty Foot because a body was lost. A diver's foot trapped in some old netting on the sea floor. The poets declare how their big souls despise safety.

2

And, three years later, a night in Bray Head Hotel, vast stack of corridors and disused ballrooms with one small person in charge and a woman screaming on the first floor, screaming and howling in drink and rage. The sea won them all in the end, the adventurers and swashbuckling poets, the patient inquirers and victims in despair, grinding against each other.

3

It became a habit on the way back to stop at Llangollen, where a Hungarian immigrant has filled an old cinema with about forty thousand unwanted books. This also is the earth, this theatre of shelving, with its prices, categories, attached tea-shop. Some people have a forward mania, which drives them into the big boss role and everything costs the earth. We should be grateful when it operates small-scale. Later we found a way of avoiding Llangollen.

4

Battles are lost and won in border-zones but creation takes place at the centre, at the peace at the centre, that is what I think. I don't care if I never think anything else in the world.

5
Long reaches of late sunlight on the narrow land, catching the western walls of white houses scattered on a territorial grid that suddenly stops at the cliff's edge. And the edge runs round the headland alive with dozing boats, white birds, children shouting. The inner edge of what we don't inhabit, and can't know. It promotes contentment, yearning, ice-cream, and soul inflation but look how the long land reaches out to be cancelled.

6
I left the car on the top of the mountain and walked across to Llanllawen, where an old woman lives in a group of three iron huts with about thirty dachshunds. She was cheerful as I passed her perimeter fence, though moving slowly. The dachshunds were an over-excited infant class. Darkness was falling on her enclosure, and the lines joining the tops of her huts, for hanging out washing or bringing electricity, were a script reading "There is one true purpose."

11. Absent from Llŷn, 1994-1997

1.

Four years pass, we don't go there. The little girl we carried across the shore packs a rucksack and goes to Zimbabwe, we don't expect to see her for at least a year.

At the airport she says, "Well, I've had my adventure now, I think I'll go back home" and almost means it, but the plane accelerates into plane zones, and the bird has flown.

Meanwhile, a small cove on the Welsh coast in the night, the sea grinding stones in the darkness, the disused boat sinking deeper into the shingle year after year.

And far from all that distance, in the waiting fulcrum we call home, a smile of trust mounts from the heart like someone climbing a cliff-path, casting knowing eyes on the connecting sea.

2.

The day after Gatwick we take a strange room in Southwold, a loft over a garage with old wooden furniture and a long window-set. It rains a lot, we wander the marshes bereft, our thoughts elsewhere.

And tear drops fall into a mug of instant coffee. But the urgent question is: did I get the message across? Daughter's gone away, before she left did I remember to tell her my story, whatever it is?

When all the pantomime is set aside, all the poetry, did I get round to mentioning the straight message which is all I have in the world, the one thing I know? What in the world is it?

Walking paths through the coastal marshes in the rain, the wet sedge brushing against us as we pass; and always before us that sadly unspeakable certainty, absolutely clear, that takes the best of anyone away from who they are.

3.

Another Christmas card from "All at Rhwyngyddwyborth."

Daughter and wife gone to Egypt. I stay and feed the cats, living alone in the small house that developed round us.

More mysterious symptoms, spinning head, aches behind the knees… Carefully preparing sautéed vegetables in the late evening.

Woke up this morning with an awful aching head, never measured the distance, never solved the far shore blues.

4.

That place there, that anchorage, its tough grass its sparkling rocks, that holds us scattered souls to a focus

And means death too, means succession, somebody's noisy grandchildren on the beach. Life is particularly insubstantial there, it flits across the landscape, a figure on the cliff-top, next moment gone. Restless, reaching sea.

Herring gulls, whimbrels, and choughs, and the small birds that flutter on the fences, riding the wind.

*

The same wind curves across the land, anticyclonic, flicking the last leaves of last year's autumn from the treetops in Cambridge, but stronger straight off the sea, out there. Crows, curlews and herring gulls, soaring down the cliffs as night comes, landing on the nest, calling in the green dark.

And the small birds asleep in the bushes and hedgerows, balanced on one leg, head tucked under wing, asleep but still focused on each other, as the wind shakes the branches, asleep but aware.

*

Aware of distance, aware of poverty, aware of hopelessness, sleeping in identity, one eye half open.

Goodnight from me here with my wine and my word processor, to the green dark out there, full of calls.

12. Llŷn in the Rain
September 1998

1. Over two mountain passes to meet up with Barny at Blenau Ffestiniog station. Already it's raining. *For Sale* signs all over the town, indeed Barny's been round the town's estate agents pretending to be interested in properties, and says they're almost being given away. But who wants to buy a corner shop for ten thousand, live here surrounded by dereliction and go barking mad in a town with a miniature railway running through its centre? Old slate quarries hovering over the houses, the books in the bookshop all damp, the tired pastries in the bakers' windows. Later we learn how these places return to their identity in bad weather, but as yet it is dull and depressing. We get through to Mrs Jones from a 'phone box: yes, it's all right to go straight there and arrive a day early. We do the supermarket shopping and drive off, plunging behind the town into the granite vale that opens down into Cardigan Bay at Porthmadoc.

> Rock and fibre glowing wet, brown and green,
> estuarine light blue under trees:
> a bright line beside us – we fall between,
> buying the future an earthen dream.

2) A take-away curry from the Tandoori at Pwllheli, which is a whitewashed brick shed just off the sad white rain-washed sea-front, across the road from a boarded-up beer-hall. Sit there waiting for it, nodding at the staff: young Asians living out here, so far from the city communities, I wonder what that feels like. Run through the rain to the car with the wrapped curry and drive on. And when we get to the caravan a shock as we come over the rise towards the farm – it's a new one! this is the third. The curry just about warm enough to eat by the time we arrive, but barely curry at all, a strangely sweet stew, which must be what is expected in far west Wales… but we're here. We're all here again.

> Solid cloud into the distance / sea blue-white
> black-tipped waves / threading back to us
> us all here all busy / reeling in night
> and small in the rain / trading histories.

3) Mrs Jones had a heart-attack but has been all right since. So she tells us, in that cool matter-of-fact Welsh style as if talking about the price of margarine. In exactly this tone she told us of her brother Geronwy's death from throat cancer eight years ago; who had been our tutor here, shyly greeting us every year, tending our spaces, naming the rocks, taking us out in the boat. No more boat. The fishing is finished. Licences have become so expensive for the one-boat farmer they have all stopped and their boats rot in coves. Government income from sport fishing, the sea reserved for the boys playing at captains. Also Mr Jones (up the road, no relation) has died: said to have been the last man who knew how to make Aberdaron-style wicker lobster-pots. Later we look at his small, tight, weather-proofed house and peer through the windows. The little triangular lawn with tall banks round it, the shed with the pots hanging up. Who will buy it? Young people don't want to live here any more: the '60s pastoral dream collapsed before the new hard domestic economy and its inhering conformism; the rich want their extra houses abroad; the locals have had enough: fishing prohibited, no use farming, sheep two a penny. House prices have not fallen, but they might.

> Raging apart the need and the cost
> hollow distances where the gull sits
> and laughs and the tides roar back
> small change wash hands take it.

And she gives us tea, and tell us where the food shop is this year (every year the food shop is in a different place) and says how the child has grown as she always does. Mrs Jones who continues year after year while grandparents, parents, brother and neighbour vanish into the landscape.

4) Days of persistent rain. Reading books or playing chess as it beats on the metal walls. It's been like this all summer, and by September no one around. I've never seen the place like this. Porth Or a big empty bay, the

shop almost abandoned, two young girls in charge of a few racks of leftovers, you can't even get a cup of tea. And everywhere you go the same quietness, raining or soon will be, Aberdaron, Nefyn, Abersoch – a few stragglers in macks passing from newsagent to grocery store and hurrying back to the car.

I remember going on holiday with my parents to places like Llandudno and Rhyl, and in those days you stayed in boarding houses which gave you breakfast and chucked you out; you weren't allowed to return until the evening meal at six. So if it rained for the week you'd had it, you stared at the shop windows for as long as you could, you lingered in tea-rooms and amusement arcades but basically you sat in the lee-sides of the sea-front shelters. You sat on a bench with half a roof over you wrapped in coats and watched the barren sea frothing or the shops opposite and the battered tulips in-between until it was time to go back. And this was people's only holiday, they worked 50 weeks of the year in factories offices and shops and this was their annual break from it. And they spent it sitting in the wind and the rain while the kids sulked and sucked sweets and cried.

But now it's a triumph, a restitution. The rubber dragons sitting unsellable in the corner novelty shop while the sea wind shakes the glass door, the guides to Celtica Mystica and works of the previous vicar dampening on the shelves, the water-colours unlooked-at, the candy-floss machine unplugged, the luminous pinks and yellows deflated. It is such a relief, that the place stands so solidly there while the season's sordidities shrivel away. Places arisen for an economic purpose and a spiritual relief, turned into nonsense depositories. And thank God it rains and rains until you think it can't rain any more and then it rains again and the truth finally unwinds: there is actually no reason to come here.

We dart about in this unreason. We nip in and out. We sit with the shore expanse before us through the window of the hotel bar in Aberdaron, the rolling waves washing the brown sand and the standard beer in the glass. We pause before the slate tombstones the biggest crowd seen in these parts for some time. Tea and Welsh pancakes at Carreg Plâs under Mynned Carreg, surrounded by people talking Welsh. Superb little salty-sweet buttery mouthfuls, and no English worker-snobs spreading their ignorance in the air, their paid-for-it-and-entitled, their contempt for the locals and the language. Outside, rain sweeping the fields and no one on the paths. Bareness over all this peninsula, but native, speaking softly to itself of the music it lacks.

Because an alien centrality took it away and replaced it with a trade in fakes which, predictably, let everyone down when fortune's pink smile faded in the slowing of the gulf stream. Fair-weather traders, find something to sell that people need.

And the wind on top of Uwchmynned is magnificent, you can hardly stand up in it. The concrete road winds up to the top, you get out of the car and whirl round and the door slams, it blasts across your ears, it hisses round the corners of the coast-guard shed (closed) information centre, the heather tight to the ground vibrating in its passage and you push through it coat flapping to the top of the slope to see Bardsey before you, riding the turbulent ocean two miles off. How the true locations are still there in all the changes of weather and the prosperity badges ripped off, how the sites were made solid enough to pass by all that, and the structures that talk us into it. And us ourselves, certainly.

> Viewing the green theatre behind the rain
> knowing our little cares will increase
> year by year and the red of the petal
> and the red of the fire do nothing but gain.

And no, we shan't get to Bardsey this year either, clearly, but the time will come. The space between it and us is too full. Like the space between prosperity and purpose, full of all that weather and most of what we are, and the silence when everyone's gone away.

> Then green takes its fair shine.
> We wondering what we need
> freely twine red thread on
> walking stick maybe the last time.

5) Porth y Nant under rain, the deserted village rebuilt as a Welsh language centre, and with a café, which even has a few people in it, staring out at wet slopes through steamed-up window, macs dripping onto floor. Signs have sprouted everywhere: *For Sale* in the towns, *Keep Off* at the edges of the land, and there is no one to keep off, and nothing to keep them off. *Private* in front of a bracken-coated cliff, and big red *Danger/Keep Out* all over the remains of the gravel works on the shore and the quarries further on. Institutions protecting themselves from claims, worried before the privatisation of law, plastering warning messages on everything in sight.

Later walking alone up the cliff steps at the south end of the bay because I want to photograph an old farmhouse I remember on the top pastures, the rain really comes on. The stone steps in the cliff, which the workers made for themselves to get down to the gravel loading bays, are little cascades. On the top the wind drives the rain hard against me from landward, it soaks my trouser legs and gets down my neck front and back and into my shoes. I pass that strange wooden dwelling like a cricket pavilion which I'd almost forgotten, and which does look lived-in, but the stone house is silent as ever, sitting there on a shelf of the sloping pastures. Standard Welsh thick-walled small farmhouse, two storey with central porch and slate roof, furnished and curtained but never anyone there, exactly the same for twenty years. So whoever owns it remains elsewhere, and the fact that it's one of the few houses without a *For Sale* sign means they at least survive, whatever they are for good or ill they haven't been dispersed or eradicated by death and change. I take a photograph of it. These things are rare.

And walk behind it across the fields to the cliff top and back down the diagonal path across the face, another workers' route, to the north end of the bay again. Stone sills over red mud. A buzzard hovering over the cliffs, and two choughs on the beams of the derelict quarry house. A mountain goat noticed high up the cliff through the café windows. A lot of seals around, one usually appears whenever we get down to the sea, and two regulars in the left cove at the farm. People move out, but other things move in.

Rooks circling the green pastures spotted
with bright red flowers / Are you our ghosts,
will you protect us? / Future love in the hands
of black armies, and wandering hosts.

6) Let the rain do its worst, we perform the whole routine, we shirk none of it. We do the full Morfa Nefyn sequence first established circa 1983: drive there along the coastal tract south of Nefyn, which is one of my strongest images of this terrain: the land coming down from the central ridge striped with stone-walled fields and rebounding in a gentle wave before stopping suddenly at the cliff edge -- a great scroll of land up the coast. Then get the fish and chips (the F&C shop itself is for sale! this really could be the last time) and take them down to the shore to eat on the rocks, dump the paper in the same green oilcan provided for such purpose for the last fifteen years and then walk over the wetness a mile to Porth Dinllaen. Low tide, we pass close under the stilt houses, some of them showing signs of habitation, mostly not. And the quietness that's everywhere has settled here too: no one in the pub or outside it. Then walk on, the little shore-side path along the edge of the headland. The wooden hut in the cliff niche, still there, someone still getting there maybe a week a year and keeping it going, bottle of washing-up liquid on window-ledge. Somehow people keeping a few things going as desertion settles round them like rain. And on past the lifeboat station to sit on the cliff-edge of the golf course (no golfers) and watch the seals coming to roost out there on the rocks. And they do, again.

Michael Haslam used to sing to these seals. We don't, but in our silent hearts we shout over to them, "Hey, seals, remember us? You haven't seen us for four years now but we always came here. And you were here in those days, seals, we watched you out there on the rocky pinnacles, your home for the night. Every year we came here since the baby was born, eighteen years and now the twenty-second. How are you getting on, seals? It looks good, there's more of you than ever. Big ones and little ones, rolling about on the sharp rock needles with nothing but seaweed to comfort your hides. Snorting and puffing and calming down as the light goes. And being there, at rest on a known point, being there tonight again. We think it's a great achievement, seals. Can you hear me? We think it's the answer."

> Remember you too were once a new-born baby
> as helpless as a seal on a rock just
> rolling around while war flew
> red banners over the green city.

7) Reading books or playing scrabble while the water hurls itself at the thin walls and the whole edifice shakes slightly. The two sheep in the field outside looking perfectly happy about it, standing still in the rain. Two hand-reared lambs who run up to you if you enter their field, two friends, two siblings… Reminding me, that there are two true world-messages, birth-joined in a hatred of injustice, but rigorously opposed to each other. The buyers and the sellers. Those who scan and those who focus. And that something else, like a sheep-ness, arches over them both and keeps them persevering in the same field. A balance, a conflict, created in this recognition which generates the tension on which the song is sung.

Only the song stands high to see
on stones of the yard on the message wire
stands and calls, brushes water from coat,
everything said returns to the throat

Making there its nest, red cell cluster that
closes the light and leaves the land
quiet under vast rain vast under spread pain
lapping the edges of a modern caravan again.

Later it won't matter what these words say
in the light of what these words see: a cat
on a wall a rook on a wire a sheep in a field a
hope lost in the pink world home to its believer.

And the long land with white houses proposes
a symmetry to your warring poses and the answer lies
all round you. A little flock of some little bird or other
over the rain beaten bushes flares and falls together.

Do so and melt. *Zerschmilts, du felsenhartes Hertze!*
Everything said runs back to the throat, and
works there a form of gain. A security brighter
than the fields, and harder than the rain.

A solitude which is gained, a safety in a shortness
of time, curved to the sky and turning round and
round again a chaconne which we bird voices
trill over in flight, settling to the bar of night.

A solitary night together, all of us. Towards
the end of which a passing luminous creature
spreads a call over the roof concerning death that cause
of fear. Wrapped in distance we count it ever more dear.

13. Llŷn, Pausing and Going

Llŷn, Pausing

That peculiarly broken ground, the turf cover always halting at an earthen scoop. Shoulders of grass above the sea clasped tight in mosses, plantains, clumps of thrift, opening like wounds to reveal the grey rock surface. The bright orange lichen on the stone roofs, the rust breaking through the green-painted corrugated iron. The tall stony banks between fields, hawthorn hedges along the roads, with elder and blackthorn, riding into stream hollows and up again. Sections planned and executed long ago, long fields riding the waves of land to break at the littoral. Solid thick-walled stone houses with small windows and front porches, and here and there makeshift dwellings made of boards with tin roofs tucked into field corners with a gate through the hedge from the road. And the lives there, entire lives which cannot be reduced to their occasions, but seeming to have almost nothing of their own, no ornament. And there is no dictionary to define the terms, of this great distance, of these bare walls, of these flat hats tilted over physical tasks.

Only the chapels, bare outside and in, with the low graves set round them, partaking of the same austerity as the fields and houses. The care for the polished wood, the rule of no ornament. A hymn in Welsh reaching us through the thick walls, pushed around by the wind over the fields as we bend over Geronwy's grave, sung plainly and in perfect steadiness. I don't see, in my fifty-ninth year, that we have anything better to offer, in the ever burgeoning contrarieties of our cosmopolitan riches, than a place set apart where someone with the job in hand will tell you it is all right, it has to be, sing together and rejoice. Or a doctor who will tell you, I'm sorry, but it is not all right.

And the choughs, not knowing they are choughs and so quite special, seen from time to time, always in pairs, floating over the cliff ends, and we notice with pleasure that they have children. They have children in foul weather, and attend to them in niches of the cliff as sheets of rain sweep along the coast. And next year they are there again, flying over the sea where seals, uninterested in choughs, cast their eyes downwards through the water, and following their sight, turn into the deep. Seeking food, as we, seeking rest, or adventure, turn into our graves.

Llŷn, Going

Going away now. The chances diminish,
of returning. I wonder if my daughter
will bring her children here, and find
a Mrs Jones still here. Me not here, me
somewhere else

Singing my hymn. Lift up your heart
and your voice. I wonder if the sound
will reach the far shore, I wonder
if the sea's continual code will ever
be broken, in English or Welsh,

Someone, dead or alive, saying, in
either language or any on earth,
that like the stars in the morning
sky we reckon to falter and cease,
and place what we know on a broken shelf

"Only remembered for what we have done."
High voices in the cove, excited at the
splashing waves, running towards them
and back, three kittens on the farm wall,
singing in the wire, love grows in the sun.

And the day grows beyond love or hope
into its result sure and firm in the
lowering farm-light. A future running
towards me across a field, that I myself
helped to grow and be, shadows on the sea.

Notes to Sea Watches

Some readers may not notice that the stanzas of *Sea Watches* are rhymed alternately ABCDEF.

I/1 pilgrim's goal. The island of Bardsey (Ynys Enlli) which lies two miles beyond the tip of Llŷn was an important mediaeval pilgrimage destination, partly because of the danger and difficulties involved in reaching it.

II/7 "I was ill…" Quoted from *Tide Race* by Brenda Chamberlain (1961).

III/2 Hell's Mouth or Porth Neigwl is an almost straight three-mile bay on Cardigan Bay with a bad reputation for shipwrecks.

VI/2 Porth Or or Whistling Sands is a popular beach bay not far from the caravan home, with attached minimal catering facilities. The sand does indeed squeak underfoot on dry days.

VI/7 "Gentle Morpheus…" This address to the Greek deity of dream and sleep is the beginning of an aria in Handel's opera *Alceste*.

VII/4. *Bryn Celli Ddu* is a prehistoric structure of the kind known as "chambered tomb" on Anglesey. The other names in VII are those of chapels of rest on the pilgrim routes of Llŷn. *Ffynnon Fair* is a fresh-water spring on the cliff face at the traditional point of embarkation for Bardsey.

VIII/7 "The shadow of the earth rises…" This is a lunar eclipse.

Other Notes

Six Prose Pieces.
There is a legend about St Merin's church concerning a thief stealing St Merin's silver bell and leaping over the coastal rocks carrying it until divine intervention dropped him into a sea crevice.

Rhwngyddwyborth ("between two harbours") is the name of the coastal farm with the caravan in which author and family stayed during the action of *Sea Watches*.

Poems and Notes.
Porth Grwtheyrn, Porth y Nant. A bay which was the site (at that time) of the derelict remains of a large slate quarrying industry and attached deserted village. Chutes and piers because the stone was taken away by boat.

"Death should not be a problem…" slightly adapted from Norbert Elias, *The Loneliness of Dying* (1985)

Overheard by the Sea.
This is the remains of a work originally conceived as a poetical dialogue between my son and my father on the cliff tops overlooking the shore at Porth y Nant; that is, eliminating myself from between them. Its fictive basis was an apocalyptic scenario, as of a destroyed country from which they were waiting to be rescued by boat.

Llŷn in the Rain.
Zerschmilts, du felsenhartes Hertze! "Melt, you stone-hard heart!" Opening of a song from the opera *Cecrops* by Johann Philipp Krieger (1649-1725).

Llŷn, Going.
"shadows on the sea" is the title of a song by Joe Skilbeck sung by The Men of Staithes. It refers to an old belief that that is what sailors' and other mariners' souls became if they did not become seagulls. The ending of *Overheard by the Sea* is also affected by one of his songs, "Heading for the Harbour Lights". The other song refrain, "Only remembered" is from a traditional Methodist hymn.

The 2007 edition included a greatly extended version of the notes to the Llŷn writings, especially the topographical ones. These notes are available on the author's website.

IX.

The Derbyshire Poems

(1975-1981)

Following the Vein, I-III

THE SPHERE descends into the cleft striking

sparks from the walls. The diameter

is fully sexual. >The miner

revolves his arms at the mineral face, the pick

curves over his head and in that wheel

the child and the old man in that wheel

the male child and the old man opposite

each other on the rim their mutual weight

conveys impulse into momentum

alternating strokes of linear time.

At each stroke the old man falls forward

and the child mounts behind him, but the entire rim

grinds constantly against the shore, the sparks

shoot off, the child dives over his head

and marks in a flash the limit of his futurity.

The miner turns his wheel following the vein

deeper into substance, he accepts the challenge:

to rouse and threaten the conditional thick in armour,

professional authority that declares love

is an event of the selfhood. This diameter

comprehends entire rift and city – the field

is tipped on its side folded in two and

petrified but the horizon remains

at completed distance, a life we can

only participate in, never be. It slopes away

beyond our cope and is subsumed in matter.

The line of farewell

                                  is a pointed arch.

UNFOLD THE line and the triangle
springs forth, apex structure dreaming
the rounded arch, dreaming us back
to earth. >As the miner bears into the face
the woman is more than at his side she is fixed
in the side of his knowledge and from that
copulation the ores are already melted the
metal runs glowing out of day's furnace
and the flames wing round him each
to each, birds of passage pulled through
his limbs. The flashing globe rolls
over the hills, circles the horizon,
aureole of the liveable space. From this
the fire-worms shoot into the sky
perch on the masthead with their
beaks unfold the centre: his right
to be there, to be this work. The old
woman and the young child, the app-
ointed equilibria: hospitals on the right
battlefields on the left: patient wounding,
aggressive healing, fair death. The sides
of the road, familial plane presenting uniform
pressure onto time, not stretched but
ranged, tenure on future drift, central traverse

across city edges. We notice then

the centre of a sphere, some distance

before our eyes, which depends on our

work for equipoise. Deferred to that point,

the dark shroud is lessened

and pushed behind.

SO, WALKING down to the Manifold the river
curves round to follow, dimly lit or
underground as it rains and if eternity
is in front infinity is behind, white cliffs
to the sides beyond the meadow trees.
Topside of the ripple reflects daylight,
the negative is concave, the whole band
flows to the side and past us. This flux is
trusted or we are at a limit. Pythagoras
showed that matter cannot be reduced
to indivisible atoms, that the course
is by definition continuous remote to
remote otherwise minimalist reduct, we move
only forwards, we only say yes.
Or no as the case may be. Which is untrue.
And how could we anyway, with that solid
bolt up the spine, set to any process worth it?
Memory of the womb, memory of the
spermatozoon striking the egg, all the
unknown fractional lives across earth and time
participating in the self but here consolidated
in the channel, a unity entirely responsible: I.
Only the present then can be finite, only
the potential can cease to be, the reward as real

as the revenge. The first strike into possibility

remains intact through the web and the narrowness

of the divide and all the torques and all the guilt

is refined out of it, we are interested

in being complete, > and in tracing the metal thread

as it darts between mirrors and surges through

to the end of the connexion; which we

don't know and never shall know but

shall be having been able to have known

and that therefore it does exist.

Tracks and Mineshafts

I

Material Soul

Given to death and life, no choice,
fallen into these terms, borne as the
tide bears the wave to its strike,
cut to bedrock, crest, charge the shore.
Given to this, life carving itself out
of its knowledge and the earth
is a cup to which the lip fits,
and the senses' final construct moves
relentlessly through substance to the houses
of light, mutual devotion

Joined to death; danger
specifies its fear, the message forms
its own access or nerve and behind
the point of contact perception opens
onto a cleared space, a settlement, holding
people of all ages together,
the whole of life, is this shift
back, this rearing

And arrival, which leaves a mark,
a birth documentation or yell echoing
down the unlivable corridors and arcades
of transitional time. Flesh scores lines
in the calcium slag of earth and the spirit
wakes, the needle enters the groove,
polar tension shakes the circuit, which
responds, gapes, tremors, issues
forth into the acts of day, for good.
Peace is nothing without this resistance,
engaging distance beyond any possible
repair to the end, the inhabited city.

And this is what we see, and live, all
round us the world arrives at its end.
Welcome it, plunge into the stone,
never to be seen again.

Eight Preludes

i

Each day some further light each day some farther dark.
Carry on go here there make a note of it what for.
Climb the hill walk down get in the car and drive away.
It is nothing to do with me. Valley stream
meadow waterfall gorge. There is something else there
nothing to do with us, that makes no difference.
We can go we can stay at home and drink tea, it is
still there. Far reaches of the Upper Manifold, where
is it, what is it, green chapel if it rains it rains.
Smear of cloud in the distance, book of nothing not
inhabited, ruins of the whole thing. Light on water
quick by blue shale cliffs, thick in fern, light filling,
bearing the sense of a curved need. Mineral vein
running down the hillside up the other side and away
over the moors, worked or not. Or not worked, unknown,
what difference does that make? Light filling the valley
with not a soul to be seen, dark beams of disappointment
filling the city streets, death shadowing the grass.
What am I then as you which otherwise stays sleeping, or
if we weren't in the dark star's way would our sense
still open beyond the ground whether we knew it or not?
No, the material soul yearns by the day's annoyances for real.
So love bears forth our joyful stake and I turn us again,
front to front to front.

ii

Night outside is the theatre of our patience
as you lie beside me in the dark loft;
distant thrust of steam locomotive in some
vast marshalling yard, cold papers blown
across the square.

Night contracts the distances of love and fortune
to a presence, angles filling the dark room
loud with inaudible instructions like an
equestrian statue in the full moon and a far away
telephone rings.

It is me trying to contact a third person
out of the past or lost in the city streets while
night's cover persists – footsteps of the heart agent
passing by ticket office and clock tower
to an abandoned station.

Then false dawn brings a nil invoice and faint lines
near the ceiling, a small child runs down the corridor
holding a toy angel, wings flapping screaming at us
not to owe – the world is wanted, and full, our full hearts
crack at it.

And famine over the earth in futile wars,
monetisation of time whereas the emptiness
is real and there is no return, no restitution.
Oh keep intact the underwing starts, the
cup carried through it.

iii (a)

A sense of urgency and the kitchen floods. Most of the time gets mislaid.

The weekdays pass to the side; called to the present we wind ourselves up and something quite remote comes out: old jazz, demolished cafés where we breakfasted in our prime, a head full of grey mornings, quick postcards, old thorns… What time do I have to get up tomorrow?

Most of the time belongs to most of the people but I can't hear you, I can't find you, hero of our time, toy of our governors, I can't read you, I can't hear you for the grinding of milk-teeth, bone against bone, teeth chewing teeth in the cavernous half-light of a bottling shop. Hero of the white line, humanity brought to the idea of itself, dying of imputative success, chewing itself to image pulp and anyway, when will a human idea ever eat real raisins or hold my hand on the way to the station when the time comes for questions? Every time it rains I know a nation is a logarithm of love, how the present tangles itself in desires, how the mess we make of it unwinds into space.

iii (b)

There is a reason
why discomfort gains the route.
The honey drips but the fire
leaps: be held out.

iii (c)

The reasons are all eaten in secret
or baked into Easter buns.
Superfluous honey corrodes
the map. We spit out pips
and fragments of grindstone
into the fire.

iii (d)

Thin liquids! give us some
annals of the orchard,
some fire laden rob.

iv

By the worm in the sky, by instruction,
the people would enter the state due them?
Unless otherwise stated it is a phantom dispatch.

Our wires live and respond; high gritstone kerbs
energy which isn't ours: we intersect, recognise
and worry. How we worry -- darkness is

Two things and one of them (ness) is light
cutting through us. No rest, no tuition,
enter the island state guided in twain.

v

I am constantly bugged by something I think I'm supposed to be saying: the philosophy of poetry or the joys of wisdom or the truth that snaps the world back into place. Where is it? It's easy enough to focus on nothing like a missing pilot and set absence in the text just to have it there before us, newly reflective; but you are elsewhere and it's very uncertain that something human is actually there at the end of this dispersed line wanting or waiting for anything on earth. Surely the fire is getting low; if we don't signal our love there will be no reason for dying. I turn to the simple sky-trapped animal, the looke in thy heart and write, bit. Plentiful and expensive. The heart, of course, is a nonexistent book in which we read the education of the world. The adventures of Bugs Hunter. What rubbish. I am not I, pitie the tale of me.

Meanwhile, someone is stockpiling sugar in an abandoned theatre across the road from where we live, and the cat returns for her dinner. Give it her, naturally. We can't turn back at this stage. Open her tin, welcome her children behind the couch, find them as good homes as time and this world afford. These necessary acts compose one by one the map of grace. Everything glows with sheer presence: couch, kittens, bugs, boredom, dark, ness, it all slowly gathers to a landscape, an inhabited and structured landscape with walls and ditches and paving by which we hold on to the world like a vast hand. And that also is love, whose grip, routed into purpose, steadies us against the earth exactly here: dispersing in our heat but consolidated by fear, the tension of the wing, that opens and closes. What wing? What rubbish again. Opposite the theatre of sugar a wing of rubbish opens in our honour.

vi

Willing also to be remembered, lost
in fairest love-task scholarships such
as bring sight to its own predilection
where the broken edges catch the light
unfolding, a tract where sense
and love fuse in the energy of script
holding the world together at that point.

And immense wastage, entirely ours
as we humanise the world and then resent it
objectify it and wonder where it's gone
and place such clamps on our speech that
most of the people become figments of something
shot past like a disintegrated pudding too late for
winter, lost in clouds of fume and dust.

But I also think of you as fairest before sight
in a vocabulary which is generally considered
nonsense out of a 13th Century context and still
fairer dark by the light that glims beyond.
Well, it is night at the crossroads and many years
since a dignitary came this way. The faces
of the houses are silent. Time suddenly rusts.

vii

Faint calls from the mines,
holes in the landscape
or star targets.

Of the heart of the earth
where the one-person is undivided
and the market serves the home.

Of the oceanic cycles
where the dream disperses into day
and we cannot rest in our value.

Of the self cast.

viii

If you want messages you must provide an orifice.
But to really want messages is in itself an orifice,
a lesion, an interruption of the diurnal pact. The future
ferments in this cleft, packed with honour and disdain,
drawing us ever larger and further on, to this self-
same world, that listens; the rest is vain stuff.

Surely it is this whole particular, this action we
are that draws our sight into the funnel, opening
and closing as the light wing flutters, back
and forth, back and forth, wisdom and rubbish –
poetry is the flight. And now if I can just get out
of this notional claw I'll find out exactly where I am.

> I'm in the dining shed again exactly up and about
> my morning task I crawl at this morning through
> the floss of dream. In a wink I fill the kettle
> and forget it. I shake the radio. I wince.
> The light outside is clearer than any hypothesis.
> The edge resounds in light because we don't linger.
>
> And off to work I go. I enter a solid block
> of morning light scored with branch lines;
> I close the door before you even wake, check
> ignition and brakes and turn again to the book,
> to the page shewn, the passage marked before.
> Fate, it says, is a professional improvisor.
>
> I duck under the brow as the overtakers
> glide past in their dream wagons: Monday
> Tuesday and Wednesday, fleeces thick in oil.
> Feeling "rushed" (like "crowded") mounts to
> a signal. I turn into a lay-by with herbage. Rain
> clouds the stream. The entire landscape is vocal.

I lean on the parapet while the police matrons
check my documentation, and listen to the story
of the water vole, his home under the bridge, the pain
of his extended incisors. He breathes under Saturn
and scurries along the bank. He eats or is taken – he
knows that. His duties end at his honour to himself.

We have considerable doubts, but raise a song
of this inadequacy the thrush couldn't fault.
And we keep it, chuck it over the shoulder for
luck and resume direction. A mended stone.
Nothing any longer bears on us that isn't ours;
nothing any longer wears us that isn't love.

Hell in some century's language is where no one
makes a life any more. We have the key to it, fast
to the wrist under the sleeve, the misplaced heart.
Then we mine into light in a way no office can
endure or regulate save the office of delight,
past and future safe in a shell and love's farther still.

King's Field

Patches of bare earth on the far hillside: abandoned mines, standing out like sores through the rough mingling pastoral surface, scorched by the core of the earth as by a passing meteor. Sites of encounter, engagement, victory and defeat, where a piece of nature split against humanity, into metal and slag.

Teeth marks on the shoulder and flank of the hill, scatter of clinker in the grass, compacted rain-washed mounds glittering with small surfaces of calcite and quartz... The craftsmen of fire departed long ago, decamped and returned home under the sunset in a dying wake of mineral flame: the fire they inhabit, and work with, treading the bright coals, walking the furnaces...

Earth substance and sky energy converge at Man, wedged in the point of creation, nuclear cocoon, handling the living gold, fixed moaning on the rock...

Until the work is completed and past, and we hold the result in our hands and our everyday perceptions, and the whole process, in retrospect, becomes an instant, a flash of penetrating fire – the book, closed, becomes one thing, the coinage fused to a crown.

Leaving us here bewildered, leaving us with a cold in the throat and a mass of sterile rock at our feet and no idea what to connect living to, no continuing occasion or ferial relief; leaving us holding a medallion against the moon, stamped with cold royalty.

As if the present is something already lived.

As if we could pick what we think we want out of the world leaving behind the hole we dug it from, let the rest fall aside, without getting caught in a speed trap of proliferating division, where sympathy is merely the recourse against a massive dispersal of substance and love strains against income to keep a few people together in true lives. Then we are outside ourselves: we have no architecture.

It is dangerous, for the world returns us to ourselves in the end, in the formats of our own acts. Intimately, eventually, the world has us as we have had the world. Right through the boundaries of our estates the world splits back at us, returns our vocabulary ground to a knife edge while the residue crumbles and shakes over our heads.

As if it were possible to gain the run-off from the treaty of stone and fire as a bystander, to make or continue anything without inhabiting the generative point, the ecstasy, and bearing its toll. As if our hoarded sentences were anything but paper hedges against the expanse, excuses for lateness and silence, thorn collars for the refusal to say.

And we hold on, fingernails tight in the engravure, as the bounty of the original act disperses through the years into cloudy smears of garden-age. Nettle, willow-herb and bindweed creep up to the mouth of the mine, smothering the work floors and smelt holes. Smoke and gauze float in the air, blotting the earthscape. It has always been like this.

Now as probably at any other place in history the trophies seem to be secreted, the currency reserved. Indolence and jealousy pull us down, we fill with disappointment, time-resentment, struggling in blatant hypocrisy to survive on input without living any real events at all, just a few token games, bitter takings we never earned. It is the language that fails.

The language lapses, families cooling and drifting apart, bitterly shrugging each other off, emotional victims of regressive economics, taking a shabby single room in a Victorian terrace to live through the clouding of the mirror, withdrawal of speech down the throat. Twist of flex in a circlet of yellow plaster-work, old carpet, naked bulb, dusty settee draped in Indian shawls: anything, a few bits and pieces, a cold fire. Work discontinued and disproved in the lost kitchen, victims of metallic ambition: experience lived as instant coin.

So there is a void section, a wastage, which can't be reprocessed back to possibility. Ice cracks the shell and cups the seed; the faintest reminder of participation floors us. All sense of belonging is suspended, "Purity of heart is to will one thing" but no extant script will recover the retrospective simplicity, the lost whole.

Leave things aside then for a term, attend to the present, the one thing. Go shopping, write a letter, go to the cinema, the art of forgetting. Ruthlessly adhere to normality as it stands at any price, sharpen senses to the weather, that alternate freezing and melting we get on the edge of North, water always running down the fields, and the world is what you see.

And sharpened to that edge, non-claimant, totally engaged in the substance of living and the thought that survives it, we begin to recall ourselves, brought home from distance and obscurity with always some 'wholeness' behind us, whole because behind us, which the world casts back in our faces as marginal loss and we dream from every night. But the only real thing is here in the hand that holds it: life focused on points of distinction.

To meet this demand a flame is held back in the eye.

There are points of light all over the valley, where the sun catches car tops greenhouses and puddles, piercing the winter haze filling the air, a body of light gathered piecemeal towards us and held there, suspended, animate light, between us, that anyone should be glad to surrender to as it throngs up and over and soars on the horizon, beckoning the night.

Casually we brush it off with excuses, headaches and liabilities, crushing the distance between us, the caution zone, to a slight thing. You and I, descend the stone steps in the hillside and pass under cloud into the real, where things also clasp and contain the light, have it in substance, and the objects of earth stand in absolute presence through light and dark, holding energy close and ripe, solid, and nothing needs be said.

Finally the person, redoubled in native fire: animal combustion but also the tip of flame held in our good-will, illumination of the heart page in a dark cell at night, to which all that cosmic display bows: the human warmth that splits the rock and melts out the copper and gold, commingling, consuming our bodies. Flame that gains as it disperses, consolidates and augments as it flares on the horizon, the blue lettering of anyone's few, accurate, sentences. And the more we distribute the more we hold, the more we tell the more we know.

Then the sun is safe in the sky and the hills well wrapped in grass and bushes, with outcrops and bare patches where the human and divine construct spat a brief statement to the ground, or bit a chunk out of the hillside. The people of the town stroll around on a bright afternoon, their protean potentials well concealed in human casing, formative / caustic energy more or less deeply packed in travelling suitcases of flesh and bone, occasionally breaking out in sparks of meaning that flash across the circuit, while a constant pressure slowly moulds and consumes the active surface of the person.

This ferment in us, belonging nowhere else, and is the force that moves us anywhere, forming mere distance into resounding arcades and terraces, lakes, rings, graveyards… and certainly cannot be contained in these lumpy sacks, walking bolehills with no fixed site in the world, fighting constantly with shoelaces tape-recorders and each other in search of a rightful being or a wrongful reward, and harbouring all the time a perceptive core that in true response opens out to gardens and edging woods, creates the world and belongs nowhere in particular.

Human body gurgling and rattling in its excess of language, that stands between us and the source of life as our only access, dithering in the way between the self and its permanent home: final pivot and moment of peace that must be all body, all nothing at all.

Don't we already know it and as if in preparation are brought constantly up against the ordinary things, that signal personal redundancy, the mass of the earth in its hideous simplicity that alone gives energy and light any substance or durability, where language crashes and revives, flesh reconstitutes itself athwart times. It is the message that exceeds us, the concept not grasped, the emptiness of total being, pure sign of itself to which such substances as metal, poetry, history, can only form the tools of an interim script. Immovable and unspeakable, the mournful dump of matter.

What can we do but set the fire through it, immediately and rightly adore the quick glitter of roadside glass as a sign of hope. For truth swells in the very instant we live it, holding sheer surfaces out to catch the soul-fire, burning seed, candlelight still as standing water under its technological canopy, waiting to lapse into the world space of a specific attention, kept alive through millennia, simple openness of response to authentic script, across wars and famines.

What if that too, upper sense of the heart furnace, in the end fails, scatters and dies into featureless geology? What if that too breaks its percepts against the things of earth, that nullify all our languages and strategies: the friendly local object which is also the death of culture, the utterly unbreathable world-thing lying there sucking endeavour towards nonentity – the stone in the field, the light bulb, the rusty stapler, the terracotta head dripping with chicken blood and wine… These things we have given our lives to and they finally sit there on the desk staring back at us entirely void of expression or promise, unsellable untelling exhibits, tools that we have set at the focus of increment and exhausted – vehicles of intercommunication from which we expect oracles. And we batter our spirits against the grey matt surface, the screen that now refuses to cast back either spring blossoms or infant smiles. We are reduced to knots of hair and gristle at the crossing point of human and cosmic wills, wide open to the annihilating denials of infinity. Of course we are, and always knew it.

And still the authentic embodiment of light playing to and from the world remains celestial whether it lasts or not, still in its torn jacket this body of thinking flesh is the song of it, the new star mounting the rinsed and morning sky, fresh from ocean, shrouded in its own time. It notifies the successor and warns the sleeper, tracing an arch across the firmament, and finally descending to its dim repose: the true moment thwarted against unbearable extent, and in painful response echoing back the form of a spiritual figure, full of beauty. The talk of the town.

Completely answering the world.

* * *

(Sacred phosphorus inside his
small head, cloaked in
snow & humus, clock intact. Brain-

glow holds morning in reserve, its own
and not the echo of any received light:
we wake up because the dream is exhausted

and falls through the slot in the door
in little bits. Likewise
we receive the day's failure
into our bed at night.

This perseverance
and fellowship with separation
operates a quite different economy
from what shows on th'electronic
balance-sheet at reckning time.

* * *

The light (this
morning) falls out of the sky
and passes into the ground
and the stone and slate of the roof

falls into heat
and number
at substance, where
shadows contrive

and the rising penumbra
intercepts
this divine speed
ay, at the forge of lives.

(Letter)

Yes, you have needed to distance, unmask, normalise. You are no longer held in that relentless intensity, your pitch has dropped and spread, you are not focused on a redemptive centre at the point of decision, yours or another's. I think it is important to know that this, your state of being, is only the occasion of what you do and not its substance. It was a 1960s confusion from which many received lasting damage, to think your fate would respond to a conditional, shorn of act as of home. And I don't see why this recovery, which is what it is, has to be represented as some kind of failure. Welcome in fact to the world, where you go on, and the double-edged images no longer cut the heart, and objects no longer (fencepost, omnibus, feather, crystal) recede. Things stay more to your side, completing. And so you move on, past the defeated and defeating questions of who you are by reflection and accession; you move to a wider, more social, and apparently firmer sphere. And it makes no difference at all – nothing changes – the blood does as much flow, the meat pulse, as much hurt as much comfort as ever, as much confusion. Whoever you are the red string dangles at your centre, don't deny it – you are no longer hurt, but hurt remains in your sense, the demand persists and pays no attention to our smooth adulthoods and their reckless persistence. The formal energies of our constitution transcribe such urgencies as reach us, drawing them to a linear journal, which is a twisted and coarse but final means of having done with it. The intensity may be the way but it is not the message; the message is less particular (who it has) and more exact: the whole sphere of singularity has to support the flashes and sediments it received under command to finish as known truths. Whatever it is (firestick, handlebar, dictionary, sea) that bears and threatens it, this craft won't be tied to selected personal qualifications of youth race temperature or history, which flaw the very singular authenticity of the structure. Surely the whole of life is the issue at every point by obtention – your crisis is a metaphor – you are focused (scissors, maypole, tumulus, gun) on a redemptive centre.

Glutton

Grey limestone ridge under transverse sweep of low cloud, full of cavities, crystals, and men sharpened to a point.

•

Minerals come slowly to fruition, across millennia: molecules of lead and sulphur riding air-bubbles in the warm waters pouring and seeping between masses of solid limestone, coming to flower under the roof of Hell. The metal trends westwards and upwards, final outcast of an oceanic pulse rising towards the atmosphere. This bright thread worms its way towards the sky along borderlines and faults in the tables of sleepy limestone, round the corner, skirting and infiltrating the vast shell-dust annals: solidified white powder full of crinoids and molluscs, blocks of pure defence. A line, then, compounded of metal, oil, and heat, traces the edges of sedimental stasis and sets up a challenge on the edge of contentment. It approaches, fastened to weightless air; it is held up to us. It glows in the subterranean night, calling us, persuading us to faster and sharper acts – a tight, iridescent vein packed with sleeping princesses and red thorns...

•

Approaching the surface of the earth, this perilous band curves back on itself, sheltered by the white rock. Gaining cavities, cracks and entire vacant layers of the stratification, it opens out into efflorescences: crystals and cave-pearls, colours of sky and flesh held in translucent stone, breaking into the spaces in formal excrescences. The metallic compound lies amassed at the centre of the cauldron. It is as if a whole warehouse of books lies under the sea, the books stacked on their sides; the pages congeal together, the languages forgotten, cubic masses of documentation totally inert. But the gilt letters one by one float off the bindings and assemble on the surface in a matrix of red and blue inks, a dazzling unreadable scum, a possibility. And waits there, as if expecting us, an ore. Always referred to as "true", the nascent language is there, and ready, as soon as our organs of perception are tuned to meet it.

•

Men sharpened to a point plunge into the earth. Flesh breaks out into hooks and probes, teeth focus in tight clusters like poppy heads. They grope in water-rooms, labyrinths, hotels with bricked-up windows, bank vaults, scenes of lust and criminal heat scored onto the walls, a whole fresco of despair. It is a lust constantly renewed, a driving force only marginally attached to gain – impersonal and irrevocable, pure species act. Men goaded to nerve heat twine with the dragon in ecstasis of parity. Set around with guard mechanisms, channelled, under command, the miner's eye catches a lustre, a hidden spark in the tensed rock which fires his anonymous soul and he sets to, blow against blow, hunter under his moon. Pressed and focused into this encounter anyone's wholeness is broken and rephrased like a larva in the chrysalis. Care is elbowed aside and behind in the fray, becoming the function of an over-language and progressively eroded as ever more refined instruments of penetration release perception from direct engagement. But by then the ore is exhausted too.

•

So like anyone going a lonely walk, head down against the blast, dog trussed up alongside, snow on the valley sides and steam in his pockets, the sterility wrought by the taxonomists stands always before him as a possible channel for his acts. There is no message for the world, there is not even any news. Scales and inscribed plates fall off his spirit into corners as he wrenches his life out of a stone vice or crumples in the attempt. Fighting the globe for the faintest sign of ore, stuffed in a niche under the fields with barely room to turn round, his work-focus becomes such complete anti-home, so specifically unwelcome, that the rest of the world, the width of day, brightens in response behind him in a fury of tears. A wholeness burgeons out of sight, in front beyond the rock, behind in the day, language of a royalty he doesn't himself in his moment speak, but works for. Life is sectioned – greatest pleasure in the sweep of earth's width now stands against an alternated blindness and rage, from which it catches a melancholy renunciation, a funereal suspension. The sweep of light across the land is caught in the cone of night and directed against the rock-face. You stand at the shouldering of this structure or nowhere.

•

And attains the un-
feared present (to-
morrow) cap in
hand, open past the
crux to full orbit,
folded in night and
secretly aglow.

The future, you see,
no longer simply "a-
rrives". It is or is not
a betterment;
tomorrow's day-
light is clearly
already there.

•

It is a matter, then, of bringing this tension, this long curve of time across the earth, this metallic arc, to a perfection it cannot gain itself, where the tightly compacted mass is broached at its bud and its flower is released into the active space of human society. The metal shoots out in pointed flames, casting off its earth; it is given birth to; its potentiality becomes an actuality; it shouts through the land. Twined metal thread corkscrews up the spine, gold emblazonry on the canopy, coins and nails. It leaps and spans its cyclic course, and falls back to earth, recombines with its sulphide and runs pell-mell to the sea.

•

Raising the question of whether it is we that are using the metal or the metal that is using us... Steel works closes with loss of 2000 jobs.

•

Man wound up to a knot of muscle, all fixed eye and lung, blind and deaf to the spreading world, stabbing and pecking at the ore, tearing it down, owl-man, hawk-man, man in despite of himself, driven into an underground language-laboratory by the ache in the clay and hammering at a proposition until it yields its full and proper sequel with all the arts of war... Man at his worst, focused entirely on the one point of engagement with the world, deaf and dumb to all the rest of the year. The only consequence he accepts is immediate gratification. The shining stuff tumbling into the box.

•

But he brings it down, he wins it, and refills the hole in time with the residue. A position is moved to a result, a work is completed, and passes out of his hands into distribution and coinage, not his concern. And he returns, day after day he returns to the workface, year after year until there is nothing left worth getting, the cavities in the hill are scraped clean and everything else is sunk in water beyond reach. The latch on the door rusts into nonentity or disappears beneath stalagmite while the door fades into a fungus-stain. His work encapsulates his death somewhere deep in the head of a casual historian or local hobbyist, strolling over broken ground. He disdains secondary pickings.

•

He continues always in the prime cause. He passes through narrow tunnels and vast slippery caverns in search of his love, following the twists and jerks of the vein, where it divides and re-forms, drawing yellow twine through his eyes by the pale flicker of his forehead on the blank walls, streaked red and brown like Sunday's dinner. Indeed everything homely is mercilessly parodied in these appalling underground routes and halls: an old mattress perched on a cavern ledge like an electronic clock at a chess match, relic of some earlier defeat, some troglodyte earnestness interrupted by the police; bits and pieces of homeland pressed everywhere into service as props and winches: parts of mangles, bed-ends and stair-rails coated in slime and flow-stone. The drowning of years moves under his feet. The palace of flesh is dark, silent, and smells of gunpowder.

•

Ruthlessly, ear-plugged, he delves for the true substance, the one result, bright and whole in the tray ready for processing into the world. Its potential harm is then someone else's burden, but at least it is the real thing; whatever Society puts it to there is no excuse to be passed back to Nature: the material was initially true as delivered. He knows nothing about all that – diplomacy, "piecemealing", invasions of ore-bearing countries in the name of Freedom, bread bleached with white lead, self colonisation, debased coin, screen illusions, enforced waste, cheap copper for the East India Company, echoic side-focus into nothing at all – he knows nothing of all that. Through the hollow climate of singularity he persists until there is no more, the metal bridges its last gap to the sea and the mines close. The reward remains in the sky for future workers: star headband last seen as a pale signature on a pardon: human privilege, the blood-leap, joyous cap. He destroys himself.

•

He works at nothing but his own death. Only the constraints on him, only the worries, humanise or harmonise his career, opening it to a possible future, by the analogy of the tilled field. Customs and combinations lift his torn self from the pit and carry it back to his family.

•

The hill, the limestone ridge, is riddle with these abandoned courses, thousands of failures scarring the walls of tunnels and shafts – tracks of the spark, the minute speck of light at the bottom of the box he sank into. His entire life glows beyond his death, like everyone else.

•

Grey green limestone ridge seeming to brush the transverse sky heavy with cumulonimbus. In that narrow, hardly distinguishable band between the ridge top and the cloud is a wind-swept table-land littered with old furniture, crumbling headgear, forgotten shafts, tumuli, TV masts, telegraph poles, engine houses now barns, neglected grey stone walling, broken ground with mounds, hollows, and crumbling banks. The soil rich in calcium encourages the growth of eyebright and dyer's greenweed. And in the failing but persistent light of day's end a grey aura everywhere as it all slowly sinks into bibliographic oblivion, closed and falling, faint murmur of traffic from the town below, scattered rooks in the air, tufts of wiry grass swept sideways... How the whole band curves and storms into the valley shaking with lies and broken promises, the whole stratum scribbled and fought over and over and completely illegible, the lights below gasping supine for information-thrills, the town pulling the fringes of distances over itself, fighting for sleep. The wind battens the grass, beats and plunges about my head as the light finally slips away and the meaning of these paltry ruins is swept over the heads of the town and away, for really there is nothing to be gained from all this febrile perseverance and concentration, there is no linear reward and nothing is secured until death.

*

The world is missed, again and again, we are busy in a darkness while the days flew over us like birds in a storm and only the total sum of a life will show a moment's burgeoning. Surely we catch the joy of it where this thread refolds on itself at love's conclusion.

* * *

A person's single reach continued to its end where it's fast to the earth possibly becomes in the back thrust and petalling of patience, becomes the shelter sited beyond this medium ground, death shining like a solid star, blasted through eternity and exclusively here as the line taut across hope is at that goodly moment inhabitable, and will be indefinitely.

•

This hollow globe is incapable of inaccuracy. Reward lines it. And at once the closed landscape wrapped in tough grass held tightly to the earth, our single star, is held among us as it slowly dawns on us, our prize is the earth.

Manifold

Green and white valley and the river
fast, double, manifold, always
full when most empty, bright threads
across the land, spring grass and
history it doesn't mean a thing
if you break the accord.

Nightscape cast in space, patches of
white rock glowing in the fuzzy darkness,
questionless, clouded eyes turned aside
and why not when we get what we are in the
end anyway, always, end up with what
we are bound to.

Duple creature, quick river every summer
vanishing into the earth, to secret courses
and underground lakes, empty bed blazed up
the valley centre, pebbles hot to the hand.
Carry them up to the summit caves,
the ox-head wake.

And in winter constant rush and throb of water against
stone, arch of sound, sides of night forming.
Our eyelids are stapled to the earth,
we are guardless and empty without you,
plodding simply back to an unnoticed room,
eyelids stapled to the earth.

II

THE LIGHT alternates, comes and goes
in days and years and yet remains
the perfection of constancy held in
the length of terrain by human sight.
The streams descend from the hills
and meander over the plain, broadening
and deepening, receiving the sun's face
and casting it back onto the side walls
of old terraced houses, slowly decaying
factories, small hospitals, brick sheds
deep in bracken and willow-herb, sites
of persistence, signs that we are
here to stay, all of us, stations
whose weathering is on record
and anchors the language to a history
of completions.

Then there is nothing trustworthy in this world
but the heartfold, the construct that endures
beyond our means. Our promises are worth
less than the cheapest fastener on the market
and the earth falls away at a touch.
                                        The city –
the plastic spoon, the double bed, the book.
What else holds us, what sparkling trellis across
the race meaning a trust we don't actually
perform – of course it breaks – we know
perfectly well where social good resides,
at the journey's end, the making quest.

And deep in a diurnal faulting, wedged
into a space making both day and night seem wide,
someone is working, peering, scratching away,
and the lamplight of a den persists undimmed

for weeks, burning brighter and sinking deeper
into the gap between two homes, where work
of solitude delves at the bases of love,
the weight and stability of the transcript itself.

To see one thing clearly we distort
the entire landscape: it bends, clouds,
dissolves and slips away to a darkness
out of time; and the one thing being known
at once radiates back its own illumination,
splaying up the cleft towards day.

The landscape is fed back to its source
at our fingertips; the one-thing being made
is hoisted up the shaft towards home,
redoubling the truth of what's there,
by what's surely somewhere,

That we have as an idea of perfection, moving
with us on the earth in a strict veracity
to which the light responds, playing
and diversifying its facets among
the town roofs, windows, doorsteps –
the realisation of potential articulated
into a document, the moral law delivered
from nowhere by an ancient child
who crawled out of a hole in the ground,
the simple tale of sunlight on the fields

That spreads over the meadows and estates
every morning, rears itself aloft
and late in the day slides sideways away
off the pointed roofs and hedge backs
it flows, and slips away, never
(in a way) to return, since we are mortal.

And fail, warp and crack like the earth.
We know what's right but the body is weak,
and shrinks in fear before the non-person,
the person nullified into command.
And there is probably some advantage in this failure,
something secret and speculative, unclear
to the self, which could end in resignation
from event, work, world or sense.

    Stay with us! Get up! There is work to be done:
    the King is sick or sad, the cabbage patch
    is run riot and the ore lies under our feet.
    And none of these stands a chance without
    specific challenge, leverage, frontal focus –
    the moment is decisive, and slips ahead of us,
    disappearing into the flux.

The roundabout in the play-park
spins on, grey sky on the paving,
the rooks rise and swerve aside.
Suburban structures: colleges, workshops,
bungalows, horizontal slabs, ashamed
of their lack of detail – strings of the heart
held taut but untouched, nothing for the light
to engage. This empty success
spins on. There's no one near it.

"It is better to fail, and to fall short, than
to succeed as the non-person. But in failing,
and being defeated by all that vacant armour
you not only further the descent into bitterness
you also gain in your way some of the apparent
and immediate rewards of uncaring: ease, self
reinforcement, the comfort of discomfort stifled.

"For goodness' sake aren't we defeated threatened
emptied enough by the world and our bodies not to add
to the store arguing with phantoms, tricks of air,
an empty suit, a manner – nothing there, nothing to be
afraid of, nothing to love. Waiting to be condemned
by an expert on heroes you don't trust, you end up
suspended on full pay. Congratulations."

EXPERT HERO judge, Spirit of the Lamp sprouting
up from the space at the centre of the person –
he arrives in the night, uninvited and unexpected,
clears the table and starts examining the books.
No, he doesn't need a cup of anything thank you.
Page after page he prises open the weatherstones,
moths and may-bugs hammering on the window panes,
he weighs our reluctance against metal and opens
the road into substance, that stretches as far
as anyone knows. And once the opening is known
someone has to go through it. If you merely play
at access the money turns to treacle.

Patriarchal, he speaks for and against us, alt-
ernates, shouts hope & failure from a stone box
in a tumulus until the sleepers can't sleep and someone
is sent out to deal with it, answer the world, Go –
Go we to seke that we shall nat fynde, the new lover
sets off in the grey dawn closing the earth
around him, pauses under the cold gatehouse to
adjust a shoulder strap, wipe a tear, enters
the wind and sticks out a thumb.

The captains of industry perceive
a roadside shadow, a flicker of darkness
against the wall. They all
head for the city.

Bone holds flesh in a cup
as does limestone, hold lead ore,
aloft, indeed up to us,
shielding the meniscus
against the weather with
a flat and bony hand. We inhabit
a concatenation –

Succession of barely noticed moments
which add up to the absolute conditional
of the person, something fixed beyond our
intervention as if it were a dream, a closed building
and the key is a bright idea somewhere
else, far away, behind a barrier. But
the barrier is alive, flesh, the barrier is us.
Which is only to say that it is difficult
to direct a life, and the heart thrives
on the fine detail at its constant centre –
the true moment at which we do have a leverage
on our existence, that holds the key, the code,
the cup of plenty to which everything turns,
pearl of earth –

Here! Ordinary! Personal! Lived!
– new and immediately full response
set in its own discovery at the out-
come of tension and resistance:
the resolution that we seek somewhere
beyond its loss stands in front of us:
the one true thing, the life being
worked. Not the whole. The present
surety. And it is held up, and calls
out to us across the bleak shores and
engine shops of the land like
an infant cry, a note that sounds

slightly ahead of its striking
resonating through an empty city.

And all the high set objectives
we read of in the white shell annals
are the dense core of nothing –
the object at the end of the tunnel
a calcium mantle, glowing erratically
in the cavernous half-light, fixed on us,
seeming to approach as we approach it,
straight before us. It must be
a distraction, it has to be a trick,
there's no one anywhere near it.

The metal reconstitutes its ore in the sad rain
and there is no enduring substance, this hard fabric
is nothing – a cloud under the moon, whirling ash,
crumpled and soggy paper in the middle of the road –
career-based decisions, uncaring circulars…

Oh bore it, pierce
that thick, insensate grin
to the quick, busy
flesh alive with distant light.

Every faint gesture rebounds on us
leaving a vacant hollow in the world:
possible, unfulfilled acts embedded
in the tissue, growth points too late –
the land is riddled with failed promises
and premature returns.

He picks his way among hollows and craters,
earth funnels of abandoned mineshafts,
bracken fields, rose bushes gone wild,
dry voices ringing in the air
exhortations to labour and be patient –
derelict electricity sheds, tram lines
sunk into gravel, grassed-over courts;
he passes rows of empty cottages,
inhabitants now hospice inmates,
boarded-up shops and brick-scattered streets,
chapels and hermitages in stony wastes
all empty, ripe for development, reflex impact,
populations blasted to nonentity.

Sky-hatred, she said, has only one object:
you and I. That, then, is the prize —
accept cash, take no porous deferment,
bone illusions, phosphor worry tricks,
takeovers, price rises, truth hijacked…
The only substance broken and not severed
shared and not divided is love.

       Bolted fast in empty night,
       only a few pointers
       on the surface of event,
       lights on the quarry face —
       will the door open and
       she be there in
       her multifloral bodice?

As he passes up into the valley, a multiplicity
opens at the terminals of vision:
the earth horizon, full of buried gold,
lit from beyond loved from within,
casting mental energy back on the liver
sufficient indeed to the single purpose of
living; nobody could deny the one desire we
ever at the most are; and begin to multiply.

The future lies embedded in conglomerate
at an underground junction where fossils
seek revenge for our very enjoyment
of the world in all our days.

We can ignore it, and do, opting for respite
but then the more of the world we scan
the more impossible monstrosities are revealed
until we bury our heads in travel like any tourist
and moan about the multiplicities of home.

And always the point of generation, turning
and dividing point, is there at the avid focus
where we fold our flesh round the blade:
total transmission. I mean death
joins us in hope.

And we can turn from failure
as from nourishment, se-
lect but not really, we are
not thieves.

We wait at the light,
we feed ourselves
to the unsevered gate,
the instrument.

WAIT FOR (each day) the light
feeding through the instrument
to emerge and fan out miles
above our heads, bearing
what we can't yet know
across the sky at speed
and leaving a faint moony glow
on our hands like a trace of dream,
a February window scene
which broke under the drill and was
carted off in lorry-loads to front a bank.

Late in its course the stream turns south
and courses to the equinox, free at last
of slopes and details it widens and deepens,
making its own way, picking up fragments
of industry, returning to source.

We spread our language through the world
laterally, drifting southwards, seeking warmth
as if unwittingly but not without hints
of requital to the world at large against
an inner vacuum, blasting copper out of
native populations like so much dead rock.

Now her beams fall unmet to ash
in the lobby ashtray,
and puny sparks of hired spite
fall onto the map,
the world's table, obscuring
all the carefully sought detail
under scars and burns
of impersonated anger. It is handed
to the archivist.

Again the transcript is netted
under preservative (sorry of her
latent fear to be the ever bud)
and this is fairly well how we live.
It is more and less like the sky plane
rotted through with stars.

The sea, that great portrayal of the sky,
bounds right across the earth and smears
the local beach with shell paste,
that settles and hardens as the waves
steal slowly back. A residue, a vocabulary.

The fuzzily scanned future of our acts
becomes a chalky rubble under our feet,
crumbling downgrade, offer and result
of protection from climate, horizontal
bone web across the rim of hope.

We mould the materials of earth to our own rhythms
ignoring the backlash – we sink into the ground.
The two-faced caretaker sleeps through a televised
transplant of which he is star victim, exchanging
his person for an image held in time, instant replay.

As if merely connecting the self
made your future, or anyone else's.

In the dim green light of an industrial chapel
the hero of this section eats Nottingham lace
at a seemingly endless presentation dinner.

Stay by me,
distracted advocate,
alternating light
falling past me.

        The hills and plains, river
        valleys, corners and quarters
        of the town, wrapped
        in early day – keep them
        free of our connections.

        Let them be what they are
        as the accounts clerk hurries to work
        on a cold sunny morning, pulling
        his coat tighter at the neck
        as he rounds the demolition block,

        Dreaming of coffee or company
        and the narrow light in a shop window
        catches a gold ring (my father,
        Manchester c.1935, wondering
        if he could afford to get married).

The flash, skystrike,
borrows me to air –
fruit never fully
accounted.

THE FLESH, skystruck,
burns me to air-fruit,
never finally accounted

and the faceless sky's face,
sharper than dawn, wider than day,
met in mid career as a bright, tensed,

slightly creaking surface casting back
the world as something suddenly there,
the danger that realises the fear,

at a touch flies open. The sky-mirror breaks
through us and the world behind it falls;
distance becomes total.

The blast shakes the hill, and caught
in the tunnel, facing the dragon head on,
the only defence is the point, hub of patience
        at the end of the sword.

(The trick is to strike quickly
and dart ahead of the outcome,
then return for serious dealings.)

(Obviously anything coming towards you armed in a tunnel is the earth, the culmination of your doubt, whatever it is. Whether it's a member of the thought police or your lover's fading eye, it's still the earth, ash and streams, forests and hills, petrol stations and customs houses and the red-brown mantle on the crest of the ridge in autumn; and anyone wearing a uniform with signs on the shoulder is claiming to be acres of grassland held together by walls and bridges and railway lines, coming towards me, left hand outstretched right behind back; family, and staff, and you, and you of only yesterday, pine trees and inner suburban gardens swaying like tassels in the pre-storm wind: it all comes towards me, and one day we'll sink entirely each into each other...)

(It's all very well knowing what the tricks are supposed to be, but something else to survive the moment. Like stepping smartly aside into a plate-layer's niche from which you may not be able to get out because you are a saintly statue. Or just going on, continuing for the present, striding on newly armed towards the green, ferny glimmer in the black distance, not at all sure whether the aggressive drunk passed to left or right of you or all round you like a waft of hot air or straight through the middle and not daring to look back...)

(From behind the earth looks very like Eurydice, on her way to the pit.)

(The earth is scared stiff of us.)

And what if we endured earth's glory
outside the museum, outside the silence,
what if we bought something of the world
worth more than a Welcome doormat?
And what if we take the pain
as a factor of resistance and
continue, under the three protectors:
road, food, house.

        The old man sits by the gas fire, cat
        on knee, fastened to the portable TV.
        All his knowledge is constantly averted
        until there is hardly anything left of him,
        and the masters of silence talk unanswerably
        in a luminous blue mist beamed at the soul's shell.
        So his dream passes constantly, wider and wider
        through him, and will, until there's
        nothing left, poor ghost.

And what if we endure
the glory of this pain
anywhere, loudly,
dazzled by the actual world
articulating light
in my eyes.

        Moving from day
        to year his cap
        is split, his heartspace
        folded in two.

YEAR CAP split heart
space folded
in half

disfavour in
the air in the air

the city destroyed by jokes.

For the breath is prompt but the limb infirm,
stay awake and keep talking, the breath
is ready but the carnival is insecure

And the shadows swirl and focus,
negative energy claims its form –
the abandoned mineshaft barking in the sky
into which this whole substance, not just
life, not just you and me, this whole physics
will one day be tipped, light and all.

The flesh is willing but the structure aches.

Our false language draws us towards the invert star
that sheds dark beams of disappointment across the towns
and those once as children so wholly engaged into life
by joy walk heavily from door to door feeling
nothing but an inarticulate resentment that makes us
pull the blankets over our heads and snarl at each other
like trapped hounds / Colourless and formless ikons
of purposeless living, a talking photograph in the
living room to which there is no possible reply;
birth blood and battles for the sake of a tin hood
that does ninety and lasts a few years.

It is not respite, it is not safety or status.
July, tops of the ash branches already paling.
It is not your hand on my sleeve at the brink.
Valley hay fields full as the sea, a fold of smoke
hanging over the market town picked out by late
sunlight and every westward surface brightens for a minute
and surely the core of active wrong emanates from elsewhere,
not in our language at all or anybody else's –
not human and not world, not sense or nonsense,
a vague threat pulling from behind the galaxies,
outside the whole swelling sphere of time, of which
we are the skin, that we hold together.

We are beset by hypnotic clouds, dispersals of substance,
drawing us towards the void, artless existence
where all human constructs are interim, dragging
on the hollow spaces in our sensibilities,
results of ambition and restlessness which we thought
we had reserved for finer things, outshot
of the earth, at our return.

Nobody's writing The Phenomenology of Evil.
Stay awake and keep talking, fill the space
with substance, like an Irish brooch, draw out
the ribbon, fold and wind it into the enclosure,
which is the house, which means communication.
Draw it from the world's persistence. Tonight's
parcel post like a lion in the forest moves
to expectation, to continuity and response,
and what if perfectly solid men, men without
compassion, surge between us, toiling to
block the line with hollow gain – Nobody's writing
The Phenomenology of Evil and a moment's honesty
clears all the space we've got.

And nobody's writing the phenomenology of evil because
nobody wants to know. Each day the darkness shuts earlier
and behind the houses in old yards and neglected allotments
moths hover in clouds of seed under the arch of nettles,
a warm fermenting vapour holds the night creatures in ecstasy
as by day the martins zoom over the stubble fields
in great ellipses darting between electricity wires
and again the earth is caught in full action, engaged against
its own inertia and which side could we possibly be on?
We continue not writing the phenomenology of evil because
we can't be bothered, because our brain cells decay too fast,
because we still have the space available of a more urgent
engagement with good, knowing that no one will ever write
the phenomenology of evil because, set in the outering vortex
we view it and there's no one there; it's a cloud of
husk-powder in the eye between two walls, a television screen,
there's not a soul to be seen.

Don't stop talking. Any error will unwind itself given the chance to stretch out, plus a good pull and a well-balanced back-tortion. But follow it through: don't just feed it new images all the time, follow strictly the tracks of your assurance down to its origin and counter – the recognition, the bit of truth that gave it a foothold on the earth in the first place.

And it occurred to me that language, spoken written or thought, unwinds a thread of perception out of one body into another (the "bodies" are compacted moments but the "bodies" are also real people) and we follow this thread across, parallel to our awareness of the present (held in abeyance, or displaced for the duration of the discourse), developing a tension between two concurrent senses of being (being here & now and being in transition). This tension forms, as its resolution, a third being, a third place, which is both leverage and resistance to the will-power which drives the whole process, and is formal in relation to the due return to actuality. What I call bodies, the origins and ends of language, might also be states, with forms, spheres spirals and cones, and the process could as well be a matter of feeding a screen, or indeed, writing a book. The book is a physical embodiment of the tension, the third mode of being; it encapsulates the transaction between direct and referred attention, it gives it borders, walls, and streets, until it is the image of the third city, the city which is neither here nor not-here. It is a city we can only pass through, because we are foreigners and cannot own or hire its spaces. It is a travellers' city, an Arabian stronghold packed with brigands and sultanas. We come here to market. Sometimes we are detained, sometimes for our own good, camped out on the maidan at the Kaid's (the author's) pleasure; but we shall never live there. We pass through this map to a new, newly gathered, entity, place or point, quite distinct from that to which the natural world would of its own accord drift, for better or worse. Every human act genetically modifies the species, since it is only at that new point (of access and departure) that we gain our formal existence, and the moment is absolutely decisive in the future of the world and fate of its bearers.

What is the point of our being at all if we cannot advance by what we have made?

You get up, gather your coat from the wall, and go out, in the middle of my sentence, closing the door behind you. And that too, I'm afraid, is a linguistic act, bringing us to a new place. Like a gunshot.

Surviving Fragments of the Solo Diatribe

… ignorance transformed by art into a damaging lie, the city destroyed by jokes …

… organs fixed: firmly and aggressively deviant, no entry, no risk, takes the skein of language and wraps it up, uses it for a, what, a belly dance? a spectacle? a sterile wrapper? Plunders the third city for reflections in symmetrical facets …

… self-dissemination, folding a tinted mirror at the world …

… without compassion, totally solid, stopping at nothing, they would fill us with their skins, the broadcasters …

… falsity made to bear the same structure as truth …

… in every way a copy of God.

and what but perseverance will carry us through this labyrinth of denial to the poles of day, where the black glass dissolves into the light and dark world: here, ordinary, personal, and lived?

Postcard: Please forgive
my silence and homily, say all
is forgotten and come back.

(Some reasons for the cancellation of the diatribe:)

Indeed there are other things too:
poems, or orders, which don't unwind
extend or delay anywhere but smite
in a flash to the centre of the mind:
You are to report to Divisional Office at once
for assessment / re-education / torment.
Delete as appropriate.
Your life is a poisonous waste.

Dead leaves in the emperor's garden,
flame and ash in one, floating
on the cold stone ponds.

DEEPER INto stone than any technology can reach
        is the stone in the heart / humanity partitioned
from itself by gut senses of uncertain belonging
        hinged on fear, the stone in the heart
on which a small bird, a finch, perches,
        tearing up the throat.
Deep clarity of pure dread, thin light cast off
        the crystal arc at dawn, floating in the streets
as the striped men arrive and knock on the door –
        whole quarters of the town change hands,
forced separation of families, lovers defeated and alone –
        chipped and scratched songs of sleepless nights
pulsing in the vein like trapped birds – whole lives
        donated to the structure, the facility.
So in our mannered fatigue we stifle the fleshly sparrow
        with relish and an iron hand grasps the heart
year after year, pitiless pursuit of reinforced advantage
        year after year drawing the human total down
into cavities of earth, dream, purposeless toil,
        concealed disappointment –
                                    Dust of millions
grey sludge of bone powder run into the fields
        where it settles and weighs into the ground,
expressing pockets of deceptive honey, glassy edges,
        flowers blurred in ice, bright winged creatures that
flash past us in the tunnel, scoring the walls,
        smell of burning on the edge of the city – someone's
bright idea, deaths of millions and for what? by-product
        of an accelerated industrialisation policy,
concerning nobody, vast unwritable acts of mass brutality
        always intended, by errors of substitution,
to do good, to bring relief.

Throw our guilt on the heap of clay stars
        and burnish love into the day.

AND THERE, at this very spot arrived at,
indeed "under our noses", resides the difficulty –

unstructured and unstructuring particular
that doesn't want to be translated anywhere
and begins the answer about wrong and guilt,

that we call "anything" in our silence,
"nothing" in our fault. There are midges
in the air tonight, it's very close

and all the intermediary separations of the
distracting world devolve on this point
of attention, unsevered gate

that re-asserts itself into script, casually
through our bodies against all the pre-
human facilities of a controlled situation –

the midges prance in the clearing by the stream,
in the sunbeam, held there by the entire universe
and I am not reminded of anything

except the
                    rotten old
                                      universe again.

Naturally it is adored from
near or far. Struck at a pitch of
valid energy the range is immaterial.

(End: underground impact course, 1-8

Seq.: the disaster opens to a new vein, 9-11 + ending)

III

HELD IN conative energy distance is acute
but the range is immaterial. And the impacted moment
settles daily into pitch as the absolute conditional
of living, the true the sonic diamond can you imagine
walking across a field without it? unaligned? future
flattened to a dead circuit of purposeless therefore
repetitive action? Nothing on earth is worth a glance
until our knowledge of it turns on the spindle
that cuts through memory and expectation and brings
the end of distance to bear on what's "under our
noses" indeed where we very carefully set it like
a gold fish in a green pond, scintilla, this
cocoon of light revolves on its axis as it holds
a human entirety in a state of transformation,
cells clustered in imaginal buds, that float freely across
our infrastructural (pain) webs towards the waking night,
there to unfold, carapace bedecked with insignia…

As anyone can see on the darkest day there are
cavities in substance, where the earth in its rush
to the day's completion tears itself apart and is
thrown against itself, rearing and falling – it seems
difficult to know how people, fixed or settled in their
various holes do steer the whole edifice by moral acts
towards its end, maintain the earth along the edge of time,
every bright leaf in sight taking the strain of galactic pull.
Housed in pockets of earth we play perceptive sense
onto resistant and laden masses at our focus,
prise open layers of rock, paper, fat, disrupt
all the sweetly bent harmonies that pull us towards
a rigid incompletion, by forcing the resolution. But listen
to the dead men mumbling and growling inside every pebble
of the vast shoreline, like a nearing bomber
or a disappointed crowd, listen to the unearthly noise…

And the saint on his tiny island in the bay
like a doctor in his surgery, islanded off
from the unhealing world and blasted out
of self regard by pressure of work – love
like this meets constantly the resistance of
matter directly as a gardener where every shrub
is won from nothing into the ancestral shield,
and the stones rise to the hand.

Sudden turn of winter in late April –
aubrietia in flower
under pillows of snow!

*

A usual day, taken up with mending.
We run through the list of jobs
and go to bed.

Only to face the entire circus.
Sleep is engaged to prospect into the hill
and does it – by the book, in straight lines,
dictionary and log tables to hand, using
a compass marked in two ellipses
and The Easy Method Surewin Pools Guide.
And sometimes gains and sometimes doesn't
but being freed, in the moment, from will,
always retrieves what is in fact there.

Organic energy tends towards regularity
and the end of that dream is law, the final
symmetry, the victory of flesh over stone.
For stone resists order and pushes down into
chaos and sameness. Flesh clears a space, a small
travelling theatre at the heart of substance which
as it goes on its way leaves a track, an engravure,
a furrow across the strata of occluded time,
traded for air and filled in with ink.
And dreams and laws with their musts and mustn'ts
in the end only delineate what is –
sentences of the Book of Reasons,
spoken by an ancient child
who crawled out of a hole in the ground.

Unable to sustain love we succumb to the strata
or tear out the jewelled ring at the centre and turn
the earth back towards us in the act of signature.

And we shall too, meet the night sky's lording
in what we bear, in every knot we wear.

THE CITY's surface and perimeter swollen
with lights, command of feeling as extended
and productive biological need, five police cars
and an ambulance, the slightest immediate
kindly act and the very gaucheness to say it.

The catalogues of favour slowly accumulate
in right acts of any scale, etymologies and
histories of musical instruments, whether in
rage or cheer we burn through the night of thought
until the flags descend on us.

All the work is directed to this grace
whereby in a moment's turn as in a year's
bulletin we are rehumoured, and cast
resentment adrift like a fishing line
in the earth's blackness behind our home.

Oh lightly as if not bothered, to justify
being this forward transaction between soil & sky
that sharpens its claws on the city walls
and laughs at the tortuous blinds of earth,
knows them to a T and adores the green patina.

Than as the candle burns lower the spoils
of chaos are set in a wicker basket and brought
to market, bearing his fatherly self for smelting,
and courage is care, care is purpose, the weight
of earth falls off.

IN THE DREAM-shaft it was faster: door in
the whole, ore-body, world-image sighted
as a warehouse of the self from which
we feed us a supply-line into time;
but that copious garden (fire and ash
crystallised in the night) is a globe
of perception under great tension that
at a touch flies open, bearing such
strength and focus towards us at speed,
faster than bone can ever withstand.

Deep well in hilltop garden as if
we could be lowered away and never
have to be bothered with love again,
but cultivate boredom in a national park,
barbed wire and binoculars, to the last day.
Look out of the window: the grass is hard
and quivers in the rain-wind.
The hilltop garden is death's own plot
where we search for our ancient child in
the vorticist angles of our immediate trade
and its histories –

Oh if you will trade me for constancy I
will seal the compact with my whole
expression, my figure etched in the
die my life sunk in the eye leaving
nothing behind, not a trace. If I were then
given fully might I be complete, un-
merged or hard bound enough at least to be
a spoken fact before the offspring of our love.

The substance, tensed and struck, flies at us –
we are cut, but can enfold the flint
in our cloth, can bear the news.

FLESH WITH
stands and stands
with
to the world's end.

Do you suppose you have any enduring structure,
anything worth offering and keeping save
the enduring imagination bearing on particulars
as loving care? Your life is an empty waste.

The royal gardens fell ages ago –
stone rings sunk into the ground, leaf debris
and moss carpets over the paving flags –
it is the world departing, folding in on itself –
the trees spread at ease and collapse: of
twelve birches, seven remain and a dove bone,
thin as wire, leans under the turf.
No spirit, no presence, no memory. Anything
seems to be saying nothing, and all this
material, stone, fibre, with no one to hold it,
rots, swirls, and tumbles into hell.

But flesh is bound
to the meeting place
of earth and space
by the point of efflorescence
between the eyes

and tries
death's employ.

Adonaïs

The second pain is the loss of pain,
the shrinkage, and survival

Waiting for time like a long sunday school procession
to meet its end –

Hospice inmates, retainers, industrial archaeologists,
busy up to the last minute

Plotting and preparing a past
for which it is long too late,

Death as the future tense of courage.
Awakened from working out life,

You brave entry
to what you are –

Crystallised blood on the lens,
windscreen wipers too slow for the rainstorm,

Big floppy leaves swept over tombstones,
and the tall grass swaying.

The Mission catches up with the Music
and we're home.

* * *

And the miners all dead, not party to any of this,
striding in vast tunnels under the earth
to and from the workface, singing
    Con los minerales vine
    Con les minerales voy

Pockets stuffed with burning jewels, trapped
in crystal, inhabitants of the deep translucent world
that is only the world we know, cast before us, cast
outside us, for our good.

Sparks of flesh scattered on the earth,
flowers, that speculate, and call and call
till there is no rest to be had, the tower flats
buzzing and flashing through the night beside the river,

Procession of tail-lights on the motorway arm,
tunnel of orange glow, sweeping past the spangled
power stations and depots, clouds of steam lit inter-
mittently from below, brief flowers on a tumulus.

We are worn to a point in the clarified dark,
flesh smoke always in our nostrils and before
our eyes, sharpening the distance towards the end,
the island home and true repose –

For in spite of everything we are together,
every single one of us, dead and alive,
and something won't let us forget it, this
endless hammering inside matter.

The outside also matters.

* * *

Full moon, limestone ridge
a grey bank against the night sky,

Aura in the trees and round
the corners of the house, not a

Match struck. The mouse
squeaks in the grass,

The cat sleeps, dreaming
tomorrow into question.

The mines – they all ended
in a silent lake.

Lines on the Liver

Der smit uz Oberland
warf sinen hamer in mine schoz
und wohrte siben heiligkeit

The smith from foreign lands
struck his hammer into my chest
and wrought seven blessings

(quoted by Novalis)

(a)

It seems to me now that any person or place we ever might suppose to identify ourselves will always be an excuse for being later than we are. To verge on, yearn for, or enter into truth supposes a distance which is not where we live, for very truth means that we are already there. The truthful distance which occupies our lives gains its language from within, as we range through from diurnal bodily pacts out to the stellar hazards of speculation, with always the same faculty of thought engagement that exposes love over the whole; and surely any wish apart from that continuous presence breaks it, and wrenches the mind into another journey towards itself. It must be elliptical, and can never arrive, if separation from the quester's own being is the motivation and stay of the journey, and defence from the world's inquests. And in that self-perpetuating self-seeking the human image finally eradicates itself, and occupies only the gap in the torque, the emptiness before the mirror (the mirror shows a beautiful garden or a child who duly responds to us or any other receding prize) and is indeed the nothing masked by writing.

But what about the journey which the unmirrored and unmirroring self constantly undertakes in its participation in lived reality: acts of love, queuing for milk, patient inquiry into the sublime, doesn't that also have its necessary script? and isn't the felt hollowness of living which writing seeks to answer something else, in that case, than a projection of the self's incompletion, a mere vacancy? What about that breath of fresh air when the self no longer sucks back its substance from alterity but betakes itself into its materials as a ready whole? doesn't the self then claim its entirety on the spot in offering itself right out? doesn't it become nonsense then to talk about the "wholeness" or not of something which is its own field of engagement with the world anyway? isn't the lack which drives us into work then something from a distance, if not distance itself? The cross of good will and difficulty realises the construct in all its detail: theatre of desire which bounds the singular space of the person as of a city. And they who freely choose set themselves on the inner edge of knowledge, and drawing their lives onto their shoulders, refusing to act as anything which doesn't completely coincide with itself, at once set deformation and absence outside and visible, and stand alone before the sphinx which is the world asking back the disowned question about the failure of love. I mean why does all the perceptual space passing through us have to come out in twisted shreds of meaning or be ruled and chopped into bars and stored in jealous caves? The world itself is not like that, but extensive at any price in the terms of its constitution; and we speak partially and commit cruelty by proxy as if we have no proper right to be here – what's the matter with us? The quest remains, not to find yourself but precisely to lose yourself into the interrogation, which as it persists in staying within your experience is that much stronger in its resistance to premature disclosure and resolution, than the selfhood coyly evading its own capture in public gardens, and is thereby disclosed and resolved in a far greater reward – the furtherance of realisable good. (There are those who will tell you, in the cloak of loveliness, that virtue is an event of the selfhood, and oh if that were possible we wouldn't need to lift a finger, we'd live for ever coiled in the dream winding backwards from the instant of good intention.) Then she gathers the past up at the hem who sets into such a venture, only the possibility of which is actually chosen, and arched against the blast is indeed the sign she makes, by which it is to be known that time is complete, and no objective will replace death.

(b)

I thought this in the process of moving house: not far, some twelve miles, eastward over England's central ridge, where it ends here in a terminal boss, a dome of ore-bearing shell-residue, a white capsule of sedimentary patience twelve miles across, patinated thin green and powered from underneath, lately christened by the tourism office The White Peak. This pendant pearl hovers above the magno-industrial parks and wastelands of a different centrality: the Midlands: flaky shale, coal mines, ironstone, potters' clay, executive dinners, that extends to east and west of the limestone, while to the north millstone grit marks complete northern refusal and reaches down to clasp the sides of the gem. A national park has quarried the King's Field down to school tarmac, but this is completely ignored. The princely townships of the plains are elsewhere, and a sense is taken of outlying stations, and a gathering ground.

Moving east, then, and setting up house well up an eastern valley-side, just off the limestone, facing west, as we had previously been just off the limestone to the west, facing east. What is behind me is then in front of me and I walk backwards into the future, a blind sense of desire which is normal to reading and thought, and having it tabulated here I take it up into the work, the figure of my spine, the S, the written creature that I send out into the dawn, eyes shaded against star-blast, tapping the ground – this is my guide.

This move, freely chosen, has me arriving here and climbing to my window seat on a diameter between two arcs: a diagonal tension across the land. I swivel my chair between west and north, and in front of me, in front of everything I say, always, is that pastoral dome stuffed with regal imminence tier on tier. It underlies my vision like a table-top mappemunde or a chest of drawers stuffed with prize money, the past halting itself at a plateau surface marked "Gently Dip, but Not Too Deep..." Ring, clock-face, axle, compass: it is complete, and it suspends vision in stone libraries of forgotten voices fluttering against the skin, shells or kisses spinning like tops in the calcium night. Anyone could last for ever in that luminescent offer of gain, following a vein further and further into the ground, fixed on a wire of discourse whatever the consequences. But the Professor of History paces the eastern highlands behind me looking for his lost child and further away on all sides is a dull rumble from the offices of time, trouble up at 'mills. The intaglio demands a living body to wear it; the moment arches to contain.

My glance westward lifts, over the hills, and comes up against something else: another band, another lexicon, another development, stretching up through the Midlands to Liverpool and the Lancashire coalfield via Stoke. It's behind me too, following the clay and coal up to Leeds and striking across the Pennines to rejoin itself. It is a motorway community where the same replica barstool sprouts from one end of the land to the other and housing-space looks like something merely tolerated by commerce. A linear labyrinth of sameness, grimly dedicated to its own furtherance in controlled energy, boxes and tubes. It advocates soul-loss, narrowing purpose and discountenance and hides its servility to fossil fuels behind a contempt for grace. I occupy an interval in this thing, a temporary fork that closes above me, an eye, with the M62 stretched across it. I sit by the stream.

For over a century people have felt threatened by this growth as if unable to breathe openly, in or out of it. But it is difficult to resent the line of semis creeping up the hillside when the hill is as blatantly artificial as the homes, which is what they seem to be and who knows what may be given birth in them? What we've done is actually all we've got: the hill is formed and clad in our knowledge whether it's a volcanic plug or a slagheap in disguise. This whole encrustation of the world is a band which is fully lived, every scar and flake is a human result, and from where I sit it looks like precisely the result of that marine fossil energy in suspension which has men mining in their sleep, the result of centuries of human accrual, society dreaming itself into astronomy. Hundreds of miles of warehouses are the outcast from a tunnelling into the hill of dreams which has no centre, so you can never arrive, and work and will become ends in themselves, for nothing.

But there is no self more industrially exploited and scraped hollow than that which views the great plains on the other side of the earth or time void of humanity and breathes a sigh of relief, as if it might be possible to act at last, on the edge of the grave. For this pressure is also a gravity and in its tense compaction this industrial displacement of settlement bears the possibility of a song sufficiently clasped in temporal awkwardness not to lure us into the negation of all endeavour, whirlpools of aesthetic solipsism. I wanted to prove that the usurped space is also in the heart from the start, under threat, waiting or begging to be colonised, so that the regret must be a guilt. The circular hilltop garden at the ends of my fingers (the space being-written, always redolent with the sharpness of death) must have (there must be) a gateway into this archive of fear, where the hand opens to validate at large the coin embedded in the palm. The creating faculty (flower and completion of the whitestone dream) would then come within sight of the dark labyrinth and propose not a toleration nor an absorption but a trade, maintaining the distance of communication, and in that light the black stone breaks into crystals from within. But to submerge, to condescend, to inhabit urban boredom in its own terms would (to me with my shelves of ancient men chuckling drunk by the lakeside) be as meaningless a piece of self-stifling as you could think of, the sacrifice of poet and labourer into the Great War and for what? The necessity (the men by the lakeside hear the word, giggle and nod) is for access to the great war that lies over all of the western world with coastal resorts as its Christmas truce, a war relayed from event to situation, in which the wastage was never greater. (It's all very well for the lakeside men, we only know them by satellite transmission and the edge is filtered out, the rhyme-scheme, the grinding work over generations; figures of ultimate reward, we get them by fake TV as surrogate parents, "round the corner".) And it is a war in which the enemy is yourself (how simpler it would be to have a simple parental enemy) contesting the right to be. As a member of this proud state I push it with my foot out of morbid curiosity. Sometimes when I switch on the news I feel like a migrating cuckoo coughing through Flanders.

But it's here anyway, again and again it is here without any previous notification and the heart inconveniently falls apart in the night. It is my own stomach I prod in the grass. And again the hand opens in social patience – it is demanded: the north wind comes tearing down the white cliff face laden with grit and smoke, a past which will not be gathered up free of guilt, and thought of the heart is also a persecution.

The primitive class-based tension across England North/West to South/East is a fake, a hat trick of northern comedians. It is not a tension of supply and demand, or raw materials and product, not since metal completed its circuit across the final human gap and the mines closed. Then anything comes from anywhere. Demand was fed back to supply long ago and the highland zone persists, on the motel screens, as little more than a packaging on urban squalor. There is some pull still between production and the vast mechanisms of safeguard, supervision and pictorial comfort, which we seemingly need in order to boil an egg, but this has no geography and both parties serve the same master: the nourishing and progression of the speed-web centres through which the dominant fuel can use us. This tension surely snaps the moment any participant looks up and wants to know what he or she is working for, and the whole of politics disappears down a hole: you are working to accelerate natural decay. The left hand smoothes the ground while the right hand waves a flag; the only reason they can't get on together is that their total work does nothing for anybody.

I wanted to add as clumsily as possible that the opposite of generosity seems to be built into this makeshift structure as its motivator (advantage), deceit as its linguistic vehicle. It becomes increasingly difficult to view the self or soul as something quite distinct from this edifice of lies, a purity soiled by its ingress -- "language contaminated by commerce" but without commerce we die. The pressure of expectancy from the world of importance on anyone's performance is a howling constancy that everyone feels and the untruth deployed in maintaining the pretence of conflict is not normally wilful, but rather hysteric and hypnotic. I would sooner believe that the uncertainties of intimate experience are themselves at the source of the fear which commerce uses and which the media spread everywhere. Then it can be recognised, since no one escapes it.

The only tension that finally matters is between this futility and its opposite, as experienced in states of hope. This true tension remains cardinal to a different geography, wherever there is space liberated for application and thought. So it is not going to be realised through the half-knowledges that entertain the visitor, but only in the mint vocabulary whereby anyone has access to reality lived as an immediacy, meaning the particulars are no longer in conflict with distance, but become substantive as the arena in which they stand increases by a dimension. No one could actually "want" to be poked awake in this way from suspension in the present; a blast of ice-cold indifference down the telescope makes us start and we want to know with some urgency what the reward is to be, for we haven't got all that long to go. We also hate it, but have to acknowledge the gentler and more persistent demand of the totality which also reaches us down the inky telescope or across the white sheets or wherever the completion of the moment finds us. And this horizontal crosses with that vertical and there we are in the middle: sitting up and asking what time it is. Across the house, the land, the workshop, the mind, this diagonal pull persists, between what we can do and how it can use us.

If my niche is brought to the fulcrum of these forces where it is my life and nothing else that signifies it, then there is hope of raising a leverage or personal balance onto natural inertia, energy so much fuller when it is spliced into care. It can only be a personal act, for we play and are strung on these tensions in a constant engagement with the momenthood of our own humanity, totally distinct, and from this action documentation and magic are similarly infantile distractions. The scale of international discourse is so slight that the self demeans itself to think of such a thing, and global market squabbles seem like faint echoes of personal acts long forgotten and superseded in the real world. It seems that a state or nation is something which acting as a person can only act at the person's meanest and most insincere. And maybe so it is if that is its function: to be our collective grasping and cheating for subsistence, our fear for survival. Isn't the hypocrisy of its claim to a function for good (so that it expands) the very point at which it causes vast and unthinkable harm? Isn't the wicked cheat of empire the reason why our comforts and benefits will in the long run fall apart leaving us at each other's mercy as public moral structures are again set aside in order to support business in crisis? I doubt if it has ever been any different.

Which is to say we are always stuck with this thing which is evil because it is never bad enough. I don't think in that case you can mend it. It's like a mass migration: you can't opt out and what you have to do is ride it – not cowboy style to glory but survive within or alongside it in order to stay where you are. There's no avoiding this literal involvement in public movement, there is no "quiet life". There is a pensioned-off condition of surplus time lag which it is an indignity to entertain, or there's the television lake village, sheer drudgery and categorical inequality in a pocket of pictorial solipsism, inhabiting only the wrapping of culture. No – we engage with the entire present or with nothing. Far from subverting or breaking the conditionals we receive as temporal tensions, the task is to raise them, to maximal balance. The tiredness, the administration, hell-bent on debasing humanity before its own facility, drags us across the world into alienated nonentity as soon as we risk ourselves into its function, i.e., project human fullness of soul into the hard, crumbling, ugly and disordered outer surface of the anthill of the state, and the lost souls who think they control it. We seem to accede to this political reduction in submitting to the choice of a career or detesting the government, but then we take the long road home. We grasp the fulcrum, and the luxuries of denouncing wrong give place to the duties of tracing harm back to its causes. And this movement, this progress that we move with, is only humanity's struggle to meet the demands of the inorganic world seeking to deploy us to its own ends. To attempt to retire from this civilising confrontation can only mean a re-engagement with materials already superseded, the tools for which have been melted down. Marching into the abandoned mine out of "interest" and watching the ceiling crack open. The music deep inside the nest is the rumble of time brought to a harmony.

Every venture we make has to be returned from, every brilliance dimmed, back to the stupid hordes plodding over the empty tablelands in search of somewhere to stop. Back to the self, back to the price of tea. Very old people often have a way of making this return quietly and unto themselves, sometimes in spite of themselves, and others may force it with yells to the same finality. I mean people can be loyal to their ways wherever they are without damaging difference, for the map is of a wholeness too strong to be distributed.

As I actually arrive here I turn my back on the forces raging across the land, and probably derive resentment and envy from them in the most casual and irrelevant performances, and am the more pursued the more I am swept wide at the splendour of the spread, the sun emblazoning the horizon before withdrawing it from sale. To bring this to consciousness is only to say what I already know, to rescue it from the sociological is only to return it to an actual society inhabited from within. It becomes moral from the particulars outwards – where else could we learn the dangers of our own acts? Harm at a distance, tea workers of Sri Lanka in our 3 o'clock trap: it is already too late, and no sample sacrifices or megaphonic expiations will do anything but damage our own language. Our acts are already at a distance because what we inhabit is the world and what we do is done in it, and to it, all of it. That part of it within our scope is then all the more the enclosed garden, the working arena, the king's field and all its demands. We sup the bitter-sweet cup of our limitation and put the long-term question, seeking the acts and knowledges which will enhance perception itself, up to its node of healing.

To arrive and stay is to accept anyone's position in the line of the unwilled tension, at a balance. "Balance" may be an easy suppressive word, a tool against the slightest trace of living energy, the sense of single necessity that drives love, but perhaps that is a refusal to see balance at all until it is rusted into position. An active balance is in constant peril which is the peril of our lives verging on entombment in the world. Any option is a pretence: bonehead machismo or arty gossamer poses, each concealing the other. In the meanest version of experience there is always a counter-valency, and the effort is, as I said, to raise the balance rather than tip it. And whatever ancient works may, by their fossiliferous distances, persuade us otherwise, I can't see this as anything but a sequence of personally lived and created acts, taking the form of an answering quest. The questing movement and the stasis of leverage and balance cohabit finely, in fact this paradox is one of our best tricks. By this we might be able to equal the duplicity of fate, the way our acts come back to us as puns and transfix us in their terms however much we shift – the mysterious disguises and metaphorical transformations of human result, its automatism. By the duplicity of script we acknowledge and rise to the mechanics of fate, hoping to maintain good (not necessarily present good) within submission to justice.

We follow our own lights. The only common directive is the highest precept. I sit here facing the labyrinth of pre-waste at its Northwest corner as the site of personal histories abandoned, concerning no one else. I am challenged by the foci of harm beyond and behind, the concealment of good within. I don't ask for this obsession but having got it there is a chance of leverage. Stationed here, I open a channel of question and answer towards a point of attention in time, along which various futures come rolling back to me. By tracking this tide onto a new present I stake out a new past in the hope of preserving what virtue there might be to survive the absolutes of revenge.

What I do is, get to the window and look west, further and further west into and through the mist of past possibilities, through these blanket terms, ever narrowing down for points of memory set in the occasion like a carbuncle, that can never change. Taking very few images in the trust that this gradual closure of the past not only widens the present but also points the future (behind me) to its singular purpose, to eliminate the veer and swing of possibility, to be the better future that follows a completion. On the assumption too that only what does reach the heart will make any difference.

To the west, beyond Stoke, are Welsh hills and the sea, and eastward behind me stretches a simple and wide monotony to the coast, perhaps the most blessed condition of all land: unexciting and open. But the past I dwell in is not so distant, and the distance that worries me is not so extensive. West and East stay with me as I move around like a left and a right, while also beyond me and fixed. It is not a problem of extent but of accuracy, and the only true spatial index to that is the night sky. About which I am ignorant, and all I can ever salvage from such dizzy attentions is that up there there are fixed points, which only move with the whole, each as fixed as, and no more than, the whole. And out of so much space only these points mean anything at all; everything else is gathered onto the dark side of the moon and deliberately forgotten as unthinkable. And the other thing that emerges is that those points are constituted, and I think this has always been known, by stories as by telescopes. Stars, molecules, and moments held in memory: they are all constituted, and they all have histories. They all open into new landscapes under perceptual pressure. We don't reach a single end.

I can ponder and plot, but like everyone else in this society I feel the star map as something uncomfortably marginal. I look at it now and then and try to feel threatened but the challenge doesn't come, and I suppose that in a permissive context it won't. The heavenly bodies pin us onto the present with a force that passes through us into the earth's track, we know that – star laser straight into the brain where the strangers are. Coming down from immensity, bearing on the present from the total, determined to make us the node of its unbearable tune, as a perfection that destroys. Under tyranny the stars are solid and their beams, dead straight, transfix questioners into instant statues. The sky map, its points unopened, is the banner of every human fixity, and all that cold beauty brought down to earth can only mean fear and cruelty. Here in this west we occupy a kind of mess in which the same kind of thing happens, more or less through carelessness, as in avowedly authoritarian states, wobbling between the permissive and the repressive as the newspaper wind blows, but the same forces operate. The attempt to lurch sideways out of the fate-trap by sheer ineptitude relies on kindly errors which can't be trusted. The pressure is still on – we don't feel it or see it, but it is there. Surely the star snares shoot down the sky in the cold fall of light as they always have, surely they aim between the eyes. We meet the distant light and cross it with horizontal spread, or set it against its anti-point, or whatever linguistic resource is to hand. But it is here that we do it, with what confronts us, within our lives. There is a mineshaft in the garden. I can see it from the window.

And on the opposite hillside the quarries begin, ripping out the landscape for road-dust, for oily money is in a rush between banks. Staked here on a suspended earth-shift I scan the western mess for what survives from it as it settles into earth. In the first movement the reaches of harm come faintly, and the Celtic hills and the counters of Fortesland alike transmit faint and impotent moans: self colonisation, forges of nothing, time ground to a rubber band; fragmentation, vacation; resentment. All that becomes at best a gloss on the sphinx, a lamination of former joys, a loss which means nothing and for which I am responsible as I perpetuate it in my regret. There is also a false pastoral (which like all ways of writing is a way of living) which inhabits this gloss and attempts to mask the boredom in short-circuited dreamwork, leafy parabolas, ontological egotism – a reductive clarity that conceals the steps and claw-marks on the surface of language. It has caused an enormous increase in rural land prices during my lifetime. It tells me in my own image that I can pass out of blame into a special self, a suspension, reflecting the formless beauty that is already-there. Magic poetry. It is not true. All that alienation has to become specifically mine before it can even be spoken – my lies, my harmings, my concealments and their fruit on the ground, my twists of meaning. Tracing the event back to its source and forward to its result you have to own it. A bringing to a point, which can never be diverted to a generality: I, unfortunately, am the point. But then the guide is not totally blind, just wincing with dazzlement and shame, just groping in a wind of stone-dust, flapping at the accusations, just fully awake and wide eyed but only responsive to actual truth like a point of light in the clouded, earthen distances. It was us who clouded the distances, and narrowed the light.

It is easy to talk of getting or bringing to a point, like admission to regeneration at a door. The self becomes the point in the hope of returning the light to its wholeness, where it is no longer an object at a distance (lamp in window on far hillside, promise, star's reflection in flooded mineshaft) but "that in which we see". The self sharpened to a point advances to meet the star-like question wanting to scatter it, answer it, reclothing space in day. That also means bringing the self to a vulnerability which drives a wedge into experience as it opens a hole in the person, for the question to reach the centre. And my resistance will be my transparency and the tunnel through my chest will be my solidity. There comes then to be another self, blunted into indolence by the act of confrontation but resting on equal terms with the active soul. We no longer expect our divided selves, however many there may be, to stay in "harmony" like some barbershop ensemble through this process where one face is the other-side of the other, the black and white of some strange cone-shaped object and aperture. Mouth and throat as horizon wedges. Be content that they do subserve the heart, and deploy it into time.

The future does not just become the past after all: it is changed to it at a specific point, and in poetry we propose the "heart", as the only human point likely to be able to meet the blast emerging from the world's pin-hole. The heart is of course the metaphor or written sign for the purposive whole (in-one, at one time), offered out because it is thereby the strongest point we have, because its sensitivity is acute because it doesn't hesitate, because it resides in thought. Each bolt of reality chimes through me provided the quality of response will open these layers of fat to the instrument within, and kindly close them behind. Perception reaches out for glad tidings but has to take what comes and break it through the frame, to ring through the person (gathered up to that point) to an unknown future. Which is to say, that such arrivals solve nothing, answer no problems, assure no one's future, adjust no one's past. Yet, in our ignorance, all that is to come depends on our reply.

The narrowed scope of pronouns in this book (mostly just I and we; later, in the poems, plus you; and no third person until the end) shows my nervousness at seeming to hope that a few domestic poems can be central to such salvations and destructions, in what must looks like a theory of election. For there is a further sense that to refuse this exposure, to refuse to meet the truth which is the term of your existence is only to conceal the fact that you cannot refuse, and you do meet it, whatever you do, with no alternatives. For instance, as you cling instead to the comforts of earth you lose everything; the message comes zooming over the horizon in the end whether you invite it or not; you come to a point; you die. This has been pointed out often enough…

And eventually, after quite enough of this cross-fire to and from the world and its representatives beyond the horizon… I tilt downwards and scan the valley below and the town that lives there, which seems a greater distance, more difficult to see, than either geological chaos or industrial entombment. If you study the town you find it is a duple thing, living its own being now and living from elsewhere in another time. At night its lights cluster on a chosen shelf of the far valley-side under the quarry waste-heaps, and string out severally up the hills. There is time at sunset, or at dawn if I were ever awake, to know the one whole sentence of its two faces, a precise transcendence of its two truths. In the point of difference, the trading-point, the coin between desire and repletion, in the hinge of day and night lies the unique language between two translations, when the lamps shining in adequate daylight take on the force of stars piercing the blue and multifarious mantle, and seem to project the potent strength of all the souls that live there, and wait their reward. And the daylight is at such times close to horizontal across it all, direct or filtered, so that the sun's fixing weight, its necessity, is cued onto the very distance we know as home, and we are firm in its tide as persisting lanterns by the strength of our wish. And so we secure a very special position which is perfectly ordinary. This overlap has us shining in our works as only solitude can, in among the multiplicity we are no longer threatened by. But that is because that compacted state, the little place all spread out below and within knowledge as the aggregate of home, is hated and feared as well as it is loved. Out there, thrust in the narrow and brief alluvium between slices of moon rock, the created home is sheltered and sheltering, but it is also the place where we cannot postpone or quarter our rivalry for souldom and its cannibalism. That is, to enter it, and call it here: then as a knowledge of the self it becomes fully alive and distinct, and the engagement is on: sparks off the head-axe, knife-work in the narrowing eye, competition, investment, and all the noble duties of affection. This is all home within its own reward, as the theatre no longer of desire but of love, the "whole" because it is so much more than anyone could want.

My response to this double door is a preparation, a turning to the wind, that I would register, and hope to carry through into act the very light glanced off the quandary and the innocent persistence that reaches next day anyway. I set my stupidity against the town's and all this purposive self-centering breaks into a fiction of appearance, and a satire of luminescence. The town makes nonsense of time by its own clock. It actually eats into the hillside in a sea of roofs, but its hunger also comes justly back on it in huge undertows. It is exactly opposite me across the fault. I am lucky to be able to witness these transactions, and have to act quickly, for the tabs are already set on it, for further development.

(c)

If it is true I am here. But where? For although I mimic some symbolic ritual of renewal with "It seems to me now…" and claim myself in the open, classic East to wish to furnish truth as firmly as I suppose I inhabit it, this hypothesis does not in fact help me in any way to be my own exactitude. I cannot keep on arriving here, where I have already lived for nearly a year: I am sick of seeing things for the first time. Sooner or later I must simply be here. Then I would be free to write myself into anonymity. Then a story could begin.

But first the written orb has to be freed from the world. For the more it is "now" and "here" the more it is "there" and to look further is of course to look closer than ever. The more the writing emanates from a totally inhabited (person-shaped) space, the more it is liberated from obligations of representation towards that particular, which appears (in full) if it appears at all, caught in the completion of the text. Who'd want to be a ring-stone proclaiming its own setting, anyway? But I don't know at all the answers that fix such a distinction and settle the wide contradictions that rage about the furnace. I don't know where the guilt of withdrawal gives into the prayer of furtherance; I don't know where the furtherance of happiness finds itself in the open clarities of pain, and is bound. I only iterate that the whole ragbag has to be fetched "here", so that my personal space, which is of course normally "anywhere", becomes so engaged in the transfer that it can only possibly be at the one point it is at, without wrecking the joys of fortuity. Elsewhere is then distinct, there are no alternatives, and there is no direction for the writing other than its own, written, destination, which is no more than the perfected and logical firmness of the links it proposes. To be nowhere else is an augmentation of the angle obtaining onto the world, by the elimination of spread. Then you are fixed in the presence, veritably driven in, and the world stands still at last waiting for your answer and is a thing of its own, in which we are included, to which none of our affective terms necessarily apply. Every preposition begins to take on the sharpness of resignation, knowing that the final or total offer can only be refused; the very width of love returns it as a possession from the stone in which it is embedded.

We know this at the edge of the person, which is where writing, among other things, takes place. This edge is furbished to a seemingly inhuman sheen as it extends into script, but the resulting compaction makes possible an entity which as it is so completely itself can begin to act helpfully, undisturbed by the incomplete and unlimited denizens of seduction, the broken edge to the public image of humanity. Then surely the central disclaimer holds us together: what on earth do you think you can act with but who you are? And that instrumentality is being-here, and to exist here in that sense is then itself the result of the exercise of love.

In suchlike considerations poetry comes into being and continues to exist (cooling) in its own right in such a way as to corrode the self-absorption which prevents people from picking up old ladies who have fallen over when they know perfectly well that they would rest better if they did.

That is to say, to further the good act, which is known by its result and by its fidelity to its own moment. Possibly poetry can set up the fiction of inhabiting the moment sufficiently to delineate the good result of its completion. The old lady says thank you kindly and potters on, grumbling about the price of margarine and the lack of discipline in schools.

(d/i)

There is a single point where the pen touches the paper, of which writing is the extension, which is the mark of the person. So much writing is no more than that (so much of my writing is no more than that) and scared of the white space behind it knows only what is in front of it, does nothing but arrive (a continual zooming-in, perhaps never actually getting there). And since that flattering self-welcoming (in gain or loss) can only intend a meaning which is never fully present (this is rather like showing photographs of your self in some remote and desirable setting in case you're not all here, or so that you needn't be) the reader can only read herself in it (can only read what she already knows) because there is no whole or sited self for the reader to engage with, no mind to encounter, no resistance to her own self-welcoming into meaning (whether she "agrees" or not, or just recognises her imago flattened into sympathetic spread). This is to dominate the reader, playing tricks with the mirror, inviting her to a determined subjective space. It conceals the fact that she is already in one.

The point of writing is not pure and it has to move. The point is a space (conceptual and metaphorical since any actual point is metaphysical) – it is a marred space. It is scarred, smeared, and faulted like a limestone dome once subject to lead mining, teeth-marks on the shoulder and flank of the hill, like a pearl which has passed through centuries of trade, warfare, and domestic unpleasantness, like the full moon inscribed with all our foolishness and error. The circular garden is the site of a constant fight or coition, which only ends at the peristalith of a hilltop tumulus. So the constituted point has to move, through the years of seasons and meanings, leaving its trace, remaining intact, becoming whatever colour it enters but not forsaking its identity. Intact through its changes because it is the fixed mark of the person it bears, and, in the solitudes of thought, his only, cold, open, eastwards, home. If such a home – the durance of the edge of a personal space distanced into a sign – is not trusted from within, how can change ever be renewal? Such intimacy is a hard, and far, remand that releases affection to its boundless exactitude.

(d/ii)

There is a single point where the pen touches the paper, which is, as it moves into its fate, the mark of the whole person. The "whole person" is a fiction dependent on an actuality, the movement of the authentic signature under trust. Reported presence need surely be no more than that, and anything that represents an author adequately crammed into a corner of that imperceptible dot. The "whole" person is then the person in extended time where he or she can be known only by in and as his or her work.

But I seem to return again and again to this act as a kinema of my own daily doings, with all the risks of coy glimpses, domestic preludes, sentiment shifting slyly towards aggression or displays of seeming integrity with no second opinion. I think it is necessary. The moving planet of the soul passes through medial opposition towards a resolute polarity, and surely the delineation of good in that course (the completing of that course) depends, at least sometimes, on a singularity that can't be taken for granted in favour of largeness. Surely the ground of the act, intimacy, requires constant renewal from the centre in favour of largesse; a constant testing of habit and manner against result in living. It could be an anchorage or land-mark in polar apposition to fixed points of high purpose in the night tumulus above us. There are ways of guaranteeing vast scale on the instant: the point of singularity is stretched out to a hieroglyphic cartouche which slots into a pre-existing conceptual width beyond anyone's actual sphere of experience: social metaphysics! Well, I admire any attempt on History and only fear that in my present state of contraction anything vaster than a goldfinch means turning aside from the heart, and the bird in the hand will pine for seed.

Meanwhile, this rectangular machine, rattling through the night, this bone-box, crashes a fully formed stigma onto the skin at every stroke: the standard letter. On what model? Who licenses these chunks of meaning? The sign is at once a shield and a majority verdict removed from the beauties of any particular human visage as it reels through time. I insist that the heartscript is cursive, bearing difference at every point and unwinding its messages like a sledge-track in the snow -- errant, and subject to the contours, but aligned. The stamping seems to reduce the act to a package deal, public from the start. I never use anything else; indeed I no longer possess an ink pen. Every word fights against its publication for access to the heart, as indeed it should. And the forward point is maintained in its own metaphor zipping here and there across the keyboard, as it was at the end of the nib.

(e)

And yet I remain suspended in front of the question. I move in, I install. I drive the world and its absences out of the house with a few practised fences: bookshelves, records, hangings. I climb to my window and station. I know the vein opposite, by its warmth and disruption: signs of life just under the horizon and further insecurities on the radio. I wedge myself into the ledge and insist on staying put, trusting that the more firmly my personal time-space contracts towards its (chambered) centre, the more fully will perception disclose the world's secrets, open as they lie on the surface of event. If I seek that disclosure I am back in the van again, in transit: nowhere. It is not itself a purpose. It must be a conditional of my being, a kind of birthright, the very script of my species. It inhabits the bright and dark fields of result.

We are constantly drawn out of this made space by insecurities and shady percepts, so that we become our own objective. Pairing becomes a mirror exercise and a whole "culture" is developed on the fear that needs constantly to be assured that if all it believes in is its own advantage, well that is all right, and important, and sexed. I will not step outside. For sitting at home quietly at work on the tracks of love is the Bible of Hell to that fabricated world of lies we are led to believe we inhabit (by image-proxy, no one has ever actually been there), instructed by the defence of defence. It is the book to break the fixed, cloudy, faces of all the spokespersons of nothing, who would have us out there to the ends of our days stoking the furnaces of the smoke industry.

But this home shouldn't be mistaken for the actual refuge I am permitted to call mine in this world, where as soon as I set foot in the door I start owing. The home I speak of is real, and physical, and mutual, and there's a funny smell in the bathroom again, but as the site of work it is not subject to the temporal conditions of an uncaring administration. Oh, I pay my concern politely: "I hope your civilisation will be better soon". I go to work. I take a walk in the abandoned quarries or a quick off-season excursion to Paris, but I don't budge. And to refuse the glass of that seeming exterior forms a different seeking, to explore the sepulchral anterooms of the heart for the world's engravings. My participation in the deception, as instructed on the screen, is supposedly provisional to the day when there is no longer any spare part of me available but I need it all gathered into the truth I posit by existing. And the punishment for this duplicity is my own obscurity and failure. Gaining the food where it lurks I at least retain the right to disclaim advantage. And it is in fact marvellous the way people all over the place hold this life unto them and run it into heaven without tax or insurance or anything but a simple number on the door. It is an elaborate script merely to notice this, and another to delineate it – the furtherance of joy, which I'm sure finds its authenticity also in the disarming validity of the expiring moan or wince of shame. And while I know that the home of writing (the third city) is set far apart from our earthly settlements and exposed to the biting and soundless air because of this, I still can't know the details of the force which finally coheres these aching distances, which can only be here on the spot.

The lines on the window are thick with this question in the conditional modes, the yearning again, the fall into possibility. Poetry may here move much more slowly than the gnomic prose of the self-lecturer with his prefatory sightings after the event; but that delay is necessary if poetry is to meet the world's resistance as a whole, at every point. The world demands its own future, through us but beyond us, every blade of grass a transaction to be thrashed out to the end for the privilege of knowing it. Muse Divine, aid us to win an acorn from the clash of spheres, defend us from fossil energy, the gravitation of distance into loss. May we keep us aligned to the final receptor, may we wrest one future from the doleful stroke: everywhere-present-now. We can make instruments to combat the arrest of good will against fear of fragmentation and spread (which is not the true difficulty), by setting the fullness of the immediate into the total as an intimacy. The world then rages all around, but we begin to hold our ground, our celestial anchorage. And it is from us after all, that the energy proceeds whose devastations to left and right we grimly discount –industrial wastelands and executive meadows, twin capitals of another false polarity across the world ever ready to sacrifice us into nonentity for a shred of pride. For in vacating and dispersing the continuous human agency that we are, we lay it wide open to the usury of our own acts and end up a mere vehicle for the world's cycles of degeneration, its massive corruption. Poetry or something steers us down the centre, powered from within, into the vale where the township lies, occasionally exploding but most of the time (and most of the time belongs to most of the people) lying there unhurriedly improvising its own fate. I like to think I encourage it, sitting here pointing west day after day, turning round at every meal.

30 Diurnal Poems

(1)
Moving eastward under symmetry towards no,
not yet home, not till I get there, the west blooms,
the sky behind me a crimson slush, a dream
of statement slowly sinking into tomorrow

But crammed with people and stories. My solo
is concerted, I feel the tab on my collar, the
spine touch, and radial, you're always there.

I stick an ex libris
over a library stamp.
I walk the dark room.
A moth watches from outside.

(2)
All that happened
and where's the poem of it?
– there in your surface speaking
your body writing your soul

Tall
and never still
like the autumn grass.

We could happen to
a Lycian double music
conjugates my throat weft:
double-winged.

Stephen

(3)
Your mother left you in care
Maybe she didn't care
Who now is to care
about you –

That you manage,
and have to bear
these dreadful puns

And cruel rhyme
since they
drive their cares.

(4)
Something intervenes – it's
clearly not our nature
to desert. I set up
the new bookshelves from Remploy,
placing the closer demands
at eye level, & somewhat faded
or accidental emissions
close to the floor and ceiling.

There is no one but you in this stanza,
sitting in a chair at the window.

(5)
Why do you drag me, master,
through abandoned industrial premises,
shattered windows, roof on floor?

What joy is there in stinting
and what can ever keep us
but what we turn out?

Unsettled, furnace bracelet,
north-west gritwind I
catch on the brow,
last syllable of wasted time.

(6)
Why do you lead me through
derelict factories, dead thoughts,
mindless compilations, 25W Pearl?

The spirits of need perch on
my shoulder but the height
gained is no one's vantage,
adjusts no one's past –

People are ruined,
live in holes in the ground
at the mind's command.

(7)
Why do you call me through
gaping circles
with every trapping comfort
of love except fire

While the proximate and named
you all the time keeps me to a greater
issue, globe in globe or arm in arm,
continuation to mind of those dazzling arcs.

The birthday

(8)
Six hours into night and I'm nearly what?
20/40-what? and what persists –
space, stars, and the singing.

What do the bookshelves care if we
reckon a loss, what does the town
conclude? And further on is what else –

Space, stars, and the track
the rider makes in the sand
singing difficulties and durations
into holes where desert creatures
deposit their young.

The post

(9)
The old postman died,
The new postman tried.

Couldn't he have tried a bit harder? Just when I thought I felt like getting something a bit important in the post or at least something demanding immediate action like a book by John Riley or a letter from Tuscaloosa there was this splat and there on the floor was a beige existence a demand an acknowledgement or something sent from an anonymous limb which didn't even have the courage to hurt me and the little boat grounds on a bank of ice-cream and nobody dies any more, there is no more horror or violence or danger, behind the little foggy window of the window envelope there is nothing at all, to get upset about.

The postmen are weeping
the pre-men are sleeping
the stars a-creeping
and I awake.

The window

(10)
One of the little panes is out – a previous occupant
stretched polythene over the space and sometimes at night
a moth flies into it, sudden thud.

cf. I think I'm "getting somewhere"
sudden thud
behind me.

The membrane holds. Black moves.
And now there's a dead moth
under the cover of Ten Years' Diggings,
a streak of grease and money dust.

(11)
Here out of my writing
your fingertips glow in the darkness
you climb into the valley

and I know my life can never be translated
out of this miserable little hole
full of novels and possibilities –
the sides of it cut my hands.

On the hard rocks of the heart vale
our sight ends. The magpie moth
lays her eggs in the wound.

(12)
Spend an evening alone,
eat cream cheese,
the organs are poor guests
to pain and starscript.

Waste an evening on limestone –
neither work nor company,
just resentment's luncheon.

Too late perception unbinds its numbers
and head contacts metal fire direct
splashing blades on passing flames
ah yes I'm blamed, too true too.

(13)
I couldn't say a thing
      the Day has proved
what, what for Heaven
        'sake the Day has proved.

(14)
The post is a tale told to get me up
up and out in the eyebright fields

But breakfast is closer without a knock
and subtle streaks delay the distance.

We should reharbour forgetting against
history, and live the trade.

(15)
Such a commotion in the grass!
Can't you see all the little mortifacts
running around, can't you see
John Cowper Powys
bending over a bracken pit
and striding off again
to the nearest stationers?

Now is the future to any past, upon us!

Can't you hear the music of the garden of the earth
running screaming from the nearest box office?

The return

(16)
From Liverpool to Leeds
a bonfire thrown on a motorway.

For a white smile, for a coated neck
we have razed dignity from our homes.

Your excellent teeth and the light down
on the back of your neck I shall remember
as long as I live. We fasten our time
to steady needs but then oversell – oh it's not
ours to question, we surely are to answer,

surely, are, a shower of sparks, to enunciate.

(17)
There are owls and townships in the night
and I'm trembling because some sales manager
said "Now look here…" on the phone.

No resolution is anticipated.
The owl, swooping over, looks ahead,
the town sucks vision down its lamps,
I quarry into night a day's end.

Perhaps it's just that after so much
rooting in humanity
we need something to dry our hands on.

(18)
There are ways of knowing
if it is true

If it is true
there are ways

There are paths across the glassy crust
that change every hour
"…and the flesh severed wholly
from fear or calculation"

To arrive, to stay,
breathless in twos.

Complaint

(19)
I'm dragged off into the world world
the one with wax ears and no genitive
no duty, no justice, no true cost – I'm
caved in! When all I need is a cave to
sit in and concentrate, a serenity, my office
drags me through the counties like car stock.
There are ways back, strategies, and
exercises. I follow the ground, misreading

1419
The Flash between the Crevices of Cash.

Second complaint

(20)
I'm offset, I inhabit the line
between you

Riven with storm centres and my
boots leak, they are ridiculous!

Speech also is a burden, one day to
conclude and pass like a car in the night

On this heavily scarred dome when the
bright ring is full of flesh

In the silence of our love every pronoun
calls down the sky our constitution.

(21)
Dust rattles down the stairwell
and is ground in.

The wind hisses between roof slates
we are smudged with the honour
of being so close.

Smile too at the sky's blade
as it strokes the heartboard
edge to edge.

Where it ends
we begin again.

Three disclaimers

(22)
I'm not this totally solid man you posit,
I don't take his praise – love
is at least specific and my great ambition
is to specify this bewilderment which
moves through me like knotted string
though at other times it is more like
being pressed onto the diagonal wires
of a harp-shaped entrance. What exactly is
like this is, for my part of it, no more than
sitting here at this nightly settlement, witness
to the changes of light where that includes
or indeed amounts to love which in its turn
involves and under certain pressures
amounts to, the necessity
of knowing harm
                        specifically
so that there are lines, of high tension,
indicating a pulling presence in the world
solid and clear, product of you and I, to which
there needs to be a response. The light falls
rapidly and the time switch achieves its
notch – the lamps come on. The response chimes
all over the horizon.
For this, I'd have thought, for the chime
of the response, a certain hollowness
is needed. But a hollowness
which contains. Contains what, I wonder.
Heart, chambered seed, stop
rattling around when I'm trying to think.

(23)
I'm not this filled person you idealise.
If we drank it, the Grail, would it act
like warm milk on instant potato and some
inner soul substance swell up and fill us to the
inner surface of the skin, so as then to
coincide with the form of the person and
we'd act as nothing but that, whatever
it is: poetry, love, truth, heart? Is this
why we court selfishly the light and heat
turned on us, the reflexive beam, because
we long to nurture some kernel destined to
replace us from within which we do or
don't call death? But what of the space, the empty
and tough vacuities which the heart needs
in order to function, and what is that function
anyway but a stopgap device between our ends?
Aren't we more likely to overflow with healing energy
when what expands within us is an activated silence,
a bolt of alien space no part of us at all, as when
we recognise the world's constant nil response to our
hearty well-meaning thrusts and shame and anger
blow down a straw into our sealed centre
the very breath of patience. Then we are
brought into parity in a flash of linear contact,
stone to heartstone down the throat, and
more than ever in years of good time
we slowly lever ourselves into balance
with the whole, the abomination.

And in the very early morning
the first lorries go out again.

(24)
I'm not this remarkable character you entertain –
my throat is cloudy, my eye oppressed,
and in English my You is diverse.

I don't anyway see how any person
could hope to attain to a greater degree
of sufficiency compaction and cleverness
than a brown berry fallen in the grass;
look at it sitting there with its maps
and its charts and its migratory tables:
it settles its fate before it starts
to a plain contingency –
it waits to be eaten. And the grey
wiry grass of the uplands
bends over its taut brow.

I hope not to become that one-off man,
speed-winner, screen-eye, professor of grasp.
But leave him alone and let him be –
let him be filled who will not fill,
let him be clever and let him be sure,
his prophetic shoes, frozen to the pebbles.

(25)
Ruined castle, ruined poet,
ruined husband

See how the earth twists and cracks
round to meet your fate,
your first chance.

Lesson, translated

(26)
At one time
I, frightened, ignorant, hardly living,
covering my eyes up with images,
claimed to guide the dying and the dead.

I, sheltered poet,
set aside, hardly suffering,
dared to trace paths in the abyss.

Now, lamp blown out,
hand more errant and trembling,
I start again slowly in the draught.

> Philippe Jaccottet,
> *Leçons*, 1966

The anecdote, the fall

(27)
Among so much natural beauty to slip
on the snow and fall flat on your back,
on the wooded hillside the trees draped
in crystal and floss, there to note
your feet disappearing from under you
and thud. And you sit up, and you stay there
while everyone fusses around, knowing
that this is as far as you're going.

"Do you feel like getting up yet, Mrs?"
"No, I don't."

The valleys spread out below, all the cakes
and candles they've hung around you for weeks
and at a certain point, thud, and that's it,
you've had enough, poor soul.

If our humiliating experiences
could be relied upon to make us humble
before something worth it,
something actually "up" like
a human soul or the length of days,
we'd live on sledges
and confuse the stars.

The town

(28)
It's a town of cake-eaters,
the houses shunted on top of each other
and sown out under the cliff – everyone
wants a slice, and gets it,
spitting still fertile seed onto coal.

I love the cubist streets,
reared up and casting the light about,
our work, our walls, all our
sight aimed at the moon-rocks
and coming back so dangerous and firm.

(29)
It's a town of nutcrackers,
solid, big chested
workers with
circular faces
faced into the cliff face
where the threat lies,
bedridden, infertile,
the Revenge of the Mollusc.

Coming or going

(30)
One thing
always only

pen on table / gathered evening

one thing wished and
one thing worth it

seedfract / matchless / gathering light

heartbeknown.

Processional and Masque

The Replies

There is a particularly bleak part of North Staffordshire near Leek where you can stand on the very edge of the Pennines and watch the illuminated or brick-crusted industrial flatlands run away before you towards North Wales or Liverpool. It is the edge of a plateau of high moors of heather bilberry and moor-grass, where denudation and burnt-out atmosphere have changed scrubland into miles and miles of growth failure. So where "wheat, rye, oats, barley and beans" were growing in 1385, with pasturage for sheep and cattle, only the sheep survive. This high edge overlooks the Upper Churnet Valley and The Roaches, with Stoke-on-Trent in the first distance to south-west. An unclassified road runs along it. The moorlands behind, about four miles wide, are part of the gritstone clasp on three sides of the Derbyshire limestone dome. To the east they slope down to the green and white hills at Warslow and Ecton, and high land prices start again.

It is an area of empty disregard, brown grey and purple against the faint, scattered, hidden greens. The convexity of uplands repels the human transmissive-receptive organism and they are felt as the back of something. The only buildings within miles are occasional stone farms tucked into protective folds of the moors, some operative some not, and one former drovers' inn now relying on car custom in the evenings. An army training camp under the edge sometimes sends bands of tender youths in khaki to roam these wastes in single file, with trucks, jeeps, and flares at night.

And yet by the side of this road along the edge, at a junction where one road dives down the side towards Leek and the other follows the top onwards, on the west and edge-ward side of this road just where the ground begins to fall away, overlooking everything, the Post Office decided for some reason to install a public telephone box. It stands there alone in acres of moorgrass heather and peat groughs, precisely 1519 feet above sea level, exposed to the constant wind. Was it put there for the sake of the army, or the sheep farmers, or even weekend hikers? Who could actually have been conceived as needing it, walking or riding down the vast horizons clutching their few pence? Anyway it doesn't work now. The 'phone is dead and there is no light in it at night. When it had one, if it ever did, it would have been visible from miles away to the west.

I used to pass it quite often driving to and from Leek. Whenever the weather was bad John Dooley might be inside it – he used it as a shelter against blizzards and driving rain. John Dooley was virtually the only inhabitant of those wastelands: a shell-shocked derelict who appeared from nowhere after the war and settled there. His single occupation was to walk the moorland roads all the time. He was always somewhere up there; any time you drove over the top there was a good likelihood of passing him on the road, even after dark. He wasn't old, though often referred to as "old" as a dissociative habit; he was about 40 and big, with a large black beard over which his eyes crow-like regarded without comment the passing car. He had a habit of stopping at the approach of a vehicle and turning to look at the driver, the way people do in the more remote villages where visitors are scarce and people expect to know who's abroad. But he was never known to approach anyone, army or sportsman or stopped car, and I believe he found speech very difficult. He was strong: he plodded unfaltering up the steepest hills and walked like a machine the ribbons of tarmac pasted on the moorland surfaces, with the same dark overcoat in all weathers and a large sack over his shoulder, said to contain empty bottles, or by some accounts, old newspapers. He slept in a hollow he had scooped out under Warslow rubbish tip. What was his daily bread, or how he weathered the arctic Februaries, I've no idea.

His presence as the denizen of those wastes was nothing to do with the place. I mean I'm sure the only reason he settled there was that no one else had. An unguarded municipal dump in Birmingham would have done just as well. He was not interested in moors, landscapes, views, walking, seasons, highlands, any of it. Among all that wilderness his own milieu was entirely industrial: he never stepped off the tarmac and he slept among old cans a few feet from a steel skip. Spring up there was a slight and delicate operation which he may or may not have registered specifically, but he clearly had his own concerns, and was busy.

The only remaining question might be the state of that faculty of him once known as the "soul", and whether that had a language. And if it had, how humanly inhuman might it be in its demand. How it might speak only of the final pact between the person and its existence, and the final masquerade of truth overmastering silence in the total image of the individual. That it might be the very voice of the not-self.

For the other thing I remembered was one night in thin driving snow and some hill mist my headlights caught him in that telephone box, staring straight out, not at me, as I veered onto the top of the climb. The reversed pierrot mask: white brow and jowls on one of the small windowpanes, the rest, with the beard and the eyes, black. And I was past in a flash, but he had the receiver to his mouth and ear.

Blackshaw 289:

The Replies

1. Walking east towards no more home,
   be careful what you think (feel, dream, etc.):
   it changes everything.

2. What we could is no doubt inclusive of what we never fancied.
   What happened is (like me) tall, and
   never still. My trust warp hates it.

3. Out of care
   I watch the lesser cars shoot past
   accusing no one.

4. I am totally unremployable.
   There is no one but me in this statement
   of error.

5. Resentment is the terminal of our decline.
   I crack it on the edge
   with "Flowing River Song".

6. Speaking as a derelict factory I think
   my mind requests what my tongue lacks:
   Air! Space! Light! Fire!

7. What greater issue is there
   than Man, tucked into the horizon
   and folded round a stone for luck. Fire!

8. Fzzz. Is there anyone there? Fzzz Fzzz.
   It is difficult enough, to love death living
   in a hole in all the rubbish at any age.

9. Someone breathed on the whole window.
    It's pitch outside and I'm not weeping.
    I itch with the ramifications of truth.

10.. Every day the light climbs the earth trembling with veracity
    and passes on. And the knowing hand retains
    a speaking coin – your move.

11. If I stick my head out of this miserable little window
    the sky clatters over us preaching fidelity
    and at night a slowly declining suspension of fear.

12. My mother and my father, my children and my wife
    lie elsewhere calling each to each. It's called
    counterpoint and I spent every last penny.

13. The day has proved
    cold, with a thick mist
    in the late hours.

14. Officially I have forgotten history
    but am remembered by officers.
    Actually God howls in the sack.

15. This box is my office. There is
    no remission, no getting through without paying.
    I pay me till there's naught left and stride off again.

16. But we cannot begin to answer until the question is
    through us. Like a little hooked noise: why
    does love fall short, who do you think you are?

17. We also are the brutality that sets
    the questions and disposes.
    Nothing, no literature, helps. Now look here.

18. Separate from sky, separate from ground,
    I say humanity is perfect. I have
    nothing to lose.

19. I have nothing to complain about. I know
    I am not to keep. I have been told. And suddenly
    the light reversed into a lake, underholding creation.

20. They said it was me.
    They said it was me.
    They said it was me.

21. In the morning I arch my back
    and prise my living between the spheres.
    We die from within, uncertainly.

22. I come nightly to my nightly settlement.
    I may be human but my heart is a dry pea
    that hurts a poor princess.

23.. There are weak places and dead spots in everything we do.
    Don't worry about them. Don't let them fool you.
    And the lorries go out again on the paths of destruction.

24. What you are doing at this moment (how
    ever) is called living a life.
    Not hoping to be, or other. Welcome.

25. There is space, and rain on the grass
    where a small house once stood,
    no signs of ruin.

26. It is possible to start again so often you
    never properly get going – writing a life
    and living a writing, of something else.

27. And there are nights with nothing but starlight
    on the steel rubbish bins. I am
    confused about this, but cannot help admiring the aim.

28. My eyelids hauled up on the pasty nightscape
    my revenge on myself by time and air
    my halt in the scar in the scar.

29. Oh trust your one possession -- of all the birds
    that I do know the one perched on my rib bone
    sings straight to the people.

30. Man in society, try to be more precise
    and also cut out the wist
    if you want to see heaven.

Notes to *Lines on the Liver*

Remploy: originally a state-owned business manufacturing furniture, set up by the Labour government in 1945 to retrain unemployed and disabled workers.

25W Pearl. A low power electric light bulb with misted glass.

"…and the flesh severed wholly…": from a story by Kay Boyle.

1419 is the title of a poem by Emily Dickinson.

Philippe Jaccottet: "Autrefois, moi l'effrayé…" in *Poésie 1946-1967*. In a 1994 printing the seventh line has been changed from "j'osais tracer des routes dans le gouffre" to "aller tracer des routes jusque-là!"; I can't imagine why.

Blackshaw 289 is the telephone number of the telephone box referred to in the preceding prose.

Some of the *30 Diurnal Poems* are not complete without the reply they receive from John Dooley in *The Replies*. This correspondence is absent from the last three poems and replies.

X

Poems, Peak District (ii)
Little Bolehill

(1978-1985)

The Idea Is

The idea is to establish fixed points in succession
like a chain of stations through the land,
processional sequence that breaks
the disorderly obstructions to desire
gathering up silver threads in the rubble that
twine together to a gleam in the distance:
the world's treasure at its final harbour.

So traverse the cloth of gold, the peninsula
bright and dark with gorse and hawthorn,
patchwork of farms and volcanic domes, all
there, rich in fish and wheat as normal but
leading somewhere, the roads sunken below
head height gathering together and joining as
the land narrows, pushes towards the sea,
the end, the island, the saint's everlasting
rest, we remaining are what it's for.

Another Week on Llŷn (Another Catalogue)

Early purple orchid. Thrift. Flowering gorse.
King-cup, lady's smock, primrose, daisy.

Conversing enmities: so that among
so much difference there is so much good will
and shared resource. Competing amities.

Lesser bugloss, spring squill, blue-
bell, forget-me-not, violet, so that poetry
is after all not a profession but a spare
minute, a small and sudden thing
extended to a lifeline.

The primrose glowing and fat in the
dark grass of the sea slopes at evening,
the noisy oystercatchers laying bets on gastropods.

Black Holes
(Summary of a talk by John Taylor on Radio 3, 6th January 1975)

Black hole destroys unity of
scientific grail quest

makes a mockery of laboured
unity of natural forces which
themselves predict necessary
existence of black hole

because force arises from exchange between un-likes

and expansion of force
demands an infinite self-mass
which can only be cancelled
by a negative infinity: black hole.

If matter were reducible to
non-constituted substantial points
time would arrest
work would arrest
and we live alone;
black hole assures continuation.

* * *

The point of generation flares on the horizon. It's
a fine evening and Kathy absolutely refuses
to go to bed eat her supper be reasonable or
in any way compromise the sovereign will,
and the leaves on the trees are golden with result.

Pots of light fall beyond our reach.
We think, and find nothing to say,
our bone heads empty of all but puzzlement
which also is something doable to perfection
following instructions from far away
which we are rather scared of and now
she says she wants a yoghurt.

The point of settlement colours the fair skin.
It is an earthly promise and a key, I wish I could
turn it in the lock of evening before the ground
slips away, before we get a chance to fill it
with care, food, concern and result.

* * *

I depend on every ounce of material
day by day, the horrible sunlight flapping
onto the library's polished floor while
Kathy makes new friends in Normanton
and Beryl teaches Indian women basic English.
The horrible bindings of the horrible directories
beautifully closed.

These planes overlap and turn towards life
in spite of the thin languages behind them.
There is facility and obstruction in every
conditional. You can't get a decent cup
of coffee in the whole of Derby and suddenly
my mind hinge swung back it was
11:15 and time.

I don't want clever poetry.
It was 11:15 and time to
do things, meet Beryl, collect Kathy,
write to Barny, work, it was
11:15 and time.

Middleton by Wirksworth 1980

The mines stand round like graves of kings, hollow mounds scattered all over the uplands – waste heaps, eruptions of subsoil, abstracted pocks and scars, sign the pastures. The thrush shoots out. The hawk fixes a triangulation against the wind. We walk on the brow of the hill among mounds and filled rakes, milky calcite in the grass, what grass there is, scattered with eyebright.

Steppe expanses: hardly a tree, scattered thorn bushes, yellow grass-stalks sweep to north-west. Rings of barbed wire round holes in the earth, traces of buildings, lines of white stones barely breaking the surface, the varieties of light in the open spread. This is our work, that we live for. It is not that garden, sculpted from terrain by careful sight, the flowers set in their shelving, tree columns glazed in standing water... all that marks distinction by long study, honour of just return, it is not that. In many ways it is the mess made of it all, the entirety of a life brought to grovelling in the earth for a mere sustenance and the upcast breaking the landscape.

Leaving this shipwrecked horizon, run to gravel, acreage of humps and holes, still faintly breathing, and barren vaults, and nothing.

Two pieces from a draft 1980s rewriting of *Following the Vein*

We fall to the earth and it's day.
The dream globe blanches, diminishes and sinks
into the cleft striking sparks from the sides,
cold flames running up the edge of grass-blades.
Rapidly then the hillside lightens, the light
begins to encompass detail – a car
starts, a kettle screams across the road,
curtains are opened and the sky rollers
mimeograph everything back into place.
Already the miner has located his night.

* * *

The blind traveller stands where the valley
broaches the hills and taps his stick
on the stone gatepost, and smiles, recognising
the dull response of lichen. For the breadth
of love there is really all the time in
sight of the end.

(Postlude)

If a code, then a code
which answers to our stature
and the heraldry of our love
constantly revisited, flashing
on the vault, the shift and
curvature, sight shielded from
pole to pole. The bees
respond to this hollowing,
the convex face of light in the
early morning, the queen termite
squirms in her heart of the structure
her code a singing that calls
every vein back to the centre,
to the gathering and compilation,
singing the waste into exile,
continuing as things stand.
Disturb nothing, leave the music
in the air, leave the forest
to its authors. We are surely prepared
never to have heard of any of it --
not to force stability
into biological time
where it already inheres as language.

Manchester, Liverpool, and Other Nights with Some Mornings

Winter mid-night outside
the railway station, dry
snow blown across the road
dark cafés and tool shops
locked glass door rattling in the wind
lamps burning deep in closed premises
distant echo of metal striking metal.

*

Night wind
buffets the streets
clouds catching some
street light slide over.

In the lower darkness a few
glowing curtains.

Vast spaces in living
considered normal.

*

The occasional pedestrian on the road's margin
sinks homeward clutching a parcel.

Empty dual carriageway under orange streetlights
pharmaceutical factories Liverpool airport and

Blocks of flats. Wide horizontal margins. We
made these things and they dismay us at night.

If we could inhabit real distances…

> *

Quiet ring-road night, a few rows
of small old terraces on the edges
of cleared spaces, vacant floodlit circus
as if our lives are swept to the edge
of a transport system.

> *

Moonlit outhouse slate roof
Glowing gas fire
Horror movie on screen beaming blue uncertainty.

> *

And a few cars do in fact go past,
and a truck, a moderate truck for once,
trucking part needed matter to tomorrow's hands,
the great engine banging, co-
alescing and rising out of earshot.

> *

White bird over the city at night
lifts and sails above the rooflines
over the hushed stirrings, the exhaust,
train-clack, warm airlift,
rides it all exorbitant.

> *

Sudden gusts of wind in the streets
waste paper scudding along the curb
dark and illegible offices.

The last drunk and the last homeless
huddled under arches, unneeded light
from a shoe shop into the road.

Locked warehouse, small lit window of
janitor's lodge, red night light
down the corridor, faint hum.

Windows and foot-level grilles coated with dirt
streetlight cast into black air
hurtling through emptiness...

In suspended hurry, banks and in-
surance offices trapped in night
where everything turns over as slowly as possible

towards the day already betrayed
already soiled against the curb
by works that don't turn, don't

bend to the puzzled and afflicted
but persist in constant paradise of
fast focus / own reward.

The bottle that rolls across the pavement
and settles, the wasted light
in its stratum, in its sleep,

lies on the stonework. The rubbish stacked up
behind the café, boxes and plastic sacks heaped
in a corner of back walls.

Dark and full night, worded against fall, fragile,
possible flower that dozily bends and
trembles beside the goods entrance.

The silence that persists above
the stifled noises. A telephone bell
rings and rings in a closed warehouse.

No one heeds it, no one there,
no transaction no gain and no disdain:
perfect perfect night

where the fox lurks and the sleeping couples lie
in their own time and the same wind cradles
the closed flower on the sea cliffs.

Now the coldest hour has passed
and the sky instructs the air
blow by blow, fold by fold towards day.

The pedestrian under the shadowed lintel passes
between office and station
and the manager deep in his cave

hears nothing but the alarm bell, messages
of fear in the night. It never stops ringing
nor true love ever tires. The night

repeats it and slides sideways. The night stroller
lowers an eye to a flicker of warmer yellow,
an opening coffee bar.

* * *

Bronchitis, headache,
Real snow at last.
The earth is a dim white sky.
Where is the speaker of the world?

Oh gently flopping snow,
Shrinking at a touch,
Yielding into the ground,
Where is the parliament of our lives?

Ospita

1.
Seeking a bearing point on hurt I find
Hollows and rooms in the thick of the night,
A building hard at work flashing its bright
Offers into the star dome. Consigned
Forward I bring my name in a sealed jar
To the steps up, pay the slight fee, assent
To slow harm by the covering letter.
Entering into purpose distance springs
Back from the horizon to hold the cup
The bitter cup but true, of flesh-driven earth
(This night is the day outside the dream, this
Tableau my government, or family wish)
And deep in the brickwork think of asters
Blazing on the far links in slow birth.

2.
I bear my coat and cast to a senior,
A new old faithful, who should know the coils
And corridors of the heart, the slender
Ghost smiling to the third tune. What is false
Be mixed in a pestle, what rings be
Represented as an inner garden
Open to Sirius, one and the same be
Ground and broiled and spoken as your answer.
The house is quiet, old radio music
In the walls, scissors on the table, streaks
Of blood in the sink. A call in the night.
I get up, white coat, glance out at the rain
On the glass, attend. What do I exchange for pain?
Holding a stranger's thin arm I turn down the light.

3.
Calcium night light. Suddenly a man
Shouts, "Orpheus!" and the dying die,
The sick sleep on, the deserted bitterly cry
And I count the call as best I can across
The fogs of routine silence; word that holds
The earth into a chiming whole, enfolds
Love in a capsule coated with loss, never
Cedes to wishful death but calls us to drop
Our trades and be again that whirring top
On the mountain ridge, screaming down river a pain
Of incompletion, fall medallion, cut
The human heart to song. And it will, don't
Turn out the light, see to the day's wounds, won't
Stop our good hands tying, that sweet moan again.

4.
A man shouts in pain, the voice constructs
A door. The god batters his forehead
On our simple attendance, the fruit
Of centuries' observance. But to eluct
Wisdom from hurt – any hospital bed
Would burst into flame at the mere thought.
The music coils within: a long solo,
And the final voice squeezed from a lump
Of flesh held over a sink said and we tried
Our best to stifle that singing, "Do
What you will to ease me over the hump
Of death I belong to the great outside.
My burning lust courses at last through Hell.
The pain of what I couldn't manage spreads like a bell."

5.
This house constructed as an escape
From harm is unlikely to escape
Its own folly as a new escape
From language and source of new dolour.
A woman shouts down a corridor
A real name: "Sidney! Sidney! Sidney!"
A door slams bone shut. I am sorry
To have life shot through by her call
I can't dream any harder the fall
Of light onto the wet leaf, the stain
Of nurture on a simple erection.
In the end she is right: the rape
Of endless joy and everyone's to blame.
Out on the lake the long boats wane.

6.
At night the walls are blank but we can hear
The plovers crying in the dark fields, their
Wings beating over waves of wheat. Downstairs
Someone opens the piano and strikes a chord
That tenses the flanks of hope. Again there
Is a silence in which the lapwings graze
The ear tips and clouded underwing
Flashes across the sky. Then where and where
In this globe of health we balance and bear
From room to room, where is a lasting thing?
Where is a good done that also stays it?
Someone attempts the new soft swing but out
In the earth-glow between mind and chest
Brilliant metallic birds like kisses dive to rest.

7.
The man dies and the bell sounds across
Grass and sea and mixes with the gulls.
The dream sleeps into the morning, turns
On its side and drifts down the coast
Under the grey cliffs and buildings
Dedicated to healing but now
Empty and dark at dawn, the sharp keens
Of the white hens warning us to be slow.
We comfort as if there were no cost,
As if pain could be stilled to patience
Separately, and the story lost.
Good men have died lost in empty time
But loading their bite on th'intrinsic nation
Steady as grade of light, or yellow chime.

8.
Time drags its heals on the dreamer who hears
His body calling him like a discant
Semaphore, a sign hung on a fruit shop
Under the castle wall. The sheets are bright,
Anger the oxide of faith and he fears
The fall into humanity, the slant
Of honey and cream; those fair lids droop
And he is solitary on the white
Road across the heath, he is close to tears
For the imperfected lives he couldn't want
To bring to their moment of concord and float
On further life. The swallows are in flight
Over the russet fields crackling with fear
As he enters the day's gate as is right.

9.
They draw his body from the centre out,
A decisive goodness. He lies flat out
On the shore counting ills. The waves enter
His total wealth into books of sand.
It's enough. They are happy to inter
His soul in lime and ash for the sake
Of a comfortable end, the winter
Of our success rebound in angel cake
But winter is true numbers that blister
From the corpse in a field, alternating
Black and white name-tags that flitter
Like sarcens in the treetops. Small birds sing
His centre into holes in the snow and grey
Doctors weeping envy send him on his way.

10.
I walked out on the morning of May 12th.
The blades were bright and coy and loud,
Thick with languages I walked without stealth
The fields of angry farmers, proud
To be harmless and legal, half and half.
No one could fathom my strong shoes.
There is no paradise but tongue of love.
I walked all day, I heard no news,
When twilight filled the air with gravities
I descended, heart full and slow
Down the dim fields dotted with stones and sheep
To the house in its bank of trees
The fire, the food, the Gurney piano,
Having my wonderful labour to keep.

XI.

Noon Province

(1989)

*Jag sjunger om det enda som försonar,
det enda praktiska, för alla lika.*

Gunnar Ekelöf

The Night Train Arrives at Avignon

Valued small acts. Arriving
from the other side of the country
to the standard breakfast,
wanting an ordinary thing
that people believe in,
such as the day begins,
keeps them on and together.
Neglecting in first light
stature or office, the travellers
take their turns, asking only
for the complete, the integral.

Market Day at Apt

How it fills the town to its purpose,
stalls heaped with olives, cheeses,
chickens and doves, fills the squares
with food and clothing, the streets with
garlic and mushrooms, ordinary things.
Sound of talking everywhere, town
at work, town alive, town open.
Cavern of image, the mouth keeps its
tone, retains its modest expectation,
pulses in tune to the pocket,
the ordinary day that earns it.
Wild lavender honey from the hills.

Fragments at Les Bassacs

(a)

A tower-house between sky and fields
with dust up to the door. This is
where we are, where we are
to be resolved.

(b) *(peering over Barny's shoulder)*

Scraping stones and pieces of earth
against cream paper you make
a drawing of the landscape,
curved into its resolution,
its resistance. Its question.

(c)

Where are we?
I am witless, cannot invoke
curious detail, eye on the sky
on the dust.

Les Bassacs (d)

The houses, fawn stone, red roofs, lean
into each other, backs to the expanse,
from the valley a fortress on a shelf
bulging and flaking. We think we hear faint voices

In the ground and between the stones,
dealing and deciding in a lost language,
a far and fragile history, for no-one
passes this way any more. Us, we

Come and go. We form a company.
We take over a corner of the structure
and peer through a new high window
onto (a clear day) bright mountains

And distant sea light. It is our passion
to breathe new air, to deal and decide
under a new charter, a human document.
Any profit we make goes to the future.

Roofwatch

1.
Day and night the sky arches over
hills and plain turning against
the earth, clouds springing
from the dark wooded edge fan
over the farmed land and at
night the plethora of stars
turns clear and sure and
compact in their terraces
above a veiled and separated ground.
O fine in their farming the stars
rally and exit all night.

2.
Full adoration without question.
The white rock breaks on the wooded slopes
over there and the sun dies constantly
over the vine fields, burning out fruit.

Repletion without any question
and no curriculum to offer the world
no credentials you would ever believe
for the sun burns cherries out of twigs

And the stars thresh mind pages
to a solitary and quiet wish
to line a space before we turn
to love's raging difference.

Afterthought

I take the lemonade bottle to the village
and get it filled with red wine (a litre)
improving (no doubt) the status of the object.

We proceed to fill ourselves.
But when we are full our generosity is only a meaning we have,
and the unfilled remains always more filling.

Stubborn Interval

I would like to be always present.
Not helpful or obedient
but there, without question
without sex without support
without supper or cigars
but without cease, again
as I am here, in this stone
stack of rooms at the foot
of the fields again and again.

For there needs to be a
(ordinary, unfilled, blue-green, etc.)
staying item, a point of
(salt wind pours over the sky)
(scouring wind)
stubborn answer.

St.-Saturnin, the Ridge

We are entitled to our difference,
in the abandoned garden above the roofs
of the town we are guaranteed separation,
to squat under the shapely dark cypress
with you there and you there
eating black olives and taking photographs
the yellow broom throbbing in the wind
the lizards on the wall of the dry cistern
darting away, the films and ads of the town
deep in us: a politics of matching
by which we are neglected
and rightly so, calling us out
of defeat to the fruiting flesh.

Meditations in the Fields

/1

Strolling in the olive groves and
orchards, dry sky and hot stones, hard
light and Ockeghem on the walkman,
I time the intervals. They are tightly numbered
and of such extent, such meeting parts
that all the time I wasted in disuse
(bed, social time, infant fear)
and wasn't treading the mind's width
is reckoned to my regret and returned
untouched to the earth, or so it seems.

/2

Gazing at the ground
wild thyme and sparse grass
the blue bellflower, *Aphyllanthus
Monspeliensis*, hanging over the stones
between the cherry trees patches of sunlight
and Josquin in the earphone I
am sold out. We receive everything
and return it, in the flesh,
now because it is charted. The flesh
fruits so fulsome and glad precisely
as farmed, didn't they say?

/3

Pausing in the hot vine fields, Brumel
through the wire seeming to say
that mutual enemies debate in the
chambers of the heart, as Dante
certainly said, and a small spirit
pleads to the soul through a thin tube:
Regain your place. And sweet and low
(as thyme fills the air) O scouring focus
neglect our substance if you will but
shepherd this instant to its kingdom as only
the sharpened spirit kens and quickly –
Shew mercy on those good shepherd on
us ourselves, the very ones who
sit alone for their receipt in a foreign field,
send us to our remembrance, it's time
clear enough through the crackle and fuzz,
death's silence leading each tone
onwards, to lock the door
and fall into human length.

The Walk to Roussillon

The red cliff in the dark green woods,
walk towards it. As you get
closer it is difficult to see.

Lines at Night /1

Back at evening, a stone room full
mainly of fireplace. We burn
olive roots, dry thyme, as night
gathers outside we finish
the wine, foot on sill.

Everything we touch grates
with dust and the fire
crackles and flares up.
The fire dies down, the fields
outside are gradually closed.
A speaking darkness surrounds us

And you are in it, and the light
you hold in there, is that a belief?
What else could it be?

Lines at the Pool above St.-Saturnin

Alpine swift (the white chested) carving the air
and a quick wind from the hills redolent of
pine and lavender rides the rocky cleft.
Skimming the surface our sight remains
unpolitically tabulated / innocent in delight –
it is perfectly right, forswearing a life
fixed in ratio to demand like a permanent
insect-target for the flashing creature.
All we ask is that the heads of the town
read justice faithfully.

What do we know of world and detail who can't
compete with the swift for vantage in the
dream of earth? That speed of gain and grace
leaves us standing, lost in our weight and
hesitance, lost in delight at the fruitless sight
of the species pilot fixing history into a dive.

But delight closes and light rises. The limbs
tremble and bow to the mind that pokes
the blazing episphere of day at its fault,
facing world torsion with what? with a politeness,
a reasonable plea: *Raste Krieger, Krieg ist aus.**
Beautiful silent answers move over the hills.

So among ruined walls and broken arches
we foreswear a hope that has no substance
set sticks on bricks, gather truthful items from
the surrounding area and cook up a sequence.

Later the lake dims, the birds retire,
the mind or something silently similar
hovers in plagal trust in the crumbling air,
talking to death at the ancient gate
where the locust pauses, and the woody stalk.

*"Hold it, soldier. War is out."

Meditations in the Fields /4

Anywhere in the world the
mind wakes while I
contemplate a field corner and now
Lassus in the speaker telling
of a rose entrammelled in the years,
surviving as so much else
continues to exist, so much
pain and disappointment
the rose we make again, that you would
never recognise or credit as that same
armonia, that unfolding, clad in
the regency of the moment –
a silent and remote
fold in the edge of the hills
where a few things grow and I
harvest exclusive result.

Lines at Night /2

Evening cloaks the ground again
and here we are in that stone room, table,
chairs, fireplace, dusty lightbulb, slightly
cooler air. And really not
trying too hard. Up on
the roof terrace five
large bats dip through
the small zone of electric light.

Thick night, lit windows,
and punctuated sky. Who
lives here and what they believe
(television, future, mask)
is held against harm
lightly if we trust the opening cadence.
And who knows? It's warm enough
to sleep on the roof.

Lacoste

The landscape is a thought thing,
it has been thought as a gift and as a burden.
We drive through someone's book to
the Marquis de Sade's castle, where misthought
has left not a trace.

House prices flutter and electronic pastoral
beats the air to no result: the true architecture
speaks only *vulgare illustre,* heart-stuff.
Dialectic, reduction, vantage, stand flat to the side,
everything except justice is an impertinence.

It is a crowned structure, a hill
rearing to intellect and lust as a burden
patiently and proudly borne, set
clear above the fruiting plain
brighter stone than star because thought
                                      flawed

Recalling Lacoste (Lines at Night /3)

Back at night in the old room,
total country silence. Dim bulb,
moth at window, bread and cheese,
Côtes du Rhone Beaumes de Venise 1985
cheap but delicately heartening.
Silent tonight, reading a pocket
guide or Dante and thinking of home.

The castle ringed the summit in white, the village
houses were its skirts trailing into the ridged fields.
One does what one can, of course, but only
what we know we do does much good.
The village dog barks twice and stops. Thin
noise of someone's music. There is
a question always at hand, sometimes a horror,
which we are entitled to neglect, with
courtesy, with caution. And could do much
more but look at the time.

Rustrel and Gargas

Mid-day heat at the ochre quarries.
We have pulled the earth aside and left
ourselves without shadow, without
that dark doubt that saves us

And stamp on in absolute certainty:
£8,000,000 for a Van Gogh.
("No cost is too high.")

Returning to the fields, the dark cherries
are dying to be pulled. In the village
the new bread swells and cracks.

Up the Big Hill and Back by Ten

Walking the mind, walking the prosody,
uphill, hour and a half on a stone track
through the garrigue and straight up the hot hill.
It is numbered. The little oaks whisper,
the numbers are there whatever you do
or say, no rests or interludes, sheer calm
continuing as the numbers last, when
the numbers are full you are there. No one
in. A bright green lizard on a stone.

So we turn, descend, count on. A wasps' nest
up a tree, a mantis' egg-sac under a stone.
Unkempt mountain lavender fields,
thyme, alkanet, early purple orchid,
remote farms up in the hills where much more
than entire lives have been played out and love
has been doubled or quartered and time clicks.

Politics is a play of fear. Fearful
clicking of time in the hills as if
a life is never enough meaning. It is
more than enough. A book in my pocket
by Dante, a pocket edition. When we get back
we'll have bread and cheese with wine
and count the day to its figured close.

Counting the Cost (Syllables at Night)

We are back and silent, no
fire tonight, dull light
of the moony bulb, the door
latched, the shutters to.

Count the silence: seven five
count the silenced, oh
millions, lost in the sky and
scattered on the earth

Never to be spoken or
known by any name
whose continuity is
with us in the night

Night of other nights
when we were silent
and the earth turned ahead of
our silent petrified thought.

Teaching us to be nothing
in distant foreign corners,
the earth turns the dark
into truth. Wait there.

The Walk Back to Gordes (lines)
or
Resolution and Interdependence

We are together we are lost
in dazzling light in the limestone
gullies and terraces of a complicated hill
in a blaze of flowering shrubs. Taking
goat paths between dry stone walls
stooping under laden branches stepping
among swallowtails we find our way
together and what does it ever mean
but action and purpose, to be together?
A stupid simple thing to say as if
destruction were not also action and purpose
and being lost among flowers.
We must get back and think ourselves
carefully apart and trade our love limb
for limb. As the swallowtails swarm.
As the dying flare.

Numbers at Les Croagnes

Reaching for food
offered I disappear
into a vetch stratum.
Stay with me, guilt
is a square plot,
an abandoned garden
or olive grove
in front of a chapel
with a locked door.
We say nobody seems
to mind. Soft wine
raises our spirits to
the foliation band.
Whoever says he minds
will be offered a glass.

Just a Song (Lines at Night /5)

Dusk on the upper fields, the bushes
and small trees clumps of blackness
in a grey haze. The walker, alone, has
slight but simple script to find his path,
streaks of paleness on the ground. The moon
encloses the air, the bullfrog creaks
in the silence, the grasses fidget and lapse.

He listens to the silence and hears
nonsense, eyeless jokes in a dark hall.
His mind runs ahead of it becoming
leader of a quiet procession
trailing down the hillside between fields
holding the moon on the end of a stick

To see his way. The message is clear
and hopeful. His best intentions mesh
with the world's world and fall back towards
his exclusion and so they must
or Death gets double six and an extra go
because the littleness of his world succeeds.
Look how he hangs from the moon!

The path leads clearly down to the edge
of the slope and rejoins the road where
it hangs over the wide valley scattered
with house lights and a steady glow
from behind the far hills. Someone has left
an old white horse in a field with food
water and shelter, standing through the night.

Notes on the Attempt
to Visit Lorand Gaspar

I want to bring everything in but
the poem wants to leave everything out
and where does that get us? Dialling numbers,
getting recorded messages to say there is
no reply. Driving an orange car
on ribbon roads over the hills between
the orchards to the coastal marshes,
white horses grazing in the grey flats,
the poem tapping its foot on the
accelerator and coughing for more fuel,
wanting to get on with the work,
wanting to move, out, across the city
in fits and starts, looking left and right
for a cathedral or a telephone exchange,
Gabrieli on the car radio saying there are
beams and levers at every point of the continuance.
And so we roll into the village square
and park in the motley of plane leaves, too
hot and dazzled to speak the language.
Where is the man with the orange poem?

The Slower Walk to Roussillon with Kathy

Walking through the fields, not to create
harm that devolves back to worlds.
A black cricket with orange knees, beaming
yellow furze, a white butterfly with black
edging and sage underwing. Listen

While I tell you. Blue iris newly unwrapped,
when you're nearer to death than birth
the coin begins to pass more openly
like the earth at a good conjunction.
A five-pointed violet star.

Then the wheatfield bloody with poppies.
I think this swelling bright horizon
holds us (passing) at our best yet
since we don't know where final justice lives
and death isn't quite enough to meet the need for it,

We care desperately to create a good
past us, taking to risk an edge of harm.
In a sudden hot hollow a mass of brown
butterflies and round the corner an
orange car containing.

The Telephone Box
on the Edge of the Cornfield

Letters and numbers spray from our minds,
settle on the wires in unbroken code. The car
sees everything with two hollow eyes
sees there is nothing to see but signs
at choices. This is what our minds
are reduced to, living in this world.

So we get out and stand by the field leaning
on the box and light breezes play the
corn like Mbira. There is red and slight
blue under-text, disclosed where least
expected from time to time.

And the heart is said to be a
rare blue object in a red matrix
surrounded by the yellow goods.
Consuming and lashing strokes. On the
border of which a mind or surface
pauses, keeping all this together.

Last Night

(1)

Stretched in the stone chamber
awake and listening
to the dark stone silence that
grew from nothing, final justice
lives in our hearts.

And nothing here is ours, we came
and went like a night moth, a few
tourists were here for a week
they stayed up late in thought by
the single lamp.

Exactly so, exactly us
fishing for quick messages
in the wind along the wall,
histories of earth that signal
to the whole heart

That the world is there out there
in the dark full of hope and
silence and calling to a
centre. A single bell rings
across the valley.

Slowly the heart unfolds, slowly
the mind weighs. Ordinary events
that hold people together and
on into day and year in
spite of loss.

Helpful and obedient too,
passing faithful to the
substance that writes itself
across the night and back to our
lives in the end.

(2)

Sensing a power that
answers death I move to the
window and nothing happens.
"A beautiful and gentle wild thing
pierces my breast"

And turns there and chambers and
libraries fan out from that
simple point and a music
farms the air. How it
bells the close!

And we are cast against
injustice in wild longing,
screw our eyes at the world which
won't settle into peace until
it is far too late it is over.

There is nothing but darkness out there
and something flies out, some creature
of breath, over the hill calling
and calling like to like
one power to one life.

As if a person could do a thing
but inhabit a language that makes sense
whose periods follow themselves in
tune to distance and arrive
ahead of harm.

Something in the dark quiet
night whispers in my head after
tearing my breast and tells me look, there is
nothing there, there is no
rose but truth unfolding

(3)

Light and substance. We are caught
in a tangle of seeking
consequence. And the winner
weeps at his success, to have taken on
earth's thankless gain.

Refuse it. Act on the very
minim of reluctance and the city
rears behind the hill –
calm terraces, theatre
of entire lives where flesh

Unfolding turns at last
to shore, to earth's arc, bright
moon on the tree jagged edge of the
black hill out there for a moment
which is a moment

Of complete certainty never to be
relinquished; heart infoliate the only
lasting or wanted thing.
And the stream running under the wall
and the paling ash

We leave behind, shoulder
luggage and are forgotten.
Leaving an empty house, the night
bird perched on the roof ridge
pealing death out

Of hiding, out of the horizon.
Then a slight paling begins, night
turns and trots down the valley, dreams
wrapped in darkness and world
break into day.

Orange to Chartres

Stay and work, stay and work,
build machines in the garden.
The leaf opens to show a chrysalis.
A tortoise suddenly crosses the path.
Oh stay anyway, work to the planet's
demand: how to pan that mothering arc
away from worlds to here, and come
to know at some impossible distance
how love comes finally to a start.

A model of the heart, standing
across the river. It shines at night,
covered in creations and justices,
opercular, a closed work, that stands
there like an old man in the sun –
a message of arcaded days, shadowed access
to what we are. And can and will.
Loved justly because a credit succeeds us.
At which the star leaps into the rose.

Slow Meditation in the Café-Bar
Les Caves du Mont Anis, Le Puy

Sometimes a feeling comes on me saying that to love the very savour of human being is such a rare thing, to love a kind of savour or centre of what we are, which is an ordinary thing but the only truth we wholly know, the only fullness without interference, our own stake in time: the person being here. It is not a sudden or dramatic thing, does not imply wide revelation, but is here all the time. And on rare occasions we notice, that there is a truth at our pivot, that it fans out through us, that we can act and speak on its tide.

And it is never quite singular, you know, never quite alone, however much we shirk the focus there is always that telling chime; to sit alone in a cave under the cathedral is to smile at a library of honesty. And welcome what we can of it. We can hardly move without that prime informer the tongue across time and worlds funnelled down onto what we perceive and learn. We cannot even guess at the weight and pressure of true souls informing a slight movement of the lower lip, a faint stirring at the back of the head moving towards language, a feeling as of the slow dropping of veils, the narrowing of world light to an entrance.

This feeling says very little, it says only that the light is not yet out and every point in the world continues to exist as every person who ever did exist had a centre which transmitted itself into a vocabulary and on into hope. Even those, I think, who preferred hurt. But it is a feeling which occurs in a pause and protected from both sides, protected and fuelled by the days and futures of searching, obedient, action. Protected from what anybody ever did by what they might. We cannot arrange for such pauses.

It says a little more too, in a kind of weariness inhabiting the resilience and ease of the feeling, almost an edge of anger to the blissful prescience like a line of shadow marking the edge of an arch. It mentions that we also hate this life and all its distracting obstacles. It says that the angels, in the tympanum, with their serrated wings, are more beautiful and more human than the dark twisted flesh of our comedians and newscasters because they also assure us that we are also not here, also not anywhere on this striven planet at all, we have already come to an end and a line and a syllable mark out the wonderful pleasure of not having to be where we are put, not having to be here in this lying cave. One window opening onto a stone wall. That is to say, this is not a mixed feeling, but a feeling with an edge.

This block of sense is beyond harm while it stays. Its tranquil inwardness offers goodness indirectly, as the world understands, shadowed in honour and fidelity, starting with those we know best. For it exhorts us to declare ourselves in full, and at an enjoining of calm by which the offer must be repeated until it is taken, falling again and again to lay the coin at your feet, to make verses. Craftily glossing the past into trust via forgetting it rather precariously opens the future through its own delicately poised moment and totally assures the hesitant bearer: *the end is in sight,* minutely, so slight it almost hurts to locate. And what is your secret then in the years to come of elsewhere and departure, what does it matter then to have gained a self rise? It is returned anyway, the earth wants it all back. Stay with what you are. Work the burden and blind fear out of continuance by no more than a noticed edge, a flicker of grass, a simple attendance. That is, to shepherd this moment to its kingdom, as we have slowly learned in centuries of script. The continuance held in the instant and helpless out of it, like a lost child. And that is to say, I know nothing but this table. On which is represented by curious skill, a pattern of welfare. A pattern of warfare. A map of faring.

Notes to *Noon Province*

Epigraph: "I sing of the one thing that reconciles, only of what is practical, for all alike."

Meditations in the Fields: Ockeghem, Josquin, Brumel and Lassus were all European composers of (mainly) church music for choir in the 15th and 16th Centuries. They are placed in order of seniority in the four poems, Lassus being the youngest. The liturgical pieces, whose texts entered into the poems, were: Ockeghem: *Mass for the Dead*, Josquin: *Stabat Mater*, Brumel: *O Domine Iesu Christe pastor bone*, Lassus: not recorded.

Lines at the Pool Above St.-Saturnin. "Raste kriege…" Sir Walter Scott, from *The Lady of the Lake*, translated by Adam Storck and set by Schubert as *Ellens Gesang I*. Scott wrote, "Soldier rest! thy warfare o'er".

The Telephone Box… Mbira is the name of an east African musical instrument ("thumb piano") and the music it produces, which, like most music, is a trance music.

Last Night (2) "A beautiful and gentle wild thing…" Giovanni della Casa, *Rime* XII, line 9: "Bella fera e gentil mi punse il seno"

XII.

Reader

Lecture

Author

(1992-1998)

Reader

Harecops

Grace and Honour
descend the hill
seeking the human heart,
brushing aside the wasps
and folding that knotted
academy in clay hands…

Our front window looked out two miles
over pasture and woodlands thick
with the sheen of equity, that eschews
greed or fantasy, its pale emblems still
shelved at the field edges fading nightly
into dream. We held onto this optimism
like grim death. We sank our trust
in curtained arbours of a stone house
and formed a child, who guided us
past the dark stores, and darker thrones.

And two miles away was a great ridge,
a dark green mass strung with white stone walls,
at its highest point an ancestral grave,
a circular fate capsule of long stones.
It was always there, though the light
came and failed. White stone messengers
pierced the night and focused the day, calling
to the mind, calling to the cupped heart,
calling together the kind forces
that hunt us to death.

Macclesfield

Mislaid purpose coated
with grime and stuck in a nest
of hill shoulders. Little red tractors
buzzed round the heads of the town
and the dark brick alcoves were
always waiting, you could
cowl yourself in one and
belong until you stank of oil.

The question was: did you care, did you
want any more than good being?
If you didn't you rested even
as the evening sunlight
sat on the doorstep with its
feet in the street and you crawled
between the slates and stars and kissed,
blind to all except detail. If you did,
you worked the circuits crying O,
baby, don't you want to go…?

A provincial voice has
total age or falls to scraps. We
took our purpose by the hand
and led it out of the factories and shops
into the nation.

Denmark

Denmark
was entirely my own fault!

I like to think I retained
a flake of grace

in the squint-mirrors and
winter glades,

the kindness hiding
in the passing measures.

I like to think
of you, now a lost name

who brought my wandering spirit
to its focus. I lost all sight

of you, but gained a northern pebble
to hold against the paling sky

and I think I did
eventually achieve

a sexual friendship that would have
turned New York green.

Bolehill

I shall never forget the grove
and the grassy mounds.
I shall never forget you
fighting me on a pillow.
I cannot thank you enough.
When the snow came
it melted (when our
tears came they
hardened)
and ran down the fields.

Egbert Street

A name becomes hearted
and sustains life.

Somewhere between loss
and gain, in that

narrow climate
the flower succeeds

that grows now
in the garden here,

a castle
against relatives.

Pastoral

Listening to Schubert's songs
sung by Robert Holl
it becomes obvious:
the hunter's call in the forest
is the kindest thing we know,
is the thing that tells us…
What does it tell us?

We are an always,
like it or not, that
is what we are. We
nourish our hunger.

Hastings

Our virtuous acts
remain with us,

everything else has vanished.
It doesn't matter

how little remains: the soul,
a tiny part of the body

and a white cat in the window.

High Lane

I wandered the fields and woods
waiting to be called back
into someone's life: the hand
on the shoulder or
the teeth on the neck:
lie back and be taken or
escape and perish.
I took a bus to the city centre.

Coming home late at night, walking
from the station through the old mines
I glanced up at the hunting lodge on
the horizon and cast my affection forward
against all caution to that cage, believing
the most logical things on earth to be
the most sensual, tears in my eyes,
knowing the prize
was not mine, well, such is
passion or day.

Through Woods and Fields

I would hunt you
to the end of the earth
and the beginning of a song
by Robert Schumann,
listening for that call in the
forest, meaning new life,
and looking
for that boat on the lake
meaning death.

After a Poem by Nicholas Moore

I repeat, the heart, the
hart in the forest,
the white one, I shall
pursue that forehead for
ever and don't care how slowly
it comes closer and closer,
that heaven to this hell.

Then it is hale and clear
and clearly us, together
in the (end) clearing.

Irish Drones

All those chanters
all faring well enough
and along he comes, what's
his name, Willie Clancie, Billy
Pigg, not Irish either and
plays as if his heart's cut in two.
It isn't. Somebody's is.

Maybe it's mine, the
listener, maybe it's us.
The as if
is a long acquaintance with the sky.

What the Fate Capsule Told Me

The hunters' call across the valley:
us, is what they're after
and can't fail either, in the end
we are theirs, and they take us.

Then the horn calls them back
to their silver folds and
the quarry rises,
white against the green hill

And turns towards us, heraldic creature with
open arms, compact of ore and bone,
living and breathing creature I have
followed all my life.

Then all our virtue stands in us,
and there is no further pursuit. Note also
the beauty when a face
is distracted from its intent.

Golden Slumbers

To reach you I would bar the fields
and turn the ores into the stream.

I would occupy the eyrie of my failure
far into the night night after night

until the ancestral bones
formed a nest for my patience

in which I would sit and couple the numbers
of my life without regret

and remember with uncertainty the world
in which we were and not,
all our loves in vain.

*

No love is in vain,
reader.

Addenda to *Reader*

(i)

Socialism (Prayer)

So many, guarding their own souls,
have truth and poetry at their edge
but prefer not to know it,
being focussed on returns.
Later, when the world is better,
all these souls will remain
as unique scripts faithfully
transcribed, after any of which
the world cannot be the same
but only a forward location.

(ii)

Aigburth (Howl)

Flower festivals, sewage
works, Chinese fish and

chips. We
lived together, sharing

our persons and
everything we were

for eight years.

(iii)

Nicholas Moore Retake (Pact)

I repeat, the heart, the
hart in the forest

the white one I would
pursue that forehead for

ever and don't care how slowly
slow it comes closer and closer

until the whole land is dressed
in the wholeness of a small animal,

a stoat maybe, a sandpiper, artful thing
that hunts / is hunted day

and night and day again until
that quiet end so fine and clear.

Lecture

Ego sic semper et ubique vixi, ut ultimam quamque lucem, tanquam non redituram consumerem.
    Petronius Arbiter

In life a cave; in death a lamp to poets and doctors.
    John Wheelright

* * *

*Wie schön bist du,
freundliche Stille,
himmlische Ruh'!*
and the lone star
wanders in the night fields
shedding silence. Don't
stop, don't hope, don't
take your coat off.

Evening's gentility
raises our prospect to the very
eye of April, the common
welcome, and we turn from
hope to where the water
wears the white rock
to the semblance of a thigh
and echo of a sigh.

* * *

Only true passion there is,
only penetration where the mind's
pale surface focuses on hope,
and in that clearing
falls for the love, the
swell of it
          as it breaks
on the world's obsidian
and the blood flows again,
vere fluxit sanguine the frail boat
splits and sinks, the child
gasps for air. The answers surely
are simple. *O clemens O pie*
clear and particular
mercy pity peace.

I Wrote a Letter from France

Here I set my suitcase down
and swear by the twin stars that
triangulate our wars, the new
meadows open their doors at
evening's end, the soft sand
slides along the river bed,
the singing night birds
plunge their beaks into comfort.

War leans on the shadow's edge
where light pours into the ground
and slides through caves. The star
on the sole knows the way,
anger locked in shadow mouths,
hope a flicker on the dark river but
well within sight of the necessary vows.
I open my suitcase looking for a ring.

***
(for Michael Haslam)

Congress of twins that
    lengthens the world
in a mournful music, send me
    back to the bench but
keep me in that fold where
    the amethyst holds and
we are sunk in the generations.
        Kit this pillow
in a fabulous lace of spittle.

Regendered

You entered me and that
point of you that means
real and future has filled
my emptiness with seed.
Now I drag in the moon's
path because I am
trapped in because and
there is a small light at my gut.

Glow Worm True Worm

Bright hyphen in the dark valley
between the path and the river,
I never even tried and the water slips
sideways, the little owls hop
from branch to branch in the dark,
living like us with what they aren't
but could be. And the stars
pulse dryly to themselves, a steady and
irrevocable calling across date and
post, across floors and shelves of
goods across the merely possible
the synapse fires as if suddenly us.

But I always thought love was deserved.
I thought it was the earth shining.

Heinrich Biber

Passion's proximity, passion's three-step
and you're there. If you're there
be there, show pluck, walk in the
streets of Laredo head high, danger
on the cuff and mortal precept.
Willing, I mean, to die for nothing
since we do and have plenty of time.
In this faint light I couldn't see
better and scratch an elk on
the cave wall in five minutes flat
because passion creates what it means
out of thin air in red streams. And turn
to the bank as the moon shrinks
and the membrane tightens across
the mossy fields, the debris of our
gain signed in passionless lymph.
Take your partner, harmonious nymph,
and treacle the earth without blame.
Out of my case I choose a clear name.

Die Mondnacht

Out in the fields behind the airport the stream sparkles in the night, bits of light fall from the leaves and the house ridges blur into evening, sugar and milk before bed. Faint voices through the night's broken spaces, speaking of journeys we shall never take, as the tenuous airships lift off one by one and disappear into the sky, heading for futures by the thousand. Where are you now?

Where are you now? How do you face the world and its night, fortune or failure? Have you had babies? Would you suck the cream off their heads and wash their shirts, would you curse the glowing sweets that rot their teeth? Have they grown up now? If I could hear you what would you say to me? Would you be now as you were then? *Eins ins andre gar versunken, gar verloren, gar ertrunken...* Would you get tipsy and tiptoe round the sleeping cows? *Bis sich jede Öde füllt...* Have we (have I) in our (my) impatience left a wasteland between us that cannot be traversed even by air?

If we see and yearn for the world's bright edges we are one. *Dich umringend, von dir umrungen... Gar in Eins mit dir geeint...* As we always were. Unmasked. And somewhere the great airships touch down, one by one. People proceed to their destinations.

Magdalenian

Hand stencils on concave surfaces at points of relinquishment. Hollow horses and bulging bovines. Desire, that claim on light between mouth and legs crashes day by day against the lens, it really is too late to 'phone. The last signature is set at *bouches d'ombre*: thresholds of lower galleries containing running water, doors into the world's black fall. A headless snake on the banks of the underground river. Absolutes move in the night in the dark back streets when everyone's asleep, relentless laceration of the necessary victim. Speech blocked, broken membrane, casual and arbitrary deaths in a war for want. We cost it all in poetry, wild notes in our dark mouths, with the animals alongside stacked red and black, small flickering shades on the walls of the river, phosphenes in attendance overhead.

Author

I eat fire sometimes. But I have to control myself because my father taught me that even a chief's son is a commoner in other lands.
Chenjerai Hove, *Bones.*

In manus tuas

Gendering touch that gathers
and cups like a boat on the
rotting sea because I tendered

all I am to your safety. We are eye
to eye, heart to purpose, bent
forward in the western wind

that blows over hard and
blanched ground towards an idea
of work as shelter.

The children raised there will blow
this distance to anthills and tie
themselves to aerials

and hunt themselves to equity
in an under-tree light loud with one
mutual cry – of succession,

dying to a rich suture of the future.
Deep then in the oily mulch a
smouldering hope, a patient ear

to another's woe and a door behind the snow.
How it seals the film of spring,
where we ride forth in company.

* * *

Pure need scores the pavement.
I know the mind is a final place
and a stone violently peaceful
to lie on, hidden in the grass
under the shadow of your arm.

The present becomes a gap
of fearful chance, older than
any church. Lights consign the arcade
to a virtual offer, begging
in the street for sacrifice.

The tired are a fine people,
hands almost touch, almost turn,
hearts almost tread.
O memoria felice! Nights at the
star loft, days bound ahead of reason.

Slowly failure becomes an honourable nation
in which I wait for someone's arm,
counting the miles towards home
while quieter waters leech the soil
and closer minds bow to the pavement,

tracing the future of mineral solutions
under the meadows of desire.
So set in the failed traffic my vocation turns
as the tired turn, downwards, dark road to a
chip sandwich, weeping prisoner almost touched.

* * *

Voiced consonants buzzing through Suffolk
to a dark road white houses when I
knew the cost I had no language,

my death spread over the fens. Love
predicates a real future or
burns to nothing like a white leaf.

My hands felt like two balloons. Did you,
yes you did, see the great flocks
of Scandinavian wood pigeons and

plovers in the ploughed fields, hundreds, in
slowly dimming winter light wearing
a question to be proud of, bending

to the day's end, calling where is the
river where is the course of us
where is the bridge of flesh?

Not here, nor worth knowing
in a society that reckons care
by tenths. The sheen of their wings

makes a sea of the field
and a person's age is a grateful fact
sailing out on it with you

sitting in a car in a dark road white
houses, bookshop open answer closed
fruitful company in a closing world.

I have to believe what the earth so
distinctly says. Settle noisily honourable birds
onto everyone's food.

As with rosy steps...

Set to a hyaline edge the dawn
light spills heavy with milk. Over the
rim it spills as it is bound to,

creeps among the grass stalks like a silent snake
as the rusty tank yells the lads back to slaughter
that they surely will on the chime of ten.

Yet it continues slowly and chromatically
mounting like a reasonable despair
that finds an answer in its own folds,

in the crests and commerce of
the shadowed fields its own voice
reaching to the upper tonic or

scooping light to the soul's mouth while
the city clocks its advantages, turned
back to back with disdain, hand in pocket.

Hand in blame. I can't exactly
unregister myself from harm as the first sugar truck
cuts across the fens one September dawn,

cold and faint, cuts purpose from act
and state in all innocence. But the light
spreads, green and brown folded in water.

Chalk under foot. *Domine libera*
animam meam a labiis iniquis et
a lingua dolosa. Chalk under bone.

Spreads and means, turning home.

E Questa Vita un Lampo

Wrap the light in tendons and no one
can take it except finally. So the world
is darkened.

Daily darkened. O blessed man,
that the self flees into
a cave at your anger and the worms

the beneficial worms bite the white rock
to a soil, that holds the stem
of a marriage cup, future prize of

written flesh. Worth every drop too
for it opens and tints at the
start of love to the temperature

of the globe and bears its illumination
from cell to cell unwrapped, casting
back from the body's reluctance a glow,

small in reach that blasts fantasy inside
out. And the occasion of this release:
a single pronoun on the doorstep begging no

more than sustenance. Claiming no rights.
Starting no fights. Elegant in rags.
Citizen of the nights.

Delphine
(extempore on a Schubert song)

To begin then if it is
      and if it is
what it does or
      not do here
or do there and do head
      to toe if it is.
For us, then, is it, alone
      worth it, is it
fading enough is it
      nothing enough, is it
doing and wanting and
      being nothing at all
or almost at all such as
      not wanting to stay in and
not wanting to go out, is
      that it? So it is
a not that binds
      and burns, but still not,
and finally withers.
      What indeed is the good
of planting rows of flowers
      and watering them if
what it all comes to is precisely not
      but what could hurt
and pleasure more?

O That Singer
(to the memory of Amédé Ardoin)

You're fallen, the street at your throat.
Denial echoes under the palate as they
queue at the bank for promises, not

believing a word. And you who believed
everything lie cast in a rail-side cot,
blood-clot on the brain and a hawk came

and perched on the wire, beautiful thing,
preening its oily coat in red and grey.
And the text of those unfolding wings

was a cloud encumbered sky over
a measured plain, immeasurable pain, where
distant travellers greet the dawn

eye to eye, hand to mouth
and never arrive. Never arrive
because the syntax is cut

just where it opens where the
wooded hill cleaves in the wind. There
we offer pittance to your archive.

And we your friends, your very
loyal congregation set our hearts back
to the living light in the far shed for the hope
the day harbours, singing and playing.

Bar Carol

There are worse deaths than singing,
worse singing than death's.
Gently over black ever
shifting water the wooden craft
moves out. The newspaper
soaked in itself, sinks.

And the city back there, circles scripted
over the sea articulating light we
adore by rote, and touched by the
tainted fall of socialistic promises
like petals of death, sign out
with a blown shrug.
                    The city divides
and falls but the world waits for ever
the great curve of thought we
slowly sail round towards singing.

* * *

And love alone, untouched by ideology,
is a rare thing that the flesh
calls out and runs to meet. There they
stand, hand in hand, watching the horses
pounding the green field at the sea's edge,
green pulse at the street's end, always and
precisely that sundering coil of breath.

And love alone, without bonus, roars
in my ear the final score. Wherever on
earth we may be in the time and
measure left me I shan't dream or
anything but honour. And silly too,
forgetting the exact ground whereon those
two eyes bought my breath.

And love aligns the bruised letters offering
nothing to the future but itself, what it
purely earns. Snow brushing the hill,
honesty of the offered arm, daybreak over
the ruins of will. So the earth lightens
to a hawk's point in the sky and a silver
cup for the loser, as ever was.
Take it this parting prize this blow.

Notes to *Reader / Lecture / Author*

All quotations in German are from the texts of songs by Schubert.

All quotations in Latin are liturgical or biblical in origin.

È questa vita un lampo: This life is (but) a flash (as of lightning) (permitting an English pun on "lamp").

The poem, entitled 'Do It Again', that came between 'Delphine' and 'O That Singer' had to be removed because of copyright fears.

XIII.

Snow Has Settled...

(1997)

Prelude

Snow has settled in the lines
of an old ridge-and-furrow system
striping the gently sloping dark
green fields, engrossed script
of duration, repetition, authority
at which that calm baby in the self
that finds it so difficult to speak
lowers an eyelid on the shrinking day
and suddenly says outright
the entire brochure of love and all.
Stay here before you fall.

Wirksworth

Now I put 500 books into cardboard boxes
and the boxes into the back of the car, hoping
springs and axle will take the weight
then walk out across the town, the fox's
lair gaily varnished today in winter light,
the cubist garden, stone walls sloping
with and across. Walk to a purpose and wait
for that pause in the business and shopping
when a spark of world falls and locks
itself behind the ear, a sky-connected fate
capsule, small as a bee's sting, groping
down the spine in search of a heart, down
the throat in search of a voice to say Make
an art of these days and people, your prime estate.

Wirksworth

Next I move 500 books like ancestral skulls from
here to there in boxes. What in the day
tells us where we are bound? The snow thrown
against the valley side, the grey
lumps of snow stuck under the grass tufts,
northern reticence and southern obstinacy.
Thin lines of supply toiling across
the damaged hills, a constant roar*, a closed box.
As if it matters what colours we wear. Battered
and resolute, resisting the cold refusal to live,
fear of ease and pleasure and the licenced
theatre of death, we continue, as if it mattered
whether the poem rhymed, whether we move
or stay, resisting the arts of silence.

(* variant: a constant war)

* * *

Relenting of durance the snow evaporates
under warm breezes and that beautiful thing
of night, the moon's crystal stage, meets
the rising day, sun-softened and neatly folded.
How the cold-lovers lament its passing, and range
blindly over the thin tufted slopes, planning
spartan endurance centres in pale concrete where
thorns stick against the wind. A strict economy:
pay for pay, nothing for nothing, setting mortars
at the faery palaces on the desert horizon
oh hating the very thought, of a spreading benison.
The day is held upright on the edge of nothing.
But as dedicated workers we learn what works best
and no one welcomes the final ice in the chest.

Further Education

Ah, to be a full citizen of here, the nation
of sheer being, the real that fits like a glove.
So where is the pass? I turned on Radio One
and an elderly man was speaking of a personal love
which had sustained him through an entire life,
moving a constant gratefulness between him and his wife.
I had to acknowledge my unworthiness of such emotion
and I asked why or how a resistance came upon us
implanting a resentment when the tie is from above
and we can't speak so warmly as he. But trust
also in a working fate we bear together, and when
the ward light blinks for one the other will gasp for certain.
And at variance become more richly equal and when
the pulse breaks for one the other will grasp for the curtain.

North End

Surely, once the mind is tuned to resolution*
there is more in the day than you could possibly say
and every millimetre of it worth recording.

Once distance is admitted to the vein its action
spreads through the sensual mass until the day
is almost as richly dight as a small poem worth reading

But not quite because much of the information
remains locked in the stones and the sky
is a book unopened, a transaction resting

On possibility and fading into contradiction
from the edges inwards. We shall stay
quiet, as if in solitude rehearsing

Until the offer of love is grounded on propitiation.
Then open and read and the grand opera does take place.
At night the earth is hollow and the sky full of lace.

(*variant: restitution)

Poem Beginning with a Line
by Nicholas Moore

Oh buzzing bee, art is a thing of love / as love
is a thing of art, they build each other. But who knows who
is the contract salesman and who is the perfect lover?
"It is what the girl wears that makes her beautiful"
It is what she brings, cattle, solid gold rings, a promise
consolidated over centuries of which it is full
as the river is full of sky. Not the slightest threat
to the self is implied or taken. Richly the promise is met
richly the table is spread and the insects forced into retreat,
the pickers and snatchers rigorously excluded from a slow
tableau where generosity is the defining percept of the other.
And this ring we carry on our bodies as we buzz round ever after
and the foul dry winds suck the pools and harden the skin but we try
to maintain our patent purpose. If there were only love it would die.

London Bridge

The townscape must in its new hour be brighter
deeper and more resonant in sense than all
the crude rocks and fibrous masses that few have ever
touched and no one could love at all. Tall
in the day's straight light the edge-lines tighten
on the elegant buildings and plain blocks, the force
of pleasure beside us compacted like marble on
the corner of the street. The moment runs its course
along the banks terraces and windows drenched
in sunlight, unimpeachable hope. Social danger
dreams also in the shadows, a not yet substance
growing hungry, that Turner with a bold hand wrenches
and smears with light, pushes and fixes with anger
in a proud, instant, mortal*, trance.

(*variant: moral)

Norwich

Grains of perception rattle from the dome
to the sorting office. We bring our plunder
to the city like cats and gain a temporary home.
The music is also the price, the song darts under
the boundary and nests there, hollow stone.
Garnered lives mount up past their own redundancy
and transcribe a damask garment, bone-
chest or triumphal vault, floodlit for our wonder.
Walking alone by the river in this curved
city, evening mist spread over the meadows,
I sense the persistence and thus fidelity we
do evince, and turning back to the station am re-nerved
against pre-death as it seems we people like tall windows
have earthlight in our substance act and purpose, all 3.

Great Eastern

Finally on the edge of night there is
only one love. We are specific to it but
not ourselves within its objectives.
The factory hums all night outside the window
the walkers come home late from the pubs
and restaurants. What we love is the earth
as the condition of our convexity and so
it is in the steady distancing and fall
of light between houses, which is
itself a meaning but not itself articulate
and calls to us between our hearts
opening as they do one toward another
one by one to duty and reward. All right,
opening to the earth at a guess of its plight.

West Side

The earth's plight is also our delight
lost in it, brushed awry by the night
of stars and factory signals, make of our
loves one love, make humus of our hearts.
And the city becomes a robe and an articulate
constant of hope, corners full now as
ever of threat in the sharp-edged night
and windowless buildings above which so
many stars cluster as almost to light the earth
by an intellectual focus. At midnight the pubs
switch quietly off across from my window,
the bridge glows under the factory. This also
is the earth's plight, the lights not quite
meeting but dying to say we know perfectly what.

Bolehill

Who is it comes knocking at my door in the night
breaking the quiet darkness, calling me out?
Brother, colleague, I am the world's dimmest lout,
why do you want me out there in the source of light
what use am I to the nascent day? And he says
he has been sent from corners of the land
to gather solidarity to a scattered band
of true souls, thinkers weeping in a maze
of brutality and he says the world is badly
balanced on a point of trust, he says the whole
world is an unstable thing, a shrinking caul
on truth and we have to meet love's demand.
In the darkness the rain falls from leaf
to leaf and beats upon the ground.

Next Door But One

Grass in snow to the doorstep, crystalline dust,
bright hills, cold house, home of a man died ten
years ago and now his wife follows, across the fields
the white fields in silence. Empty house, open window
and that rumble always filling the valley, drone of time.
A new silence held in the magpie cave she
made there, packed with buttons and cloth, trophies
of persistent economy. Now the rooms are bare
and you and I we are pushed out to our centre by this
clarity, the yellow gleam on the tempered snow,
out of our country fears by the ancestral trellis.
Dark branches cross the stellar axis (for we love
what time denies) and slipping on the ice I bring home
the dead wood, the result. The fire at time's heart.

Little Bolehill

The stack of days is useless, there's nothing,
the days are nothing in the pocket no books
on the shelf: a white wall and a black kettle.
You can think & feel freely but there is nothing
left of the day to have or write into a book
or stack away, finally only a cup and a kettle
that we take with us into the garden where nothing
grows except statues and ideas or sometimes books
but a real enough garden with leaves. Put the kettle
on the brick-lined hearth to simmer as the book
says and pour slowly, hot water on the leaves.
Perhaps it is a life's richer act to wish nothing
more than its creation out of nothing
of a real and final thing as true as leaves.

Midsummer Common

What were the victory fireworks like in 1945
if you didn't believe in the war but loved
the people and their victory? The sky
scripted in hot lights, the sky full
and veiled rim to rim. Oh to escape
under the edge of night, red hair streaming
in the wind like coals in a world fire, a fire
to heat the world's best wishes to a red
glowing ardour, the great ring on the bone
and purpose of love for the field is full
of folk, firework, seedscape. And return
as a soldier returns, to what? There is something
further out in the dark than the painted stars,
something that also hates us and our wars.

Cambridge Blue

The book stands, as closed as nature.
Caught in a star mat, domes half
sunk in the fibre, we set it down as pure
transverse agony, trying not to laugh.
People view these double leaves and scream
with what I don't know, delight anger fear
boredom. The knife is flecked with cream
and the heart wobbles like the foam on beer.
Torsive* answers flatter the west horizon
tight as thorn-gags, anchored to stone,
orange above and grey below, flat on
the closing sky that burns us home.
Danger of melt-down everywhere you look.
Nature smiles, as closed as the book.

(* variants: torsile, tortive, tortile, tortious, tortuous)

A Shropshire Lad

That great land is here when we die,
multiple sky brought to our feet
blown there piecemeal, North quartered West.
And that starless zone speaks us out,
a dark patch cut into the night
as a name called, a fallen guest.
This can't change: so the meet
and divide of the world rings high
on the clock tower, so too we cry
ourselves through chains of flesh heat
by centuries, arch in the East
through which the truth is a bullet
and a desert throne. We cut us in.
All sweet dapple falls to the margin.

Dublin

Venus is shrouded and the dark houses
contradict life which contradicts itself
in a mass of talk through a bar doorway.
It fades, white moon, white statue against
black wall, cut of equity. Canal moon
floating in fuzz under Ballybough Road,
corridor of glow between cliff houses,
leading surely to the end of itself
and a drunken cripple in a doorway
sings his Irish heart out as if all the
gardens of memory lost in the moon
could lay this mist and clear this cruel code.
Suddenly I was a red horseman
helping a blind man to cross the road.

Dublin

Day is occluded and the night walker
shields his mind from the museum of loss,
the circus behind the contradicted door
or collapsed against the wall, needing help
and saying nothing, like a white statue
in a black canal. A shudder tears through
society, unnoticed, the walker
drops tears into language quietly for loss
of equity, and passing the closed door
of a bank where someone has chalked GOD HELP
THE BLACKS IN SOUTH AFRICA the statutes
of his helpless trust declare themselves through
again that dark canyon where windows
glow as day stars, clenched rose.

Fontaine de Vaucluse

Here where I half am, city-fled, set on
the hope of breaking that wall,
city-followed, city-led, city all,
sitting in the round stone square not alone
but only half hearing the constant falling and
doubling of water flickering on stones. Gent-
ly trading town, long wooded river cleft
in the hill to the resurgence, the strand on
the edge of despair where they came and stood
in season, Dante, Petrarch, others, half
here and what would be the point of being more,
what the frosty outcome of forgetting?
An old man gathering herbs among the trees,
wedge of city ice sparkling in his head.

Loft

I was resting quietly in my slight knowledge,
barely support enough to any human freight
through the world and the clouds! the clouds
shooting across the dark sky and as soon
as we notice the clouds moving the edge of
our tenure starts to erode, they skate past
and we're suspended in the bounds of a cosmic
sandwich, something God planned for lunch.
And I am far too sober to confront that great
display of uncaring with a wedge of unique
script – which is what it takes, mounted
from the very rooftops, beaming in state:
that when it comes to the bite (calmly) we seek
further than cloud, appetite uncounted.

Hackney Loft

The clouds, yes the clouds shoot
under the sky brown with town light
bearing our purpose away across
the horizon as if it doesn't matter
and what can we bring against it
but a darker hedge of thought,
rain, mass, burning coal.

Or a saffron headband, mute
while it lasts, fading light
consumed in the street: the loss
of our years doesn't much matter
if the day is borne out fit
to die as indeed it should.
Hail, heart, decisive goal.

Parker's Piece

What were the victory fireworks like in 1945
if you didn't believe in the war but loved
the people and their victory? Hoping perhaps
these would be the last bangs, this the last
time the sky was shot with fire and the man
with red hair find his rest at length,
lying like evening on the earth, alive
and achieved, at full, like flowers, like red
tulips in full bloom and begin to lapse
openly back into history, a dark green bed.
What reason is there why each and every one
shouldn't inhabit a working peace that ends
separately, as we carry our peculiar fates
forwards through the smouldering gates.

First In Last Out

Life waves us in the wind which arcades
down the coast rousing the waves, striking
the measure. That is how orderly we are.
The body means but the mind laughs it away,
shaking that mean thing in the wind.
Who knows what heat lurks in the islands
over the line or how to know what purpose
we are set to? But certainly stopped
is better than small when the heart leaps
to be voiced in the trees of the mind
swaying in the wind, fixed in dreams
that rise slowly out of the restless town.

Equerry to the poem, I divide equably.
Quietly too, not to alarm the family.

S. Cecilia in Trastevere

What moves between bright thoughts and finished body?
Music's Idea turns in the clouds and she
lies on the floor, denied her time, face
turned away so as not to view her own pain.

What moves between is all we live, heavy
and light banked in winged tiers, that we
carve our eyes through day to day, kiss
the bed and back to the devastating sight again.

I believe in a centre to the wasted life
that is carried before the world and holds love
through distance and strife towards a
perfect reconciliation however many times
occluded in failed responses finally standing
whole and obvious, like an orchard in the rain.

S. Maria in Trastevere

Final beings in a golden field, ravenous concavity,
glowing up there in the darkness, impossible promise
sucking our very breath to their eyes, every single thing
that's worth a thought burning away and there it is.

So we have it as we don't and wish it as we
tear it apart and suffer the weight of
divided light on our dark stinging
eyes at the sudden cancellation of hope.

I wander in the darkened city thinking
I know no purpose to this thread of being
or where it shall come to an end. The shops
and taverns gleam to the side of the way,
the central distance stays empty until that
lucent shield cuts it clean, I hope it is.

S. Pietro in Montorio

Leaves and dust flying in the road. Deny
any perfection which is not made, which
curves not back to hold mental heat
to the dark ground, the bright stone.

It is all burning chaos, it all wastes
force to suck nothings to a point except
that one grace we own and are, to meet
cosmic dispersal at a still, equal, dome.

I stand in my absence in front of a thing
that stands in its presence and fits it
to perfection. The city is a tensed texture
behind me as far as the eye can want to see.
The sky curves less kindly, the planets greet
less formally the pitted world than this crown.

Dar es Suriani

Dug into the gaps between nations,
inhabiting the frictions of light,
keeping the sentences locked

Until they're needed.
Keeping silence, Lebanese
wine in the cellars

Reserved for visitors,
hiss of blown sand against white
walls, the messages cased and locked

And passed from life to life in
silence, the syntax unbroken, the fruit
held from its unknown result.

Patience and fortune at rest
on a thread, a spring in the desert.
We repeat the text again and again

At first light and evening
because it is true because
it cannot be moved or pictured.

A stone breaks in the west, a bud
of dust on the horizon meaning
trouble as the sky crashes

Daily to our feet. Our transmission
is fixed and immediate, solitude and obscurity
make our beds. A stone breaks

In the east, army trucks file
past from the horizon spreading
doubt and fear, the dust

Of their passage glitters on the floor.
We scoop it up and blend it with
goat fat to make a binding paste

For the books in the library
that we can't read. We bury
the dead, they haven't got time.

What else can we do? What is
left of us after they have all gone
is a body faithful from its centre

Further than it can see
as we toil at common tasks
absorbed in our procedures

Hardly aware of the uncertainty
and ecstasy hoarded under the text,
the fuel in the cellar that

Fires our fate, to maintain
beneficence without object and virtue
without enemy and cry in the desert

For he is mine and I am
his again and again in
love and war. At night

The stars screen our orders
and the small fire in the clay room
burns prepositions. We squat on the edge

Of the inhabitable, guarding a vacant tomb,
strictly in position and engaged, ensuring
that the only possible result

Be the exactly possible outcome
as the flesh line is held straight
and true here by the equinox,

And however the earth is wasted
in speed and excitation, here
it is altered, it is given

Back before it can be spent.
Heart levels cross at night
in the stone shed alone with love's answer,

True loves at war,
ours and yours. For we meet, serve,
and retire for good, as you know.

Château Musar

Everything inhabits the thinness
of a plate of light. We are informed,
twice crossed and helplessly
empowered: it's all for us,
we are why it moves, and it does,
with and against us, slowly
turning the crystal. O Lebanon!

There is nowhere else. Virtue in battle,
large white clouds sailing over the hills,
a forward thrust and a downward sigh,
peaceful wine.

Château de Muzot

Thick walls and thin ceiling

Heavy ground and light tread

Walking to the cupboard for a bone.

Hergla

At night the dead are lungs of the mind
male and female, left and right, breathing
in and out and calling over the sea towards
the answering place, hovering wings of despair.

Day is blue and white, blue for hope and white
for protection, with red carpets flung
over white walls and women in red robes
strolling the streets and heat filling the air

Until the light is switched off and the dead
in their wing-shaped graveyard hover again
over the sea shedding sparks of distance, and return
each morning, bringing what answers to the mind?

Bringing sad certainties, shrinkage set against
fear, black twists of industrial soot on
the white pages of books by which we learn
to stay where we are and live towards another's hope.

And listen very carefully to the real sky always bright
and long, filling the green question with yellow light.

Djebel Bou Dabbous

Shepherds like posts, with little ragged flocks
of brown goats, over the plains as the sun arcs
across the sky from one side to the other.
They stand there like statues in parks,
that stillness, "Where even today a God might enter
and not be diminished."

The shepherd's heads are full of Arabic,
prayers, curses, calculation, save and stitch
like all of us. Heads full of breathing.
The only God space I know is made in script
as a rich hollow at the heart of meaning
that can't be finished

And finishes us, shepherds, poets, freaks,
persons of the people set to watch
the frail resource. We signal like brothers
across the plains and run our longings
into musical continua as the hawks hover
over all we mean, guarding our edge.

Djebel Bou Dabbous

Of what are we ashamed? We are still enough
in a world made daily more expensive. We stop
the car and take out a basket and spread
a cloth on the ground. We have cheese and biscuits
figs and mineral water, we share them together.
A feathery breeze touches our heads

Like an idea of completion: acts that pass
well into the world beyond our short and
faltering lives, acts of trust in sudden
fits of star-hurt and deathly patience
claiming nothing but the limits of a tongue we
openly declare, small in the peaceful deserts.

And all round us as we sit there in the puff
of wind small flocks of brown sheep stand
quietly browsing across the long plain
of thin grass, with their masters. *Mes petits,*
we are ashamed to be alone. O my gossips,
the God hollow throbs and hurts.

Ghar el Melh

The light that sits on the edge of the leaf
in the gardens by the sea without limit,
the words on the ground crisp with response.

Again and again from item to item it shines
across the road and out to the harbour's white wall
open to distance, unwilling to domesticate.

Real gardens by the sea, growing vegetables
and fishermen camped in reed huts, riding
social injustice like a big wave: with glee.

The white houses wedged into the cliff top,
the sky lens focused on the ear, that hears
dominion on the wire and shudders. For the world

Is a house too big too small, hope is directed
to the fertile courtyard but the streets end
suddenly in the grey dust where no one lives

And tracks turn down to the sea gardens at day's
end, brightness blazing across, continuing
to shed acute definition you love-torn spheres.

Leaving me to think that the mind's track on
soul-light is instrumental to the earth's
equilibrium, as I have grown older.

Saint Louis' Island

Again the bright teacher opens his book in the sky.
pauvr'âme solitaire how you loved the fullness
of the city, the new light heating up the old walls
the wine of amity, and thoughts of home
as a distant portico full of tiered wave-lights
and sexual reward. Taking the price lightly
you certainly wrecked yourself on point honour.

In memory of you I carry the heart monstrance
this bright morning through the wet streets and
over a bridge into the stone crown. Aren't I also
the disqualified lover of vanishing states?
Aren't we all? Beams and signals hover and cross,
the wide eye of the street dweller calling to
the vertical fantasie of state O my lost brother!

Our forehead mansions, our genital smoke,
and fortune is what we dare to ask, not for the
self, that sore, for the life. The vane
skreaks in the wind tossed off the cathedral,
the shops open and tense like bees in amber
and fast in the new day where first and simple things
are true, be grateful for every other.

Saint Médard's Quarter

                They come to market
and sometimes it is a fake market with
nowhere to place your trust. They throng
in the tight streets, they sway and blush with
festival but mutter "jew" behind the coin.
You can get what you want here and cheap if
you turn quickly as they half-speak "immigrant" and
smile. The language is laid in strips
and the gain spins off distant war.

Aside from the market is a meeting house
or inner garden where the cheated can find
some company and thought of recompense
passes from table to table in the loud smoky air.
So better clouded we tune our hopes down
to earth for our own sakes, how else
will anyone thrive in this quick bare
time we have? Sense of lasting friendships
and mutual fruiting across difference, is the civilised star.

Saint Séverin's Maze

I can't wait to get out in the night crowds
and I do, sharp-eyed I weave the streets.

Un sandwich grecque at the stand, this is
the bright capital full of people, this is

Why.
And a slow Chinese cake.

Suddenly the lit zone ends I am trying
to work out a few things among stone walls, the sky

Writes a thesis in manganese dioxide
at the closing of the gates.

Something fine, all dangers past,
turns me home. Something not-fine bars the way.

There are people sleeping on the pavement in the rain.
The water runs off their backs into the gutter.

Causeway

I defy your bloody language. I cast
my whole life at your delay. My lapses from care
are a perpetual night surrounding my mind.

Pascal's Corner

When then does the society of solitude give space
even to its own history? The dark and quiet back
street. I stop at a small wine shop I remember
from six years back and again buy one cheap
rather unusual bottle and clutching it walk on,
the long boulevard past the prison, the hospital,
the observatory, shadowed by approaching night.

> City walls at the limit of script
> Hard as the space that hardens round
> The heart since there is no help,
> That has worn us since death became
> The door to nothing. Until we turn
> Towards home again and angrily cast
> Our whole lives at this dark delay.

Darkness falls from the sky, leaving it
light, above the long boulevard. On the
left the prison wall called Health, to the
right among trees a hospital called Grace
and further on the observatory where we turn
away from everything we know in our haste
to love. Hill and valley echo with delight.

Street and station say it is all right.

Notes to *Snow has Settled...*

The title of the book was originally *Snow has settled [...] bury me here*, which consisted of the first three and last three words in the book, but the last poem has been thought better of.

Midsummer Common and Parker's Piece are two areas of open land in Cambridge where kinds of festivals or manifestations take place.

Three poems are titled after mediaeval churches on the left bank of Rome. Santa Cecilia has a magnificent but ruined Last Judgement fresco by Cavallini and a touching statue of St. Cecilia in death by Stefano Maderna. Santa Maria has a large 12th century apse mosaic ("a row of figures before a solid gold wall"), and San Pietro, which overlooks the whole of Rome, has a circular chapel or tempietto by Bramante in its courtyard.

Dar es Suriani is a monastery in the Egyptian desert, important in the transmission of ancient Greek and Arabic texts.

In Djebel Bou Dabbous (i) "Where even today a God might enter..." Rilke.

Château Musar is a Lebanese wine label. Château de Muzot in Switzerland was Rilke's last home.

St. Louis' Island: Île Saint-Louis in Paris, where Baudelaire lived.

Index of Titles

30 diurnal poems	425
'A mist coming in…'	135
'And now he swings over to the bitter left…'	79
A Day	90
'A person's single reach…'	363
A Repetition of Machado at Porth Grwtheyrn	280
A Shropshire Lad	581
A Song to Conclude	224
A spring on the upper slopes of Mynydd Anelog	274
A story told of Anglesey	142
'About this evening…'	58
Absent from Llŷn 1994–1997	311
'Across the axis…'	174
Across the Island	170
Adonaïs	400
After a Poem by Nicholas Moore	532
'After which to fall howling…'	205
Afterthought	480
Aigburth (Howl)	521
All Saints	21
An American Photograph	59
'And after the spasm…'	207
'And again those bright calculations…'	229
'And all through the day…'	107
'and by the way,'	28
'And it is true…'	191
'And love alone…'	551
'And the miners all dead…'	401
'And there, at this very spot…'	392
'And this is where the colours come in…'	196
'And we do get somewhere…'	192
'And what do we love…'	201
'And's henceforth…'	184
'angel of the north…'	144
Another week on Llŷn	456
Arbor	220
Archilochus	152
As If Sonnets (The Lost Pamphlet)	25
'As it might be possible' (The Fighting Temeraire)	134
As with rosy steps	542
At Pott Shrigley Brickworks	63
At the Café	94
At the Children's Playground	92
At the Labour Exchange	95
Bar Carol	546
'Becoming as time fills out…'	187
Between Harbours	301
Birth Prospectus. The End of Us	231
Blåbærvej	150
Black Holes	457
Blow Blow Thou	216
Bolehill	518
Bolehill	562
'Bronchitis, headache…'	467
Bunker Hotel	226
Burnham Beeches	35
Bus across Mid-Sussex at Night	52
Cambridge Blue	566
Canzon	243
Care of the Body	217
Causeway	590
'Cavalry exercising…'	193
Château de Muzot	582
Château Musar	581
Climacteric	214
'Come together in the fields…'	186
Company	246
'Congress of twins…'	532
Counting the Cost	495
Dar es Suriani	578
'Deeper into stone…'	391
Delphine	562
Denmark	517
Die Mondnacht	535

Djebel Bou Dabbous (i)	584	Hackney Loft	572
Djebel Bou Dabbous (ii)	585	Harecops	515
Doing Nothing in Particular	101	Hastings	519
Dream 29/xi/1966	40	Having Breakfast	91
Dublin (i)	568	Having Dinner	96
Dublin (ii)	569	Heinrich Biber	534
E Questa Vita un Lampo	543	'Held in conative energy…'	394
Edward III	221	Hergla	583
Edward IV	222	High Lane	520
Edward V	223	High Lane 1964	22
Egbert Street	518	'How can they live…'	84
Eight Preludes	339	'How insistent it can be…'	185
Emilio de Cavalieri: Lamentations	60	'I am from language…'	83
Essay on the West Window of Killagha Abbey	242	'I depend…'	459
		'I feel terrible…'	200
'Expert hero…'	370	'I live with the child…'	51
First In Last Out	574	'I shake with the gifts…'	203
First Third	213	'I should be asleep…'	89
Five Serious Songs	115	'I sit in the café-bar…'	157
'fixed points in succession…'	277	I Wrote a Letter from France	531
'Flesh with / stands…'	399	'I'm prepared to believe…'	183
Folded Message	172	In a German Car Park	225
Following the Vein	325	In a white van…	275
Fontaine de Vaucluse	570	In Bed with You	103
Four Dream-and-Waking Pieces	36	In manus tuas	539
Four Round Dances	118	'In the dream-shaft…'	398
Fragments at Les Bassacs	477	In the Pub	99
Free ramble over the Archpoet's *Aestuans intrinsecus ira*	131	'In what sense to know'	239
		Instructions for morning	143
'From the window…'	146	'Into twilight…'	182
'Full moon…'	402	Introitus	45
Further Education	555	Irish Drones	522
Further to Cavalieri's Lamentations	62	Is this Düsseldorf or Kiel?	227
Gallarus	240	'It's all going on up there…'	209
Getting Away from Wagner	136	Just a Song	498
Getting Up	90	King's Field	349
Ghar el Melh	586	Lacoste	491
Glow Worm True Worm	533	Last Night	502
Glutton	357	Last Quarter	215
Going Home	100	Late autumn, the peninsula on the turn…	278
Golden Slumbers	524		
Grassy Lenses	171	'Learning to (speak…'	85
Great Eastern	560	Les Bassacs (d)	478

Let us all	161	'O see like a silver ship…'	137
Lines at Night 1	486	O That Singer	545
Lines at Night 2	490	On Behaviour, after reading Herrick	54
Lines at the Pool above St.-Saturnin	487	'One of the screws…'	108
Little Bolehill	564	'Only a week after…'	107
Llŷn in the Rain, September 1998	310	Only the Song	321
Llŷn, Pausing and Going	322	'Only true passion…'	530
Loft	571	'Open the curtains…'	173
London Bridge	558	'Or the house is a mountain…'	84
'Love – the open air…'	87	Orange to Chartres	518
Love Poem	24	Ospita	468
Macclesfield	516	Other Poems written on 11th May 1968	107
Magdalenian	536		
Manchester, Liverpool…	463	'Out into the open…'	56
Manifold	364	'Out of (quit)…'	190
Marine Resistance	130	Overheard by the Sea	300
Market Day at Apt	476	Parker's Piece	573
Material Soul	337	Part of an Inferno	36
Meditations in the Field 1-3	483	Pascal's Corner	591
Meditations in the Field 4	489	Pastoral	519
Memoirs of the Highland Zone	139	Pieces fragments and notes	282
Middleton by Wirksworth 1980	460	'Please don't tell me…'	180
Midsummer Common	565	Poem Beginning with a Line by Nicholas Moore	557
Mornings with a Walkman at Rhwngyddwyborth	288		
		Poems written on 11th May 1968	79
Music, wife, snow outside, a lot of old books	50	Polecats' Song	252
		Porth Grwtheyrn	279
'Name and place forgotten…'	195	Porth y Nant	281
Next Door But One	563	(Postlude)	462
Nicholas Moore Retake (Pact)	526	Prelude	551
Night-watch notebook	284	Privately	20
'No one comes to terms…'	85	Processional and Masque (The Replies)	443
North End	556		
Northern Harbour	162	Puisque j'ai perdu	47
Norwich	559	'Pure need scores the pavement…'	540
Notes on the Attempt to Visit Lorand Gaspar	499		
		Recalling Lacoste	492
Numbers at Les Croagnes	497	Regendered	532
'O my eyes hurt…'	178	Relenting of duress…	554
'O my hands hurt…'	202	Rhwngyddwyborth 6th Sept…	276
'O my head spins…'	204	Richmond and Kew	33
'O our intimacies…'	82	Roofwatch 1-2	479

Rustrel and Gargas	493	Terrestrial Home	88
'Ruthless, you find it…'	181	'That it is not so simple…'	128
S. Cecilia in Trastevere	575	'The blind traveller…'	461
S. Maria in Trastevere	576	(The Cancelled Diatribe)	387
S. Pietro in Montorio	577	'The city's surface…'	397
Saint Louis' Island	587	The Day Fishing	219
Saint Médard's Quarter	588	The Encyclopaedia Office	30
Saint Séverin's Landing	589	'The figure of hope…'	86
Sea Watch Elegies	293	'The flesh, eyestruck…'	381
Sea Watches	255	The Idea Is	455
Seafront	74	'The light alternates…'	365
Six small prose pieces formerly attached to *Between Harbours*	309	The Linear Journal	175
		The Lost Conditional	110
'Sky streaked with rain…'	149	'the mist full of caves…'	140
Slottet	159	The Night Train Arrives at Avignon	475
Slow Meditation in the Café-Bar Les Caves du Mont Anis, Le Puy	507	'The point of generation…'	458
		The Return, the Silver Bough	38
Snow in a Silver Bowl	64	'The screw that holds the window shut…'	113
'Snow is falling…'	149	'The sea is flat…'	112
'Snowdrops and crocus…'	230	'The simple pulse like a train…'	179
'So many cathedrals…'	188	The Slower Walk to Roussillon with Kathy	500
'So while it seems…'	199		
'So, walking down…'	333	The Song Sung	218
Socialism (Prayer)	525	'The sphere descends…'	329
Some pieces of The Irish Voyages	240	The Telephone Box on the Edge of the Corn Field	513
'Someone touches my shoulder…'	177	The Translations of St. Columba's Sea-Watch	298
'Something follows me…'	108	The Twelve Moons	68
Sparty Lea Epilogue	57	'The universe is not contained…'	84
Spitewinter Edge Lookout Prose (untitled)	405	The Walk Back to Gordes	496
		The Walk to Roussillon	485
St Merin's Church (i)	271	'The wind across the chimney top…'	127
St Merin's Church (ii)	272		
St Merin's Churchyard	273	'Then back to the mainland…'	189
St.-Saturnin, the Ridge	482	Things Saying Themselves in Llŷn	291
Still and White	238		
Strange Family	121	'Though really I don't…'	206
'Stream…'	198	'Threats and promises…'	156
Stubborn Interval	481	Three Poems after a literary convention in Ashdown Forest	53
Summer	37		
Surviving Fragments of the Solo Diatribe	388		

Three-part invention for John Dunstaple	114
'Through the day's obscurity…'	149
Through Woods and Fields	521
Tidying Up and Going to Bed	102
'To back up…'	53
'To blaze through language…'	82
'To cut notches…'	81
To live trying	161
Toy Music	251
Train	55
Train skirting the South Downs	53
Two Machaut Songs	120
(two poems and a letter)	354
'Unfold the line…'	331
Up the Big Hill and Back by Ten	494
Valley of the Moon	145
'very early morning…'	141
Victoria: The Shadows	129
Visiting Other People	98
Visiting People	97
Visiting the University	93
'Voiced consonants…'	541
'Wait for (each day) the light…'	377
Wanderers Nachtlied	23
'We are at large under the white beam…'	160
'We become extensions…'	34
'We don't belong in language…'	109
'We fall to the earth…'	461
Wednesday Supermarket Poem(s)	156
West Side	561
Wetton Mill New Year's Eve 1974-5	228
'What condolence the earth has…'	80
What the Fate Capsule Told Me	523
'Whatever you do is right…'	109
Where was I?	19
'which murmuring encloses…'	139
White Arrows	158
'Wie schön bist du…'	529
'Wind on glass…'	75
Wirksworth (i)	552
Wirksworth (ii)	553
'with its unexpected vistas…'	197
'Year cap split…'	384

www.ingramcontent.com/pod-product-compliance
Lightning Source LLC
Chambersburg PA
CBHW021756220426
43662CB00006B/75